DEAD VOICE

Dear Julie, please
accept this book
as a token of
admiration.

RV .
New York, 2022

THE MIDDLE AGES SERIES

Ruth Mazo Karras, Series Editor
Edward Peters, Founding Editor

A complete list of books in the series
is available from the publisher.

DEAD VOICE

LAW, PHILOSOPHY, AND FICTION

IN THE IBERIAN MIDDLE AGES

Jesús R. Velasco

PENN

UNIVERSITY OF PENNSYLVANIA PRESS

PHILADELPHIA

Copyright © 2020 University of Pennsylvania Press

Published by
University of Pennsylvania Press
Philadelphia, Pennsylvania 19104-4112
www.upenn.edu/pennpress

Printed in the United States of America on acid-free paper
1 3 5 7 9 10 8 6 4 2

A Cataloging-in-Publication record is available from the Library of Congress
ISBN 978-0-8122-5186-9

Ce livre est dédié à Aurélie Vialette et à Miguel Velasco Vialette

Not all things are blest, but the
seeds of all things are blest.
The blessing is in the seed.

This moment, this seed, this wave of the sea,
This look, this instant of love.

—Muriel Rukeyser

CONTENTS

INTRODUCTION

This book is an investigation into the methods, decisions, and theoretical perspectives that underpin the creation and writing of an all-encompassing legal code, the *Siete Partidas* (*Seven Parts*), although it is not an exhaustive study of that code.[1] It is, rather, an examination of some of the code's technologies and techniques of codification. In that sense, it opens up a larger conversation with the theories and techniques of legal codification in other languages and cultures during the Middle Ages and beyond. Ultimately, this book is a study of the question of what it meant to codify law in the Middle Ages and what problems this question gave birth to, along with the technical strategies that lawgivers and law scholars offered to resolve those issues.

These techniques and theories of codification fall under the notion that gives the title to this book, *dead voice*. As we will see in more depth in Chapter 1, "dead voice" is an expression used by many theologians and lawyers during the long Middle Ages and was introduced by Alfonso himself into the text of the *Third Partida*, Prologue 18.[2] The expression (*vox mortua*, in Latin) may refer to many different aspects of legal writing, and it is always set in opposition to some sort of oral witnessing, or *living voice*—a kind of oral witnessing that seems to have appeared during the first or second century of the Common Era.[3] Procedural lawyers and law scholars used *vox mortua* to refer to written instruments, and Alfonso enhanced it in a way that I find particularly productive. As I will argue in this book, this enhanced concept of dead voice as a means of regulating legal writing at both the normative and the documentary levels will give us access to larger issues in the process of legal codification. For instance, this legal codification productively utilizes fictional devices, establishes legal temporalities, gives birth to a specific form of legal subject, and includes a legal rationality based on philosophical corpora. Dead voice is the gravitational center and the general name I give to some of those techniques and theories of codification.

One could think of the *Siete Partidas* as a constitutional code that was intended to present a theory of power and the rules according to which all other rules must arise. Alfonso inscribed this theory of power in and as the legal system itself, so that legislation, codification, and power theory cannot be separated from one another. The code also includes a full set of laws of all the branches of ecclesiastic and secular legislations, both public and private. In that sense, it is a code that mainly contains canon, administrative, procedural, civil, and penal law and legislates across these legal divides. As part of its legislative impulse, it also regulates its own legal science—its philosophy and theory of law. Again, these theoretical elements are part of both the legal text and the act of codification. Such complex codification required an innovative architecture.[4]

The main characteristic of such architecture was a technical tour de force—that is, in its use of the vernacular. The *Siete Partidas* appeared in a world in which vernacular legal writing was chiefly reserved for local regulations, whereas legal science and codification normally ran in transpolitical (that is, crossing different polities), arguably universal, languages (Latin, Hebrew, and Arabic).[5] The legislator decided to code the law in a vernacular whose legal vocabulary and systems of expression were technically limited. Only certain kinds of legal objects had been previously articulated by this vernacular legal language, including private acts taking place in relatively Latinate vernacular expressions. Across the Iberian Peninsula, some *fueros*, or local regulations, as well as charters regarding the foundation or population of a town or city (*cartas pueblas*), customary law in Castile and Aragon, legal responses, or even the proceedings of *cortes* (the itinerant meetings between the king or the regent and the other orders of society) were indeed published in the vernacular from the late twelfth century onward. Likewise, the important compilation of Visigothic law known as the *Liber Iudiciorum*, or *Lex Visigothorum*, was translated during the first third of the thirteenth century under the rule of Ferdinand III (r. 1217–1252) as the *Fuero Juzgo*. The vernacular royal chancery started during the kingdom of Alfonso VIII (r. 1158–1214), to bloom only during the kingdom of Alfonso X (r. 1252–1282).[6]

Despite its vernacular articulation and unlike the local examples given above, and also contrary to the idea that some scholars of Roman law, including Manlio Bellomo, have entertained, the *Siete Partidas* was not intended to be a document of local legal significance but rather one that would inaugurate a new kind of universalization—and therefore a new thesis on transpolitical empire.[7] The *Siete Partidas*, indeed, were born in the juncture of three extremely important events: the beginning and end of Alfonso's imperial ambitions and the administration of new territories and political entities after the conquests of Muslim independent cities and kingdoms (ṭawāʾif, or taifas) in the south of the peninsula and across the region known as Sharq al-Andalus, which encompassed the Iberian eastern Muslim domains.[8]

With the purpose of providing this new kind of universalization, the legal vernacular needed to constitute its own technology of codification, which is a central component of dead voice, or legal writing. This technology entailed developing a systematic legal lexicography as a part of the codification process, and this legal lexicography pervades the whole code.[9] It is a lexicography that could not merely be based on translation from the other more universal languages but instead needed to provide a new conceptual map with its own order and structure, and its own material representation.[10] While the definitions of concepts in the *Partidas* mention their Latin, Greek, Arabic, or Hebrew genealogy or etymology, the codification always leads toward a vernacular updating of the legal concept, not a direct usage of the original one.

The rewards of researching the technologies of legal codification are various. First and foremost, this research allows us to delve into emerging theories of constitutional power. In other words, it allows us to understand how the process of creation of the legal mainframe set the heuristic and hermeneutic borderlines of legislation and codification: how the legal conceptual map shaped the liminal vocabulary for creating and interpreting the theory of power itself. Accordingly, such a theory of power with constitutional value will configure both the autonomy of the legal discipline it elicits and the rules of creation and interpretation that operate in the world interior to such a discipline. This is important insofar as we can see how the entire set of theories and techniques encompassed by the constitutional impulse become difficult to separate from the very legal discipline; in other words, they feed each other, they support each other.

In addition, we can study the ways in which facts, actions, and subjects, both actual and potential, become legal matter. Indeed, this is important for understanding the pervasive process of juridification of the world—how every single experience becomes susceptible to being narrated and interpreted according to juridical models and languages. We can study the processes whereby the law (both its constitutional value and the legal discipline) either appropriates or colonizes the other disciplines and bodies of knowledge.

The juridification of the world, however pervasive it is, cannot work solely by means of juridical logic and legal rationality. The process of codification I am studying here also codifies affective and emotional regimes of the legal subject and their own constitutional value. As I will argue in this book, with support from primary sources, the constitutional value of affects and emotions implies a whole legal theory and a set of techniques to convey to the legal clients that the law is their own public responsibility, that they are bound not only by the knowledge of its existence and the understanding of its text but also, and primarily, by their ability to feel with it, to describe the world according to the language of the law and with its epistemological regulations—namely, how to perceive through the senses as they are regulated in the law itself. This is what makes the law really meaningful to the people: that the people are responsible for an aesthetic (perceptive, cognitive, judging) participation and collaboration with the law.

In this sense, the juridification of the world by means of this affective, emotional, and, in summary, aesthetic regime also configures a legal subject. Part of my project delves into the characteristics of this legal subject and examines how this process of subjectivization entails a specific concept of empirical sovereignty (in a context in which sovereignty is always thought to be outside empirical realizations, as Hent Kalmo and Quentin Skinner, among others, have studied) and legal thinking.[11] Empirical sovereignty implies a concrete set of techniques for perceiving and conceiving of the center of jurisdictional power on the part of the legal subject. Legal thinking implies the necessary abilities to interpret the world with the tools provided by legal vocabularies, legal materialities, and legal gestures.

We are looking at a legislative drive that shapes the semantic and pragmatic, as much as cognitive and empirical, senses with the purpose of building what we can call legal sensibility. This is the affective regime that emerges from this process of codification. In other words, the lawgiver is also interested in legislating how, under what conditions, and to what extent the client of the law (the "people," as the legislator defines the whole community of legal subjects in *Partidas* 2.10) must feel and be affected by the law.

The techniques and theories of law codification include the creation of sensible legal devices that are part of the very legislation—the material conditions in which legal objects are given form, presented, submitted, and so forth—in order to have legal force. These legal devices challenge our regular conceptions of the material text. They are material in the sense that the process of codification explores the material conditions of the production of text as a weaving together of many different elements expressing epistemological collaboration. Such material forms may include text, cords, seals, images, and the different writing materials (whether paper or parchment, color, etc.) All the elements within these sensible legal devices must be interpreted and studied as bearing legal value, not as mere accessories to the legal text. This sort of material text—what I call here sensible legal devices—is also the result of processes of appropriation of disciplines external to the law but ones performed within the legal discipline—history, philosophy, biblical knowledge, and so forth. The legal material text is, indeed, a legal epistemological device.

As will be argued in this book, this way of appropriation of nonlegal disciplines by the legal science is central to the techniques and theories of legal codification performed in the *Siete Partidas* and is only understandable within a much larger discussion about the autonomy of law that had been taking place in the Mediterranean basin since the eleventh century, with some of the most important expressions coming from the Iberian Peninsula between the twelfth and the thirteenth centuries. The techniques and theories of codification elicited by this debate, which I will conceptualize as the debate on perplexing legislation, will lead us to conclude that Alfonso's codification participates in this debate by embracing its challenges and including all those external disciplines as part of the legislative impulse.

The Law-Scratchers

Let us imagine the following hypothetical situation. Written laws and legal documents fall in the lap of different individuals or organized groups. These powerful individuals or groups are not necessarily lawyers themselves, nor are they necessarily in the legal profession. They claim to be part of "the people" in general: regular clients of the law from varied social and economic origins. As such, they are concerned about the law and about the way it applies to them—for, indeed, law is not just the concern of professional lawyers but affects everyone. These people also feel that they have a say in the production of the law. Some even think that they may have the right actually to evaluate the law and, eventually, have it changed or change it by themselves, because while the law is a monopoly of the systems of government, the people themselves are an essential part of government given the social, political, and economic role they play in public and private life.

In this hypothetical situation, they then proceed to read the laws and the documents, and they *do* the following: they erase the parts they don't like, mostly those that interfere with their individual or collective idea of sovereignty; and after erasing the words, sentences, laws, and documents, they rewrite the law, replacing the parts they did not like with ones that they consider more adequate, that is, more advantageous to them.

The hypothetical situation I have just described is not hypothetical at all and has happened not only once, but many times. Perhaps it is, in fact, an ongoing situation, so much so, that the legal text has become an active and metamorphic object in which the law is not necessarily considered a durable code but a process, a series of drafts and palimpsests.

Indeed, a more condensed and objectively referential narrative of similar behaviors was recorded in the opening passages of some of the early manuscripts of the *Siete Partidas* as authored by King Alfonso X of Castile and León during the second half of the thirteenth century.[12] Early redactions—that is, the first version or manuscript editions of the *Partidas*—decry that some people (he calls them *gentes*, which is different than *pueblo*, or "people") in his domains (*señorío*, which also means "the king's jurisdiction") used to unlawfully scrape away the laws they found to be inconvenient for them: "*Las gentes* [the people in our domains, in a nontechnical way] used to scratch [the manuscript containing the laws] and write on top of them that which was profitable to them at the cost of harming *los pueblos* [the people as legal subjects], taking the power and privileges of the kings and appropriating these for themselves, which should have never been done."[13] The scratched "laws" Alfonso refers to were legal documents, *fueros*, local charters, regulations, and *privilegios* (what I always translate as "privilege," according to Scott's translation of *Partidas* 3.18.2) predating his legislative impulse and his kingdom—that is, the legal labyrinth that he, as a king, was bound to inherit. Those laws were mostly written on parchment, and Alfonso was probably conveying the image of hypothetical, unnamed persons literally canceling words or more extensive sections of text with the help of a scraper.[14] Although neither an inexpensive nor widely available material, parchment is not difficult to restore, and recycling writing materials is an old and common practice—the one that gave birth to the concept of palimpsest.[15] Probably using a solution high in calcium to refill the wounds inflicted with the scraper, these opportunistic law-scratchers restored the parchments they were using before rewriting something else on top of them.

Furthermore, the parchments on which the laws were written had other nontextual elements like hanging devices and *jurisgraphisms*—graphic elements with juridical value. These nontextual elements could also be affected by the intervention of the law-scratchers.[16] Some—such as seals and cords, or certain designs including the wheel (a graphic device consisting of a chi-ro chrismon) of the *privilegio rodado* (wheeled privilege), or certain kinds of crosses—were intended to bear witness to the authenticity of the legal object and invest it with a sacred quality. Other elements, including miniatures, are more difficult to interpret in their relationship to the law but are still central to the process of codification, legal writing, and dissemination of the legal object.[17]

Scratching and rewriting the law involved different kinds of intervention with and modification—or falsification—of the legal object. Michel Foucault's reinterpretation of the notion of *illegalism* is helpful in understanding these.[18] In the absence of a stable regulation of the materiality of legal communication, the clients of the law have a larger area of movement where their activities are neither legal nor illegal, and they can create habits, customs, or ways of doing things; these illegalisms, which were exploited by even the highest powers (as we will see even with Alfonso himself), are extremely productive and can be used in writing legislation that will turn illegal*ism* into illegal*ity*. This raises two questions. The first is, what is the meaning of the integrity of the legal object? The second is whether such integrity constitutes a necessary condition for the constitution of monarchical jurisdiction and sovereignty. In other words, the main questions at stake are these: Where is the sovereignty and jurisdiction located? and What is its relationship with the very materiality of the legal object, its codification, and its dissemination and preservation?[19] These questions are central to understanding the regulation of what we call in this book dead voice—that is, the techniques of legal writing and models of material codification of the law.

The short law-scratcher narrative we presented before connects the modification of the materiality of the legal object with the undermining of monarchical power. The narrative appears in the first redaction of Alfonso's *Siete Partidas* and can be found in the prologue to the legal code preceding the *Partidas* proper, known as the *Espéculo*, or more fully as *Espéculo de las Leyes* (*Mirror of Laws*). It is difficult to know the point at which the law-scratcher narrative was exchanged for a different one that appears in later editions of the *Partidas*. If we accept Alfonso's chronology of the *Partidas*, the project was finished in 1265. The text, however, was revised and corrected several times after that date, probably as late as the 1270s. It is not impossible that editions after 1265 had already dispensed with this narrative of the law-scratchers in order to include a different one.

In the new version, which would accompany the *Partidas* from around 1270 onward, the people in the king's jurisdiction were no longer referred to as law-scratching subjects who undermined the monarchical right to a central jurisdiction. Instead, they were presented in the new prologue to the *Partidas* as "big hearted" and "loyal; and therefore, it is necessary that loyalty be kept with truth, and strength with right, and with justice."[20]

One of the codices containing the narrative about the law-scratchers, now preserved at the British Library, is the only manuscript that can be dated to Alfonsine times. It is also one of the very few manuscripts containing *jurisgraphisms*. The first set of four illuminations, which I have analyzed elsewhere, are powerful visual concepts centered on the monarchy as the source of jurisdiction.[21] In them, the king is the ultimate author and interpreter of the law, even though he seeks confirmation from God directly and without mediation. Alfonso is represented here as the physical origin of jurisdiction and sovereignty, while the other powers of the kingdom occupy their own spaces behind the monarch. Indeed, both the reference to the law-scratchers and the illuminations show the real interests of this legislator—to find ways to establish the origin and the center of the legislative power, and the construction of a central, and concentric, jurisdictional power.

The foremost question is how can this link between codification, the material integrity of the legal object, and the constitution of a central jurisdiction be created? In other words, how can jurisdiction be made visible, tangible, and sensible? How can sovereignty be made empirically present? These are, indeed, questions that leads to another one: how can a legal code be written that can grant the king these juridical and political ambitions while curbing even the possibility of people in his jurisdiction erasing and rewriting the law? In order to do that, I argue that it was necessary to create integrity and autonomy for the legal discipline itself: the precise identification of what is law and what is not, of what has legal form and what does not, of what is legal language and what is not, and, above all, establishing the rules that govern the internal functioning of the law and legal science. Such creation would foreclose the possibility to interpret as law something that lies outside the code and outside the rules for legal creativity that are expressed in such code—which, thus, would have a constitutional value, as a rule of rules. But, how is such autonomous legal science to be created? What are the techniques of law-writing and law-saying necessary for this purpose? Do these techniques also entail techniques of government? Do they entail techniques for the subjects of the law to feel that they must take care of themselves in any particular way? This book advances some answers to this set of questions.

Becoming a Lawgiver

Alfonso X, the king who denounced and intended to ban law-scratching and turn this sort of illegalism (something that has not been considered by the law) into an illegal activity (something that has been considered unlawful by the law), was himself a law-scratcher. One of his first legislative actions took place on March 24, 1253, ten months into his reign. The Master of the Military Order of Calatrava brought to the king's attention that his brother, the *infante*, or Prince Henry (1230–1303), had deposited in the Calatrava castle two privileges (*privilegios*) from their father, Ferdinand III, granting Henry territories around Lebrija and Xeres.[22] Alfonso and Henry's relationship was extremely belligerent, and Alfonso could not accept that their father had given these lands to his brother. Two members of the Calatrava Order had brought the documents to Alfonso's attention while he was in Seville. He acknowledged the receipt of the documents and declared that as soon as he received them, "I tore them up."[23] This is an extreme—if not literal—form of law-scratching.

During the first years of his rule, Alfonso performed as a law-scratcher in different ways. He sometimes destroyed documents; sometimes he confirmed other documents after reviewing them. At times he added a seal to the document submitted to him, while other times he did not. And on a number of occasions, he simply left in a state of historical latency documents and legal claims inherited or put in his hands from different archives across his growing kingdom. All those confirmed and altered documents, the ones I call revenant manuscripts in Chapter 3, constitute the very first legal concerns and experiences of the king. They are the ones that turned the law-scratcher into a lawgiver—a legislator.

Becoming a legislator implied, for Alfonso, becoming what we can call, a *fonction législateur*, or a *mens* (Latin for mind)—that is, giving a single, personal, proper name to a larger and more complex workshop composed of many *individuals*.[24] The workshop included an undefined number of authors, compilers, translators, textual specialists, scientists, and other intellectuals and scholars from many different cultural backgrounds, languages, and faiths, all working together to build the intellectual, scientific, and scholarly immensity of the Alfonsine Era.[25] Therefore, when we say "Alfonso" we are referring, indeed, to the function, to the *mens*, and to the *escuela*, or workshop. But we are also saying something bigger than that. It is well known that each of the *Siete Partidas* begins with one of the letters of the king's name, and that, therefore, the name is the acronym, a *heptagrammaton* that gives rise to the code itself and everything it stands for.[26] Everything comes back to the name, to the individual, and from him, to the era itself, to the periodizations and temporalities of which Alfonso is, as well, the *heptagrammaton*.

Apart from other shorter or more circumstantial pieces of legislation, four major legal codes can be attributed to Alfonso: the *Fuero Real*, the *Espéculo*, the *Siete Partidas*, and the *Setenario*. It is possible to argue that the last three are, in fact, the same project—although they reveal the complexities inherent in the process of construction of the legislative code, the processes of perfection and change.

The chronology of these codifications is still difficult to settle with any certainty. There is some consensus among scholars, however, that the *Fuero Real*, the first legal corpus, was completed before 1255, when it was probably given to the city of Aguilar de Campoo. 1254 may very well be the year of the general edition, with its broader establishment in 1256, continuing more or less uninterruptedly until 1272, the year of the crisis between the king and the increasingly powerful cities.[27] We measure the establishment of the *Fuero Real* by the number of cities to which it was granted as a legal code. The implementation of the *Fuero Real*, however, continued afterward, well beyond Alfonso's time, often as a legal and political bargaining chip with cities, brotherhoods, or other political entities. Indeed, the *Fuero* was put second in the hierarchy of legal sources in the *Ordenamiento de Alcalá* of 1348, coming right after the *Ordenamiento* itself.[28]

The *Espéculo* which was referred to as an existing legal body in the proceedings of the Cortes of Zamora celebrated in 1274, seems to have been promulgated in May 1255, according to the excellent analysis provided by Jerry Craddock.[29] Many scholars agree that the *Espéculo* is a first attempt at the construction of a central body of monarchical legislation and that, as González Jiménez points out, "most of its materials would end up being recast and integrated in the *Partidas*."[30] However, the differences between the *Espéculo* and the *Partidas* are profound, and they cannot be explained by only considering the *Espéculo* as a tentative work, an unfinished first try.[31] There are, for example, key political differences in the way they regulate the social order of the kingdom, and the codifying techniques of the *Espéculo* are not as theoretically inflected as those of the *Partidas*.

Scholars of the *Siete Partidas* seem to agree that the latter code had an imperial motivation. The *Partidas* were conceptualized as the Alfonsine legal initiative after the embassy from the Republic of Pisa visited Alfonso in March 1256 and asked him to submit his candidacy for the vacant office of emperor of the Holy Roman Empire.[32] The chronology presented by the *Partidas* themselves seems to be reasonable. The technical works of Jerry Craddock and Aquilino Iglesia Ferreirós yield a clearer panorama of the creation and dates of the different versions of the *Partidas*. Despite other discussions and the convoluted hypotheses presented by Alfonso García Gallo and some of his disciples, the *Partidas* would have to have been initiated on June 23, 1256, and finished on August 28, 1265, and whereas it is clear that there are two editions and other revisions, they all pertain to what Iglesia Ferreirós conceived as the internal evolution of the Alfonsine legislative effort.[33]

This chronology is entirely acceptable. But there is a larger chronology of legislative events that also needs to be taken into account. We know the process of establishing the *Fuero Real*, but for the other works, we mostly have circumstantial evidence or internal references that begin and end in the texts themselves. Considering a larger chronology, it is important to note that the legislative impetus behind Alfonso's work belonged to his father, King Ferdinand III, who kept alive Alfonso VIII's chancery and its innovations.[34] Ferdinand III also pushed for the enforcement and ultimate translation of the *Liber Iudiciorum*, or *Fuero Juzgo* in Spanish, from 1243.[35] It is not impossible—actually, quite the contrary—that the search for a monarchical monopoly on legal production was already in the minds of both Alfonso VIII and Ferdinand III.[36] In this sense, Alfonso presented himself as an epigone rather than a reformer. His epigonism was also a way to honor the towering political legacy of his father, to whom Alfonso refers constantly as if asking for his approval. As Ryan Szpiech has recently suggested, Alfonso, by presenting himself as the father's disciple, begat his father as a historical figure, thus performing at the same time a productive character of the son.[37]

Consensus becomes more tenuous when scholars come to consider the chronology of the *Setenario*. Some, like Jerry Craddock, Georges Martin, and Gonzalo Martínez Diez, see it as the last and most personal and intimate legislative work of Alfonso's intellectual impulse. According to them, it would have been written in Seville, during the two years of exile preceding Alfonso's death in 1284. In the end, the book would have remained unfinished and sent out into the world before its time. Others, like Fernando Gómez Redondo, consider that the so-called *Setenario* is nothing other than the first attempt at writing the *First Partida*. The book had all the defects of an early attempt at codification, and in the end, both the text and its septenary structure would have been reused and subsumed in the *Partidas*, whose general prologue does praise the count of seven, and turns it into both microcosmic and macrocosmic generative structures.[38]

In my opinion, both positions miss the challenge of reading the chronology of the *Setenario*. The chronology of the *Setenario* is, indeed, very difficult to ascertain, but it is obvious that it is in close relationship to the composition of the *Partidas*. However, I don't think the manuscripts of the *Setenario* reveal that this is a more personal work, inflected with a certain melancholy, unless from a cavalier and teleological perspective. Perhaps it is; perhaps it was composed in exile—and it probably was, if Craddock's examination of the evidence is correct. However, the interesting thing is that the manuscripts of the *Setenario* reveal that the project was quite different from the *Partidas*.

My position is that it is a later work that stems from a completed version of the *Partidas* and that, drawing on this completed version, proposes a new approach to the law based on an unfinished graphic presentation of the legal conceptual map. Indeed, the manuscripts seem to be drafts that explain to the workshop how to deal with the concepts central to each legal statement, putting those concepts on separate lines and surrounded by a box. This presentation of the draft had the probable purpose of explaining to the artists that these concepts needed to be illuminated, maybe in the way some Jewish manuscripts from the Middle Ages isolate and illuminate central concepts of the Torah or the commentaries.[39] In this sense, the *Setenario* would be something like a précis or a handbook. As such, it could be interpreted from the vantage point of the techniques of reading, meditation, and study. It would, then, focus the attention on the concepts themselves, and if the boxes in the draft manuscript indicate the intended positions of miniatures, perhaps it also focused on visual, even if abstract, concepts.

What this chronology reveals, regardless of its exactness, is that the legislative momentum began for Alfonso some time around 1254, that is, during the complex process of the repopulation of Seville and other territories conquered from al-Andalus in the south and the Levantine coast of the Iberian Peninsula (Sharq al-Andalus), a process that spawned a very large flow of documentation, including the establishment of local charters and jurisdictional competences. This process of repopulation required changes in toponymy and in the very organization and subdivision of space, as well as a full inventory of properties, buildings, and, among other things, crops, trees, and vineyards. The repopulation and redistribution of lands initiated, as well, a jurisdictional reorganization; for example, on November 25, 1253, the city of Carmona was put under the local charter of Seville and the *alcaldes de alzada*, the judges who can constitute a court of appeals. The very document granting this royal provision explains that they are following the example of Talavera, which was put under the local charter of Toledo's jurisdiction.

If this legislative impulse began in 1254, it was largely finished in 1265, a bit over ten years later. It would have coincided with one of the most creative periods in the Alfonsine workshops. The invention of new legal codifications happened at the same time as the workshops were compiling, critiquing, and translating Arabic texts,[40] by which means they were culturally suturing the newly conquered territories to the rest of the expanding kingdom.

During those long ten years, the legal workshop undertook two completely different tasks, including, on the one hand, the creation of a very effective, metabolic municipal code, the *Fuero Real*—"metabolic" because of its capacity to change each time it was instated in a different city. Changes entailed the combination of *iura propria*, such as customs of local charters and privileges from those localities, with the monarchical normative principles and the centrality of the jurisdictional idea with which it had been conceived. The *Fuero Real* was an extraordinary tool for negotiations between local powers with jurisdictional privileges and the central, growing monarchical government. The timeline of *Fuero Real* enactments exceeds the biological life of Alfonso X, extending well into the fourteenth century. With the *Fuero*'s wide dissemination, the later Alfonsine workshop, as well as the king's successor, Sancho IV, prepared a companion piece to interpret the laws from this code—a companion known as the *Leyes del estilo*.

On the other hand, and at a much slower pace and with much less contemporaneous impact—but with a very durable influence in legal thought throughout the Alfonsine Era and beyond—the workshop undertook the task of composing the sequence *Espéculo–Siete Partidas–Setenario*. Although there is no direct evidence for this, my hypothesis is that a separate workshop of miniaturists and artists was working on the manuscript of an already outdated first version of the *First Partida*, usually called *Libro del Fuero de las Leyes* and now preserved in the British Library. The work's being already in progress could explain that the resulting codex can be dated to a time when there were already new versions of the *Partidas* in circulation.

During these ten years, Alfonso became a lawgiver. This conversion from law-scratcher to lawgiver is hard to perceive in all its importance without debunking the idea of the *Siete Partidas* as a *summa* or encyclopedia not entirely focused on legislation. Throughout this book I hold that the *Partidas* are, from start to finish, a code of legislation—one that includes not only real rights, obligations, norms, and other legal actions but also its own legal science, its own rules of production, interpretation, dissemination, and permanence. Indeed, becoming a lawgiver implied, for Alfonso, the deployment of techniques of legislation and codification that would foster his ambition of a central jurisdiction and a central and exclusive legal code that had all the necessary elements to be received and acknowledged.

Indeed, becoming a lawgiver in Alfonso's case superseded his then-current legislative models: proposing a new legal language and building new ways of constructing the communication of legal materials. He did it at the normative level, as much as at the level of the technologies of documentation, and in both cases not only included the content but also legislated the aesthetics of the legal object. For Alfonso during those ten years of activity, becoming a lawgiver amounted to embracing the productivity of a perplexing technique of legislation in order to universalize the law and the language of the law from the vantage point of the vernacular.

Corpus, Corpora

Libraries around the world hold about ninety extant manuscripts of the *Siete Partidas*.[41] These manuscripts contain several versions and variants from the thirteenth through the fifteenth centuries. At the end of the fifteenth century, manuscript dissemination among professionals was replaced by mechanical reproduction of the early editions. This replacement was technically efficient. Mechanized production began in 1491 with the edition Alonso Díaz de Montalvo published in Seville, which was intended for practicing lawyers—thus with additions and concordances to other active legal corpora, including the *Copilación de las Leyes del Reyno* (Seville, 1484), which Montalvo himself had been commanded to create after the Cortes of Toledo, in 1480.[42] A few years later, Montalvo himself produced another edition of the *Partidas*, with an abundant apparatus of glosses in Latin, that he probably intended as a textbook for students of law, as the *Partidas* had become part of the university curriculum.[43] The president of the Council of Indies, Gregorio López Madera, prepared a new edition in 1555, during the regency of Juana de Austria. While Carlos V and his son, Philip, performed the ceremonies of abdication of the political body of the former on the natural body of the latter, the *Siete Partidas* upheld the theory and practice of monarchical power during the period of the regency.

While the Real Academia de la Historia produced a new critical edition of the *Siete Partidas* as late as in 1807—which became the preferred edition—the 1555 edition was already considered to be best and most comprehensive within ten years of its publication. Surrounded by hundreds of glosses and followed by commentaries and other independent glosses, the 1555, or "imperial," edition had become the repository of a centuries-long tradition of legal discussion throughout the kingdom and the Iberian empire.[44]

The history of the *Siete Partidas* remains largely uncharted. It is also so long and convoluted, and so expansive, that the production of a stable text became, very early, a legal need and a tour de force. According to Title 18 of the *Ordenamiento de Alcalá* of 1348, King Alfonso XI had already initiated this philological and legal operation by situating his great-grandfather's code in a prominent place in the hierarchy of legal sources of the kingdom. He recognized that the *Partidas* had never been promulgated before and that they had not been "received as laws."[45] Alfonso XI, then, had the extant manuscripts collected, and after comparing the different versions, he had them amended "in some required points," and, he continues, "thus harmonized and amended, because they were drawn and taken from the sayings of the holy fathers and from the laws and sayings of many ancient wise men, and from *fueros* and customs of Spain, we now give them as our laws."[46]

That the *Partidas* had not been hitherto received as law means that they had not been promulgated, that their existence was that of a codex rather than that of a code. "Reception," as in "received as laws" here, is a technical term that indicates the process of recognition of something as a constitutive part of a legal tradition. This is the same expression that is used to explain that the "reception" of Roman law in the Iberian Peninsula, and therefore the reception of the *ius commune*, begins with certain legal codes that are sometimes *iura propria*, like the *Fuero de Cuenca*, or more general legislative projects, including, of course, the *Fuero Real*, the *Espéculo*, and the *Siete Partidas*.[47] This is what "reception" means.

There is, however, another sense to the notion of reception. For there is, indeed, a reception of the *Siete Partidas* in the sense that they were transmitted and copied; they were used and translated in Catalan and Portuguese, at least partially.[48] They were, therefore, part of a discussion, and definitely part of a legal debate in which they were not deemed winners. Even when they were received *as laws*, they were received only as suppletive law, in the lowest place of a hierarchy of legal sources. So, there are two receptions of the *Partidas*: one that is not *as laws*, from approximately 1270 until 1348; and another one *as laws*, from 1348 onward. Since a law published on February 28, 2015, still uses the *Fifth Partida* as its legal foundation and rationale, one can say that the expression "from 1348 onward" is quite precise.[49]

Even once received as laws, reading the *Partidas* is quite a challenging experience. The *Second Partida* is frequently invoked as a mirror of princes, and therefore one piece of machinery within a long and discontinuous tradition of discussing the techniques of good government.[50] Other *Partidas*—like the *Seventh*, which is devoted to criminal law and the penal system—have been read as renditions of particular social struggles, like the titles regarding Jews (24), Muslims (25), and heretics (26), that come together in this part of the legislative code. It is common to consider, alternatively, the *Partidas* as a source of information or, conversely, as a text that seems to be completely out of line with the society that supported it—or rather did not. In other words, traditional perspectives of the *Partidas* make it difficult to understand that the *Siete Partidas* are first, foremost, and even exclusively, a body of legislation.

The most durable official text of the *Partidas* is the one transmitted by the 1555 "imperial" edition, which was perpetuated by the editor's grandson, Gregorio López de Tovar in 1567 and then reprinted many times, with or without new prologues and appendices, well into the eighteenth century. Its official character was reinstated in 1867 by the Spanish Tribunal Supremo, after the short official tenure of the 1807 text by the royal *cédula* (a kind of decree) of 1818. The *Boletín Oficial del Estado* reprinted the 1555 *Partidas*, with accompanying laws, in 1969, 1974, and 1975. The law from February 2015 also uses the 1555 edition.

The vastness of the corpus is comparable only to the number of textual issues arising from the study of the history of the textual tradition. I will always give the references according to the 1555 edition, which I will compare with the manuscripts and other editions where relevant. I will sometimes focus more specifically on particular pieces of the manuscript tradition, as I do in the chapter on friendship (Chapter 4).

The Alfonsine Era

On a couple of occasions, I have mentioned the Alfosine Era. This was how the Muslim and Jewish astronomers in the employ of King Alfonso defined the new astronomical and historical era in which they worked. The point of this era's departure was, geographically, the city of Toledo and, chronologically, the beginning of King Alfonso's rule. Although printed editions of the *Astronomical Tables* included a chart with the equivalences among the different calendars,[51] neither the astronomers nor King Alfonso himself thought that this new era would replace all the other eras. It added something new to the other calendars: it introduced new elements into the history of humankind, and, in a certain way, it challenged present and future subjects to identify those elements and to describe themselves in the light of the star alignment called the Alfonsine Era. The Alfonsine workshop—the whole world of intellectual research and production surrounding the king and summoned by him—intended to populate this era with historiographical accounts, scientific research, and poetic, visual, and musical creativity, and, perhaps more important, a powerful legislative drive that intended to change the definition of the clients of the law and their relationship with the lawgiver forever.

The existence of an Alfonsine Era is an interesting trope that figures our understanding of the meaning of our work and our interest in focusing on the Iberian Middle Ages. The Alfonsine Era has an intellectual and historical character that worked in the short term, by means of the specific events and productions of the Alfonsine rule (1252–1282), and still works in the *longue durée*, because the Alfonsine textual and intellectual products are in a constant process of critique and re-elaboration that has lasted several centuries. Quite pointedly, it still does (remember, the very recent law based on the *Partidas* mentioned above). Likewise, the Alfonsine Era had a broad geographic presence that included the newly conquered territories of the Iberian Peninsula, political influence on other Christian kingdoms of the same geographic area, and of course, the different moments of Iberian expansion in the early modern period. The *Partidas*, as it has been studied, has marked the legal history of the Americas, the Philippines, and other polities across the globe. In countries across the Americas, the process of independence during the nineteenth century was fulfilled only with the participation of the *Siete Partidas* in the process of implementation of new civil and penal codes, after the widespread *Código de Bello* from 1877 onward.[52]

During the Alfonsine Era, the *Partidas* intervened in the debates taking place in many different spaces and traditions regarding the constitution of the legal discipline. First, in the debates of the Muslim world between Persia and al-Andalus, several thinkers, including Ibn Sīnā, or Avicenna for the Latins, al-Ghazālī, and Ibn Rushd (Averroes for the Latins), questioned the degree of autonomy of the legal discipline. Second, in the debates of some Jewish intellectuals regarding not only the autonomy of the legal discipline but also the relationships between written law and oral law and the common history of both, a debate championed by the Cordovan rabbi Moshe ben Maimon (Maimonides) involved discussions between al-Andalus thinkers, the Jewish intellectuals of southern France, and others across the Mediterranean basin. Third, Alfonso's legal work also intervened in the discussions about legal science and legal codification that took place in Christian Europe in relation to the study and marginal commentary on the corpus of Roman law and the corpus of canon law. To those discussions and to those practices of glossing and compilation (from Azo of Bologna to Accursius and from Johannes Teutonicus to Raymond of Penyafort, all between the twelfth and thirteenth centuries), Alfonso offered a set of new techniques and theories of legal codification. Finally, the Alfonsine Era intervened in the relationship that many polities—including the kingdom of Aragon and many domains in France, Italy, and Germany, as well as the very kingdom of Castile—entertained with their local and particular legal regulations, for instance, with the *fueros*, customary law, or even specific regulations that had replaced broader codifications, as happened in 1251 in Barcelona, when the more universal and imperial *Liber Iudicium* was replaced by the local *Usatges de Barcelona* by order of King Jaume I. In all these senses, the location of the Iberian Middle Ages constitutes a privileged vantage point from which to understand the Middle Ages and beyond.

By far, the most important reason to choose the Alfonsine Era as a vantage point is of a theoretical character. To be sure, it provides a historical and historicist knowledge that cannot be neglected in the study of medieval law and medieval intellectual and social history in general, but it also provides us specific perspectives on a number of issues whose theoretical relevance cannot be overstated. Two of them need to be highlighted. First, the analysis of the *Partidas* and its techniques and theories of codification shows us the processes and strategies whereby a legal discipline is designed to create specific institutions. Such institutional creativity is central to understanding the ways rules of law work from scratch and how they administer power and foster methods to create (legal) subjecthood. Second, as a complex process of codification that involves not only verbal representation but also material legal text, the *Partidas* gives us special access to the formation of legal vocabularies, legal materialities, and, what is more important, what I will call in this book "legal thinking"—that is, the different processes whereby the law and the legal discipline colonize society and public, daily language.

Perplexities and Incoherences

"My speech," says the rabbi, lawyer, and doctor Moshe ben Maimon, better known as Maimonides (1138–1204), "is directed to one who has philosophized and has knowledge of the true sciences, but believes at the same time in the matters pertaining to the Law and is perplexed as to their meaning because of the uncertain terms and parables."[53] The idea of perplexity (*ḥairah*, in Arabic), implies a specific feeling of loss and disorientation in front of the law for all those who cannot avoid reading and interpreting it while philosophizing and submitting parables, metaphors, and other tropes and fictional devices to proper exegesis.[54]

In the twelfth and thirteenth centuries, perplexity was not only a feeling but also a gateway to sin. For Christian theologians, the *perplexitas conscientiae*, or perplexed conscience, means that one has located oneself in the middle of a dilemma (as Dougherty has expressed it) that will always lead toward sin—so the person confessing the dilemma to the priest needs to know the lesser sin in order to choose.[55] This idea of perplexity is less philosophical in nature, although it is connected to Maimonides's sense of perplexity by means of the fear that one will sin.

Maimonides's ideas on perplexity cannot be disentangled from the debates taking place in the Mediterranean basin on the possibility of using pagan philosophy and pagan modes of thinking in order to read and interpret the Law. Persian philosophers like Avicenna (980/370–1037/428) or al-Ghazālī (1058/450–1111/505) debated those positions in several treatises that were discussed across the Islamic world, including the Iberian Peninsula. In al-Andalus, the debate took place mostly, but not exclusively, in the Cordovan environment, in which both Maimonides and his contemporary Averroes (1126/520–1189/595) were initially active. This debate was well expressed in two works, the *Incoherence of the Philosophers*, by al-Ghazālī, and Averroes's response, *The Incoherence of the Incoherence*. These works, as well as Maimonides's *Guide for the Perplexed*, were not only widely disseminated and read but also translated into Latin, as *Destructio Philosophorum, Destructio Destructionis Philosophorum Algacelis*, and *Dux Neutrorum ac Dubitantium, seu Perplexorum*, respectively.[56]

In this book I will frequently talk about the *Siete Partidas* as *perplexing legislation*. Indeed, I contend that the practice of dead voice, according to Alfonso, is a way for him to indirectly participate in the Mediterranean debate regarding perplexity and incoherence. Instead of proposing a theory of how to interpret the Law with the collaboration of philosophy and exegesis, Alfonso goes one step ahead in order to embrace, as I will demonstrate in this book, the productive character of perplexity.

This productivity means, therefore, a specific practice of legal codification in which philosophy, fictional devices, and exegetical procedures collaborate in solidarity with the production of the Law. The combination of law, philosophy, and fiction is Alfonso X's response to his foremost challenge. Alfonso suggests a legal code that will keep its integrity over time, that cannot be altered, and whose content at the level of both the letter and the spirit of the law will be remembered.[57] This is Alfonso's main concern for dead voice, as we will see in Chapter 1, as well as for the articulation of an aesthetics of law (explored in Chapter 5 of this book) in the process of the construction of a vernacular jurisdiction (Chapter 2).

Argument and Chapters in This Book

The argument I am going to build in this book is that the response to these issues and their challenges is the deployment of a technique of codification that, using an Alfonsine expression, I call dead voice. Dead voice is the juridical institution that governs the production of legal norms and documents with the force of law. Alfonso defines "dead voice" as "writing," and so does the index to the *Partidas* prepared in 1576 by Gregorio López de Tovar to accompany the imperial edition of the *Partidas*, which was published by his grandfather, Gregorio López Madera, in 1555.

This juridical institution of dead voice, or writing, is in its turn governed by a *fictio legis*, or "fiction of the law," according to which what has been established according to the regulations of legal writing is as if it were new.[58]

As we will see in Chapter 1, this *fictio legis* has consequences for the conception of both legal writing and the temporalities of legal writing.

Dead voice is, in fact, not only writing but also a writing technique or a series of writing techniques, some of them explicit, some implicit in the code itself. I use the concept of dead voice to evince a theory—a vision—of legal codification. One of the key elements of this set of techniques is that they involve an emotional tension, a new relationship between the client of the law, whether professional or not, and the law itself. This relationship is an affective one. In other words, dead voice involves an affective set of techniques for legal codification.

To achieve this, I argue, the legislator needs to reclaim the very concept of legislation and redraw it from scratch. The result of this redrawing of the legislative techniques gives rise to what I have called perplexing legislation—that is, fighting the affect of fear to sin—by including philosophical bodies of knowledge and fictional devices as constitutive elements of the legal text.

Dead voice is about how to think about the law from affective and perplexing perspectives: the legislator uses the articulation of perplexing legislative techniques as a way to codify an affective legal system in which philosophy and fictions incorporate aesthetic devices at two levels—that of perception and Artistotelian aesthetics, on the one hand, and that of the aesthetic character of poetic and narrative or literary resources, on the other. An important part of this argument is that dead voice involves the creation of a legal aesthetics—a legislative system in which the people are responsible for the perception and integrity of the legal code. In this legal turn, which is governed by Aristotelian aesthetics, the perceptive subject, the one in charge of sensing the law and its political consequences, is *the people* itself, defined as the "sensitive soul" of the kingdom. This sensitive soul is required by law to perform both external and internal sensory operations—externally perceiving the proper work of the law in the world, and internally thinking and memorizing the full array of legal statements at both the normative and the documentary level. "Memorizing" here does not mean "to know by heart" but rather to be able to remember the ways in which the law presents itself as a law and the ways in which this law-being-law indexes the origin of sovereignty.

I contend that this sort of dead voice and legal aesthetics have the purpose of building juridical persons within a vernacular jurisdiction. The juridical person (legal subject, *persona ficta*) is the result of extending legal aesthetic responsibilities across the territory, the new political space, in a capillary way—getting to the last corner of the newly conquered regions, cities, and other locations that constitute emerging centers of power within the jurisdiction and that therefore constitute new issues in the theories and practices of jurisdiction and sovereignty.

In order to understand those issues and their political consequences, I am suggesting the concept of vernacular jurisdiction. Indeed, dead voice is a vernacular institution, a technique of codification based on the invention of a vernacular juridical language. This vernacular juridical language universalizes the legal code—dead voice itself—across the kingdom, breaking with some of the then-current legal diglossic systems, since the law and the clients of the law expressed themselves in different languages.

The final consequence of this complex argument is very clear: a piece of intellectual history, and the intellectual implications of a legal project, cannot be disentangled from the social and political implications this project has. In other words, the only way in which intellectual history can be productive is when it becomes so profoundly embedded in social transformations and political contestation that they cannot be told apart. Of course, my argument focuses mainly on the intellectual part, because I believe that the study of legal codifications has neglected some of the questions I am raising in this book.

I have divided the book into five chapters. Chapter 1, "Dead Voice," delves into the regulation of legal writing. The regulation of legal writing entails, as I argue, the configuration of legal temporalities, legal materialities, and legal subjects that are closely intertwined. I will contend that the intellectual support for all this is the creation of a legal philology—an art of production, transmission, and control of the legal material text. This legal philology and its disciplinary responsibility was held and enacted by the growingly pervasive activity and presence of those strange legal philologists who fell under the general category of notaries (and that includes many kinds of professionals). I demonstrate how unveiling the political strategies underwriting a dialectics of voice (that is, the antithetical relationship between dead voice and living voice that would call for a synthetic solution) challenges the common distinctions between oral, unwritten law, and written law. Dead voice is a response to the struggles between customary legal systems and the revolutionary drive to codify the law while maintaining juridical procedures based in living voice.

The second chapter argues that one of the central consequences of a perplexing codification based on dead voice is the production of what I call vernacular jurisdiction (which gives the chapter its title). Vernacular jurisdiction is a visible, empirical model in which sovereignty and jurisdiction collaborate in order to redefine the environment where the law applies. This is also the environment in which the process of codification becomes the agent of universalization of the Spanish vernacular as a legal technical language.

Chapter 3 is entitled "Revenant Manuscripts." This chapter argues that dead voice lives through manuscripts. These manuscripts have archival, documentary, and even literary lives that are separated from the biological lives they refer to. They are presented, submitted, exhibited, and argued in circumstances in which they perform acts. They are preserved not in one but in many archives at different times. They also configure a documentary poetics (a term that comes from Emily Steiner[59]) through which they colonize other disciplines and even common, everyday speech. In sum, revenant manuscripts produce, I contend, "legal thinking" within the vernacular jurisdiction, that is, the interpretation of experiences as legal experiences, something that fosters the colonization of society by legal language and the appropriation of other disciplines by the legal discipline.

One of the intended consequences of perplexing codifications and dead voice is, as noted earlier, the articulation of an affective regime. This affective regime is part of the legislation—the legislator inscribed it in the law *as* law. In Chapter 4, "Legislating Friendship," I focus on the Title 27 of the *Fourth Partida* that concerns legislating friendship. With the purpose of legislating friendship, the lawgiver uses philosophical corpora and fictional devices that allow him to constitute a jurisdiction and legal thinking based on an institution of nature that works because of love relations (a love, of course, juridically defined). This institutionalization of nature that works by means of love is the result of a legal fiction. This legislation of friendship is particularly important in the context of the division and repopulation of the newly conquered territories during the thirteenth century and the redefinition of the expanding vernacular jurisdiction.

The fifth chapter, "Sensitive Souls," analyzes another facet of the intended consequences of codifying the law with philosophical corpora and fictional devices. In this case, I analyze the ways in which Aristotelian aesthetics were mobilized with the purpose of redefining the concept of people. The relevant legislation defines the people as the sensitive soul of the kingdom and endows them with the aesthetic and cognitive responsibilities of perceiving, thinking, and judging the stability of the political space. This aesthetic legislation fosters what we call a politics of the soul, that is, a redefinition of the

CHAPTER ONE

Dead Voice

Handbooks on diplomatics often refer to the following mythological narrative: documents, like history, are a remedy for forgetfulness.[1] This idea is as old as written language. It would be enough to remember the crucial moment in which Socrates hit back at his interlocutor, Phaedrus, repeating King Thamus's condemnation of the invention of the arts of writing, which were presented to him by the followers of Theuth as an "elixir," or *fármakon*. For Thamus, this is only an art of forgetfulness, which justifies Socrates's saying that "you have invented an elixir not of memory, but of reminding."[2]

The notion that written culture does not guarantee memory, but only the fragmentary accumulation of reminders, constitutes a critique of the way in which the archive, and therefore power circulation in a society, keeps track of subjects, actions, and events. The archive gives the impression that within its confines one can have a glimpse of things as they have actually been.[3] However, this impression falters when we look at the profound incompleteness of the archive and at the formal presentation of many of its constitutive pieces. The archive contains reminders, bookmarks, and markers in general, along with an extremely formalized language. The impression of a complete archive also falters when we look at other archives, those that are outside the official, original definition and deployment of the archive—archives that live in performance, that live under colonial oppression, or that live in private spaces; archives that are sometimes silenced forever.[4]

The previous remarks also raise a general line of questioning: Who are the persons who populate the archives? Who are the archivists, those persons in charge of making the necessary exchanges between the objects and persons who populate the archive, and those who, on the outside, may need to know the lives in the archives, for very different purposes (including, of course, the writing of history or the writing of stories)? Who are those who produce "reminders," and under what circumstances do they do their work? What is the relationship of those persons and institutions with the institution of the legal subject? Do the archival reminders and their avatars change in any way the formation, definition, and abilities of legal subjects?

Indeed, written documents are a repository of memorable events, even if the event is as trivial as a contract. Like other recorded sources, however, they don't register the full account of more or less amorphous events. Rather, as partial reminders of concrete actions and negotiations, they shape our understanding of the events by verbalizing them. The documents also create a correspondence, an equivalence, between the material set of characteristics of the document itself and the role the event to which they refer ought to play in history. The documents also inscribe actors and agents in the archive and in history, turn them into juridical subjects, and assign them different functions, thus also creating their own narratological rules.[5] All this happens at the level of sets of events that, by means of this documentary poetics and rhetoric, become legal events. Legal events do not have a limited and continuous life—their activity is discontinuous—and do not need to coincide with the span of a biological life. Legal events—which are, as we will see, always new, always present—determine their own era, their own temporalities, and their own lives within and outside of the archive.

From the Passage of Time to Dead Voice

Indeed, for notaries and chancellors during the twelfth and thirteenth centuries, as well as for some legislators, documents were a remedy for forgetfulness.[6] This is what some documents convey in their *arengae*, or preambular addresses, in various types of *diplomata*, or charters, and in the best-known bodies of legislation. These kinds of texts needed to create the usefulness of the document in an era in which the living voice was the preferred procedural and contractual resource.[7] Whereas oral performance during trials or in the realm of the contractual has its own time—for it lasts as long as the utterance and the procedural time last—written documents create the illusion of an everlasting event.

Time is the central concept that underlies all discussions between those bodily voices and the silent voices kept in writing and on recording devices. While the former belongs in the time of the procedure, the latter prolongs this life beyond procedural time, thus proposing a different history of time. That history is the result of overlapping natural time, the time of life, the times of the trial, and the time during which the document may continue to be active as a powerful reminder of an event presenting itself as always new. All the techniques to remember things have, as their ultimate goal, to manage time, to measure it, and to submit to a specific rhythm—the rhythm of the ritual, the rhythm of the court of justice, the sacred rhythm of *cursus* and rhyme, pronunciation, liturgy, oath, and so forth.[8]

Let us look at an example from the chancellorship of Diego García (1140–1217/1218), during the kingdom of Alfonso VIII (1155 [r. 1158]–1214). Chancellor Diego García was concerned with remembrance and documentation. The following *arenga* comes from a document dated June 26, 1193, in Burgos, in which the king awards the Monastery of Oña a tax-exempt concession: "In the name of the Saint and Undivided Trinity, the Father, and the Son, and the Holy Spirit, amen. Against the many dangers of the passage of time, we have diligently armed ourselves with manuscripts [*cyrographorum*], since the mother of oblivion is antiquity, step-mothered by the slipperiness of memory, and also because those things that are being established [*statuta*] today in way of benefit might very well vanish if we do not consolidate them with a charter."[9] The elegant Latin and material accuracy of these charters bespeak an investment of talent and funds that cannot simply be dismissed as a mere formula.[10] It is true that many of the ideas contained in Diego García's document can literally be found in other *arengae* from other chancery documents throughout Europe in the Middle Ages.[11] Diego García, like other chancellors, expressed his concern with legal remembrance and with legal forgetfulness. This is why he does not talk about writing in general but instead about *chirographs*—that is, a kind of manuscript contract frequently used for private affairs.[12] By the same token, he is concerned with statutes, *statuta*—things that have been established, the resulting benefits of which must be consolidated with the help of charters. The main piece in his *arenga* is, however, that age is insidious (*uetustatis insidias*) and that if antiquity is the mother of forgetfulness, the frailty of memory is its malign stepmother (*nouerca*).

What matters in Diego García's *arenga* is the devastation caused by time on the one hand, and on the other hand, that legal writing can actually repair the decline of things that matter, in particular those that bring some sort of benefit. He uses the word *beneficio*, which may refer to a very precise notion of good deeds in exchange for services given; this kind of *beneficium* normally had an economic character and very often included enjoying plots of land for life. Against time's damages, even against the very concept of the old (*vetustus*) and the ancient (*antiquitas*), the law may impose a different time, a restorative character, an ability to consolidate the past into the present.

This set of ideas was useful for the chancellor, a major notary in charge of the production of documents.[13] The documents are also theoretical devices insofar as they inscribe in both their text and their material characteristics their intended durability, the conditions in which they were produced, or the actors who produced them and approved of them. A document is not only a *dispositio*, that is, the final disposition or norm established by the text. For the chancellor, and for the king for whom he was acting as a notary, this idea about how the legal object can control time—not only memory of things that happened—has major importance, and this is why it needs to be disseminated at the top of the document, right after the formulas of sacralization of the document itself: sacred time and legal time gather forces marking the beginning and the genesis of the disposition itself. The disposition can actually have force because of this sacralization of legal time.

This treatment of time can also be useful for the legislator. For Alfonso X there is a distinction to be made between the bodily interactions of living legal subjects and the reminders, the systems of documentation stored with the help of recording technologies, including, of course, the arts of writing. He mentions this difference at the beginning of *Partidas* 3.18, where he—perhaps echoing a distinction introduced by the law scholar and bishop Guillaume Durand (1230–1296), as Raúl Orellana suggests, but more probably following a common model in procedural law—announces that "since in previous titles we have talked about witnesses and investigations that involve a manner of proof conveyed through living voice, we are now ready to discuss all kinds of writings of all type that may be that from which any evidence of truth-finding may arise, or which involve other kinds of proofs that are called dead voice."[14]

Why was it necessary to devise the concept of dead voice? In the same section of *Partidas* 3.18 Alfonso states that "the antiquity of time is something that makes people forget past events. Therefore, it was necessary to invent writing, so that whatever was made in previous times, did not come into oblivion, and so that men would know, through writing, about the things that were established, as if they had been made anew."[15] Alfonso X and his grandfather's chancellor seem to be in absolute agreement: time has teeth, so to speak, and eats up things, facts, and figures. In order to avoid oblivion, writing became necessary. This writing is what Alfonso X calls dead voice.

There are a number of subtle innovations in the way Alfonso explains his legal perspective on writing and remembering. The most important of these innovations is the introduction of the clause, "bien como si," or "as if," to state that writing conveys established things "bien como si de nuevo fuessen fechas," "as if they had been made anew." This linguistic operator introduces a *fictio legis*, which actually serves as the buttress of the law. Whereas the document expresses a theoretical perspective on time and law, *Partidas* 3.18 regulates time by means of this *fictio legis*. Past events must be remembered by means of writing; this is certain. But the law gives an entirely new dimension to these events: writing turns them from past events into new events. This *fictio legis* turns discourse into legal enforcement.[16]

Among the things that must be remembered in the document, perhaps the most important, is language itself. Legal language and its characteristics are part of the legally established things that time may eat away. Legal language needs to be remembered by means of both documents and legislation. Legal writing relies so much on technical words, linguistic formulas, and material forms of transmission because these create the impression of continuity between legislation and documentation. Among them, the linguistic operator of the *fictio legis* is an essential linguistic device because it is the one that makes—so to speak—the miracle of law that consists in turning a presumed fact into a legal norm, right, or obligation. This device of the *fictio legis* marshals the ways in which legal writing remembers language: not only as a series of formulas, expressions, or topics but also as an army of linguistic operations that change the substance of the expression of an event into the event itself. Here we are talking about a particular, realistic turn, or, if you wish, a legal reification: discourse is turned into things and human relations that have actual uses, even if they are presented as events from the past.[17] As Yan Thomas demonstrated, this is perhaps the most important among the *opérations du droit*.[18]

The law does not refer indiscriminately to all sorts of events, but it does to those that are at the core of public and private relations among the people of the kingdom: "Above all so that disputes and agreements [*posturas*] and everything else that men undertake with one another, among themselves, are not doubted, so that they can be honored in the way they were established."[19] This legal statement presents a phenomenological approach to public and private affairs carried out by individual men and women. The events it refers to are not just any kind of events but, rather, those that, by means of the law, become the object of public and private recording: disputes, contracts, and *posturas*. The word *postura* is of singular interest. It translates the Latin word *positio*, from which the very idea of positive law springs. Here, *postura* is something that one puts forward, a gesture as much as an utterance. *Positiones*, or *posturas*, insofar as they involve an agreement, can become law, written law by means of the document—the document itself becoming, thus, a jurisprudential source. Notarial arts and compilations of documents include those kinds of sources as well as their models and jurisprudential character (the legal concept "exemplum" includes both meanings, plus that of "copy").[20] They can be found, in particular, in institutional cartularies. The way in which these cartularies compile the documentary sources, the exempla, is not narratologically neutral, because the order of the documents is presented in a modified way in order to create a coherent and cohesive narrative of the legal privileges of the institution.[21] It is, however, rare that general codifications include compilations of this kind. They normally defer to a different jurisprudential archive, to a different source of *pleytos* (judicial cases) and *posturas*. The *Third Partida*, however, presents the archive of *pleytos* and *posturas*, both as models and as jurisprudential resource, as part of the legal codification itself.

Because the document and the process of codification are in such close relationship, the general political and ethical character of the law also encompasses an ethics of creating and writing documents. Indeed, the lawgiver focuses on the ethical consequences of these texts in order to establish a link between the ethics of legal writing, its legality, and its understandability: "So much well-being stems from writings, that they are beneficial at all times, insofar as they remind of what was forgotten; they also serve the purpose of asserting whatever is carried out anew; they also show the straight path to follow what is right. It is lawful that they are made according to loyalty, and without duplicity, so that they can be properly understood, and that they are complete. This relates specifically to those actions that could bring disputes among people."[22]

When the legislator emphasizes the *derecho* (right, but also law as a discipline) and the *lealtad* (loyalty, a word that comes from Latin *legalitas*) that must drive the writing of public and private affairs, we see how the previous phenomenology of writing and everyday life turns into legal regulation. Only this type of legal writing can be deemed the origin of public and general well-being—insofar as public and general well-being are presented as legal consequences. The goal of this regulation is to configure a public and private record that can be perfectly understood. This is totally new in regard to the theoretical elements in the *arengae* from the charters, for instance, and it will help make the court of justice altogether unnecessary.

Such writings have clear criteria of intelligibility: they must be easily understandable in accordance with the laws contained in *Partidas* 1.1. In these laws, the legislator determines that laws must be written "sin punto" and "sin escatima" (without excess or lack), as well as in a language grounded on monosemy.[23] Like the laws in *Partidas* 1.1, here the legislator insists that these writings, which produce public and private well-being, must be "cumplidas" (complete), in the sense that nothing from the *postura* and the *pleyto* can be left aside or taken for granted. This completeness will mark the extraordinary repetitiveness of public and private records and documents—and, like formulas, it fosters the sense of continuity within the archive.

At first, Alfonso seems to be discussing writing in general. Indeed, he defined writing as an unqualified activity, as the one that can fight time's teeth. From a rhetorical perspective, this is an effective way to create an argument: this definition encompasses all sorts of writing, investing them all with moral character. This first definition of legal writing has a powerful cognitive effect in our understanding of the second definition, in which the legislator tends to refine or to restrict the sort of writing he intends to explore. But in the general argument, the second kind of writing—that is, legal writing—has already become part of that all-encompassing set of features of writing in general. When the lawgiver comes to make the necessary distinctions, there is already a general argument on writing: "A written document, admissible as evidence, is any instrument drawn up by the hand of the notary public of a council, or sealed with the seal of the king or that of any other authentic person, who is worthy of being believed, and great advantage is derived from it."[24]

The prologue to *Partidas* 3.18, was referring to writing in general, while in this law (*Partidas* 3.18.1), the legislator asserts the idea that *escriptura* is in fact a concrete production that may produce evidence or proof, or help in the search for the truth. Moreover, writing has a singular auctor: namely, a public scribe or notary, or any other "authentic person" whose signature or seal produces belief.

In subsequent titles and laws from this *Partida*, Alfonso delves further into his configuration of the arts of writing. It includes, of course, models of letters, formulas, forms of expression, and even names that make the association between the models and the actual archive credible. Likewise, it includes shapes, forms, materials, graphic elements, or things that include neither writing nor writing material, like seals, colors, or cords. The titles that follow *Partidas* 3.18 are specifically devoted to the agents in charge of mandating, editing, keeping, and disseminating this full universe of dead voice. The laws in these titles are in charge of creating and defining the tasks of the *authentic person* and how the authentic person is also accountable for the correctness and the truthfulness of the layers of dead voices that inundate the documentary world of private and public affairs, in particular *pleytos* and *posturas*. According to Alfonso's regulations in the *Second Partida*, the officers of the king are indeed parts of the king's body, who are sent throughout the kingdom not only to protect it by affirming the presence of the kingly jurisdiction but also, and perhaps more important, to disseminate properly created dead voice so that it becomes the fabric of present, past, and future—but, by dint of the *fictio legis* governing dead voice, always new—legal interactions (*Partidas* 2.9).

The Registry

We already know the narrative on some manuscripts of the *Siete Partidas* and the *Espéculo*: the legislator proceeded to write a legal code because the king became aware that subjects of his kingdom had been making it a practice to scratch off the surface of parchments on which laws had been recorded in order to write, as they saw fit, some other version of the law on those same parchments. This, he continued, created a situation in which law itself was undermined and the people suffered because the law resulted in the reduction of individual and collective rights and even in the entire lack thereof. Furthermore, the very concept of power as a central jurisdiction devised by the king, Alfonso X, was endangered by this practice.[25]

The narrative of the law-scratchers is not there without reason; it was far from being a commonplace. When Alfonso was crowned in 1251, he had to start a long process of confirming charters and privileges that had been previously given or confirmed by his father, Ferdinand III, or by other kings in his lineage. During the first years of his reign, noblemen, citizens, and the clergy submitted brand new documents to him in which they claimed old privileges, rights, and exemptions.[26]

There was no means by which to verify those documents' authenticity because the originals had supposedly been sent to the claim holders by kings preceding Alfonso by several generations and were kept in cartularies and other record inventories by monasteries, cities, and lordships out of the king's reach. The regular containers in those kinds of archives were not only book-shelves that held the carefully crafted cartularies, but in some of the monasteries—including those of Santa María de Carrizo, Triantos, and many others—also sometimes sacks. The interested parties did not even need to scratch the law to forge a document—it sufficed to create a new document and call it an exact copy of an original or of a copy of one. Any philologist is aware that there is no such thing as an "exact copy."[27] There was no trace of when and where the original document had been created, since the use of registry books was not yet enforced.

In the beginning, from 1252 to around 1255, the registry book was an instrument for keeping track of what a particular scribe or scrivener had produced during his professional life. The first legal code promulgated by Alfonso X, the *Fuero Real*, instituted the creation of the registry book for all public scribes.[28] Each scribe had to keep one, so that upon his death it could be collected by the king's officials and given to his successor, who could then seamlessly continue the previous scribe's labor. The book became a sort of documentary legal body that would pass from natural body to natural body, thus creating the impression that law and order outlived the frailties of biology.

The system was highly inefficient, however, because although the *substantia facti*, or substance of the act, was recorded according to notarial models, these were still lacking a legislative framework—that would only come with *Partidas* 3.18. Therefore, the style in those entries was still that of the notaries themselves. Furthermore, we know they would be under pressure from interested parties.[29] Even with the enforcement of the registry book, the law was still erasable with a parchment scraper.

The system changed around 1255. At that time, in the *Espéculo* (4.12.7), Alfonso introduced a new category of scribe, the *registrar*. The registrar was in charge of gathering the whole body of documents created by public scribes so that the king's archives could keep an authentic record of all public business.

The registrar and the registry book are two chief pillars of Alfonso's armoring of the law not only as a code or as a text but also as an incredibly efficient apparatus with a backbone of notarial arts, concepts, and subjects. With this backbone in place, the law became much more difficult to erase under the scraper. Scribes and registrars were advised to be suspicious of scratches and erasures when they examined documents and registry books (*Partidas* 3.18.111; 3.18.118–19; 3.19.12, etc.). They became experts in paleography and codicology, and they were the ones who had the authority to determine how many hands had participated in the creation of a single document, or how old the script was, or when a tear in a paper or a parchment invalidated the whole document, or whether a scratch or a cancellation had been caused by mere corrections or whether they hid a rewriting of the document or of the law (3.18.118–19).

Scribes had to work like modern textual scholars and philologists do. When they see a textual witness (let's say a manuscript of a certain poem), the Lachmannian or neo-Lachmannian philologist thinks of it as a derivative of an archetype (called Ω), from which the original (called ω) would also descend. Both the archetype and the original would be closer to perfect, with fewer variations than the textual witness, although they, archetype and original, may be induced from the different witnesses through a series of technical procedures (generally called ecdotic or stemmatic).[30] Scribes were also required to look at the document at hand as a representation of the original document from which the copies could have derived. In this sense, scribes were the ultimate gatekeepers not only of the archive, but also of its historical and genealogical integrity.

As we know, in the language of Alfonso's *Siete Partidas*, judicial research was divided between oral confessions and testimonies, what the law calls *viva voz*, or living voice, and the *voz muerta*, or dead voice, the written juridical culture, including all kinds of archival documents. The scribes were the guardians of the kingdom's dead voices.[31] Those voices do not have sound or bodily presence, but they are supposed to be permanently linked to the integrity of the kingdom. On the surface of parchment, fabric, or paper, they became instrumental in defining the relationships between the kingdom's subjects and the exercise of jurisdictional power.

Dead Skin

We should never believe a dead animal skin. Whatever is preserved within such a piece of material is just as dead as the animal itself. If one should like to record anything previously voiced by writing it on the skin, the result can only be a dead voice.

This is what the canonist and Pope Innocent IV, Sinibaldo dei Fieschi (1195 [p. 1243]–1254) claimed at some point in the first half of the thirteenth century. He was referring to the use of written documents, the parchments themselves, and their legal relevance. For Sinibaldo, there was nothing as compelling as the witness's voice—the confession—obtained through a thorough *inquisitio*, an inquest, which elicited an instant reaction. Only the physical presence of the confessing body, and the physical pressure on this body in the particular space created for interrogation, could produce the truth. The document removed this presence and erased it. Everything else could be forged. The body could not.

This is, at least, what the 1555 glossator of the *Partidas*, the president of the Council of Indies Gregorio López (1496–1560), suggests, when he quotes Innocent's words in his marginal gloss to Alfonso's law on dead voice.[32] Gregorio López was an extremely cunning and learned jurist. He was probably quoting from a reliable source—most probably an index, a compilation, or some other scholarly product.[33] Innocent's words, however, are slightly different. In fact, the pope is commenting on his predecessor's *Decretales*, in particular book 2, title 22, chapter 15.[34] There, Innocent discusses the question of who has the authority to name notaries ("Quis habeas potestatem faciendi tabelliones"). He briefly discusses the current opinions in order to determine that "nobody can name notaries beyond the pope and the emperor."[35] The following words in Sinibaldo's text are what may have confused either Gregorio López or his sources: "One must not believe a letter made out of a dead animal without some other sort of appendage."[36] What Innocent means is that the notary has the civil and metaphysical task of attaching such appendage to the dead animal skin so that it does not go against civil law and against nature. Because of the importance of the notary's task, the utmost and most extreme care must be taken in his naming—because he is, indeed, the agent of truth.

It is at this time that the notarial arts were first being widely developed and used in cities like Bologna, Paris, Orléans, and Genoa, among others. Scribes and notaries from these cities, conscious of their growing power, began to create gilds and associations during the thirteenth century.[37] They were not necessarily lawyers. Some law professors and glossators, from Accursius (1182–1263) in the thirteenth century to Gregorio López in 1555, considered that scribes—"non . . . tenetur scire iura"—were not required to know the laws.[38] To consider scribes and notaries as artists, thus far from legal experts, was a way to curb their power; a difficult task, if we consider that their art is what maintained the integrity of the archives.[39]

Sinibaldo dei Fieschi, thanks to Gregorio López, passed as a lawyer who argued against using the written document as *proof*. ("Proof" should be understood here in a broad sense: as a piece of evidence presented at trial, the deposition of a witness, or a document supporting other transactions taking place outside the courts of justice.) At any rate, he would not have been the only one to do so. Jurists from the thirteenth and fourteenth centuries considered that those documents had acquired a performative power so strong that they could be deemed *chartae miraculosae* (miraculous documents) and *supernaturalis* (supernatural)—for instance, as Sinibaldo himself states, they could turn an infamous person into somebody reputable.[40] Oftentimes, these lawyers would assert that such documents and their use were to be classified as both *contra natura* and *contra iure*.[41] It is not a coincidence that in some narratives on diabolical pacts written during the thirteenth century, the contract between the devil and the shadowless soul-seller is considered to be a chirograph that ended up being recovered by the Virgin and destroyed as a false and useless proof lacking any notarial validity.[42] Civil legal scholars from Azo of Bologna (fl. 1150–1230) to the school known as *mos italicus* (the Italian way) of Bartolus of Saxoferrato (1313–1357) and Baldus de Ubaldis (1327–1400) still argued against the legitimacy of the written parchment as proof well into the fourteenth century.[43] The reason was simple: the art of forgery was, at least, as perfectly designed as the art of letter writing.

The criticisms against dead voice provoked different kinds of responses; however, the fact remained that no legal transaction could make do with only *vivae voces*, living voices. Without written support—the *fármakon* evoked by Plato, a poison as much as a medication—the procedural law would self-destruct. This is why documentary handbooks and the notarial arts blossomed in the thirteenth century, among them, the imperial notary, law scholar, and judge Rainerius of Perusa's *Ars notariae*, around 1235; the notary Salatiel's (d. 1280) *Ars notariae* of 1240; the Bolognese jurist Rolandino de'Passeggeri's (d. 1300) *Summa Totius Artis Notarie*, around 1255; and the *Speculum iudiciale* of 1271, by Guillaume Durand, which was reedited in 1296.[44] These texts were instrumental in the creation of the typology and models for legal documents and became a source of formulas for the chancelleries of many administrations throughout Europe. In their attempt to systematize the field, these notarial arts tried to control the *miraculous* and *supernatural* of the dead voice and restrict it to a series of elements and objects that would turn the dead voice into something we, tongue in cheek, can call voice preserve, or mummified voice.

Rainerius, Salatiel, Rolandino, and Durand were well aware that although a typology of documents was a means of channeling public voices, it was an insufficient instrument for restraining all the material issues encompassed by dead voice. For this reason, Rolandino, for example, deployed in chapter 10 of his *Summa* a relatively imperfect system for detecting document forgery and preventing it.

Some parts of Alfonso's *Third Partida*—especially Title 18, where the code regulates the material problems concerning dead voice—were drawn from these works, particularly Rolandino's *Summa*, and later versions of the same *Partida*, were perhaps drawn from Durand's first edition of the *Speculum*, or, as I said before, from a common model.[45] Alfonso, however, was by no means the conventional compiler: he recycled whatever he was able to get his hands on in order to make it work for his particular purposes, erasing all traces of his sources afterward.

There is something more important: the notarial treatises were scholarly suggestions for a plausible typology of letter and document writing. Alfonso's *Third Partida,* instead, was the law of the kingdom. Dead voice therefore was a legal institution working de jure and de facto, and not merely a theoretical suggestion or the construction of some unspecific condition of possibility.

Authentica Persona

The link connecting dead voice and the usability of the written document lies in the concept of *authentica persona* invoked by Alfonso in *Partidas* 3.18. This notion is uncommon and only occasionally appears in some clerical writings from the Middle Ages. The expression usually indicates the capacity of an ecclesiastical hierarchy to provide credentials in order to be represented elsewhere by somebody else—a proxy. In this sense, *authentica persona* is the ultimate source of authority regarding a given *scriptura*. Whereas for earlier authors such as Arnulf of Reims (tenth century), the notion underscores a collective and collegiate authority whose legal force is represented by the totality of their signatures, for later authors like Eudes of Sully (late twelfth century), *authentica persona*, as with Alfonso, points to an individual.[46] In other words, over time, the notarial idea of an *authentic person* became an individual rather than a collective source of authority or authenticity.

Rolandino de' Passeggeri expands the notion of *persona authentica* with purposes that exceed the notarial realm. Late in his work, he began to make this expansion by defining the very concept of *persona*. At the end of the

Summa, he added a short treatise, *De Notulis*, which he originally dedicated to the *notula* as the clause that authenticates a particular contract. Here, Rolandino deems it necessary to define "person" by establishing the different characteristics of the *juridical person* (the legal varieties of sex; conception, whether inside or outside wedlock; condition: free or slave; authority and power; filiation; and age).[47] Moreover, Rolandino defines the concept of authentic person in order to include those functions in charge of transferring the public record to make it available wherever it could or should be enforced, with particular attention to the key institution of the *exemplificatio*, that is, the copy (or in Spanish, *traslado*) of the document.[48]

Persona authentica or *authentica persona*, depending on the particular source, was the institution that granted the creation of a public person. By doing so, the institution established the *form*, the *mask*, that could be exhibited before and within the law.[49] This public person was the artificial result of the process of purification, by way of removal, of physical and biological conditions from the legal subject; separating the natural person and removing it from the actor called legal subject or artificial person (*persona ficta*) would allow somebody to acquire a presence within the spaces and times, the stages, where one becomes visible in public existence ruled by the empire of the law.[50] This kind of purification is one of the strategies of legal subjectivity under sovereign power—that is, kingly power.

To achieve this purification, the legal language used, among other strategies, the *census* and the verb *censeo*, which in the procedural language conveys the way in which a private individual must present him or herself in the public registries.[51] The public registry, therefore, became a public costume, the process of modification and accommodation of the individual to the regime of *authenticity* regulated by the law. If we conceptualize it with Erving Goffman's sociological and anthropological theory, we could say that the public registry is where the difference between performance and existence becomes erased: in the registry, all persons are juridical persons.[52] This notarial and public idea of *persona authentica*, which is linked to the public registry, is the one sported by Alfonso in his *Third Partida*.[53]

Alfonso, in turn, complicated the definition of *persona*. The strictly notarial issue examined by Rolandino in both chapter 10 of his *Summa* and chapter 3 of his *De Notulis* ("De personis et personarum divisionibus," On persons and kind of persons) becomes a broader problem in Alfonso's *Partidas*. Alfonso, of course, defined the juridical person in the notarial and procedural realms. Furthermore, Alfonso's work entailed a permanent performance of the "public" person and a permanent hermeneutics of this public disguise or public mask of the individual. Indeed, in the prologue to *Partidas* 7.33, Alfonso reminds the readers that "in every single one of the seven parts of this book we talk about the persons of people [*personas de los hombres*] and their actions," and that this interest in the legal subject, and not in the natural person, is what makes the reinterpretation of language necessary.[54]

This particular attitude is central to the kind of codification encompassed by the *Partidas* inasmuch as the resulting code compiles not only the laws that must be enforced but also the doctrine and theory of that law and the constitutional theories of power and power relations—which in Alfonso's lexicon is stated as *señorío*, or lordship, a synonym of jurisdiction. The precise system devised by Alfonso can be understood as a multifaceted form of redefining the person in front of the different fields in which the law redescribes public life: in the face of clerical and ecclesiastic powers and structures (*Partidas* 1, 4, and 7), in the political and administrative realm (*Partidas* 2), from a natural legal perspective undergirding all sorts of alliances (*Partidas* 4), as a notarial and procedural person (*Partidas* 3), in the face of economic exchanges, contracts, and the like (*Partidas* 5), in the rhythmic-copulative regime of succession (*Partidas* 6),[55] or as a penal subject (*Partidas* 7). Among these redefinitions of *person*, however, *persona authentica* stands out because it is the one that pervades the archive, the one that actually populates the archival construction of the kingdom, not only synchronically but, more importantly, diachronically, for the *authentic person* is also what remains as the truthfulness of a public or private document.

One could wonder how *persona authentica* compares to, and eventually differs from, the well-known principle of authority, or *auctoritas. Persona authentica* is an institution that produces and multiplies presence (the presence of authority, perhaps), since instead of pointing centripetally to the *fons et origo* of authority, it allows and even requires the presence of authority to arrive, like capillary circulation, at the furthest ends of society in both space and time.[56]

What is at stake is the production of presence of the *persona authentica*.[57] Such a presence concentrates the heuristic and hermeneutic issues encompassed by dead voice. The *persona authentica* is the material and formal processes whereby a juridical person can replace a bodily, biological person with documents. The displacement from *bodily* to *juridical* is what makes the redefinition of *person* necessary. Such redefinition takes place within the law and its material requirements.

The regulations from the *Third Partida* produce the presence of both the *authentic person*, as the repository of public truth, and the person, as the subject of law and its truth. This presence is produced for the clients of the law: they are like walking archives that carry the documents with them, in their hands, on their bodies. And so we see what they do when we read some of the dorsal notes or protocols in which the notaries explain how and why a document had to be copied—as we will see in Chapter 3.

Title 18 of the *Third Partida* records a typology of privileges and letters. In addition, it performs an exploration of the existing archives to draw particular cases from them, with names and last names, to serve as models for future writings. It should not be confused with a jurisprudential archive, where the content and the sentence are at the forefront of the project. This is pure form. In addition to general models, written on behalf of "*fulano* and *fulano*" (the Arabic indefinite pronoun used in the Spanish vernacular to refer to "someone" and used in other notarial compilations),[58] Alfonso also uses the archives and the books from the register to demonstrate the extent to which form can populate the archive with authentic persons.[59] This part of the law is not given as a general, cold account of raw materials. Instead, Alfonso sets in motion disembodied individuals that become, by dint of their presence in the legislation, authoritative dead voices, cases in which the proof has been completed and truth has been established ("cumplida la prueua e creyda la carta," *Partidas* 3.20, prologue). The code presents the material objects once they have been completed and tried by time, once they have the force of law and can become legal doctrine.

Effects of Form

Insofar as Title 18 contains a typology of what falls within the limits of the privilege and the letter, it remains on the positive side of the archive and thus expresses what the archive actually contains—or contained. The law, however, is larger than the empirical manifestation of the archive. The law explores the negative side of the archive when, by investigating the aim and scope of forgery and falsehood, it states the necessarily hypomnemic character of the archive.[60] The archival hypomnesia amounts to acknowledging that not all kinds of written records can become a part of the archive—not all of them are memorable. This negativity is a form of productivity—it buttresses the limits of the archive.

In its negativity, in hindering the archiving of some written objects, the law becomes a topology of the *persona authentica*. This topology is like a magnifying glass to help the lawyer in the process of dissecting privacy, in looking closer to unrecorded voice, a voice that can be considered neither dead nor alive, a hypothetical voice created and construed by undefined natural persons acting in their own private spaces, with no intentional relationship to the public realm of documentation. The law, then, abandons the encodable territory of the letter or the document in general in order to exclude what "persons write in their private notebooks" (*Partidas* 3.18.121), trying to determine the reasons why, in those private records, an individual would chiefly register false facts and figures, if they are indeed false, or at least irrelevant. Those private accounts include lists, notebooks, quires, leaves, and other writing materials that the law has painstakingly defined from the beginning of *Partidas* 3.18.

Private accounts, however, also include apparently alive voices that convey what people are able to remember, how they remember it, and how they tell it. If the *persona authentica* is a public institution that produces presence, the private account, or the *libro de memoria*, as well as personal narratives, *cancel* public presence. Because they fall outside the archive, they cannot be considered *testimonial*, they are not witnesses—not even textual witnesses. This sort of *memory*, as revealed by the law, can never create an imbalance within the archive inasmuch as form protects the archive. The effect of form glues the hypomnemic archive together. Form is exactly what privacy and private memory lack: if the archive is form and its effect, what lies outside of it is lack of form.

The effect of form extends a protective armor on *authenticity* and *juridical persona*. Effect of form is dead voice itself. That's why Titles 18 to 21 of the *Third Partida* are so intensely concerned with materials, colors, metals, and seals—the whole and precise art of producing a document, or, in other words, protecting the physical integrity of the written document. The title is heavily interested in controlling the process by which each document becomes a *persona*—and hence by dint of form the archive explores the trope of anthropomorphism. Anthropomorphism also has another Greek name, prosopopoeia, from πρόσωπον, which is translated in Latin as *persona*.

Barbara Johnson considers that "to use an anthropomorphism is to treat as *known* what the properties of the human are."[61] I would venture to say that the *Third Partida* uses anthropomorphism in order to define the properties of the person before and within the law. In this case prosopopoeia is indeed a trope—a change of direction in which pieces from the archive are considered to be metonymies of persons. The tropological qualities allow for the creation of moral relations (*bondades* and *noblezas* in Alfonso's vocabulary) between the person and the authenticated document informed by the descriptive power of the law.

Anthropomorphism as a trope, however, is quite special in Alfonso.[62] I would call this trope not merely or generally anthropomorphism but, rather, *andromorphism*. This other change of direction is a crucial thesis concerning the processes that regulate the archiving of the memory of the kingdom. The trope does not simply personify the objects in the legal topology of *juridical authentic person* and the dead voice: it originates in a male version of the document, and it creates the authentic person conceived as *male* only. The legal code only includes documents and contracts signed for or by men, and the whole theory of law codified in the *Partidas* explicitly excludes women as agents in legal transactions with the sole exception of two laws that use the female name Urraca (*Partidas* 3.18.95–96).[63] Urraca also happens to be a royal name, that of Urraca I of León (1081–1126), whose existence is linked to the production and confirmation of documents by her own hand, as represented in the manuscript known as Tumbo A.[64]

The andromorphism of the *persona authentica* is furthermore related to the models set in motion by Alfonso for monarchical central jurisdiction, especially as they appear in the *Second Partida*, the one concerning political and social law, which is written from the standpoint of administrative law. The *Segunda Partida* explores the king's political body and his *oikos* (household), buttressing the kind of modification of the monarchical power theorized in the constitutional and jurisdictional sections of the law. This political body is both secular and male, and no expression of the monarchical voice can be interpreted as a female actor, agent, or counterpart. The monarchical presence throughout the jurisdictional space is consistently masculine. This entails a systematic relocation of the king's body across the geography of the kingdom: the law creates the *men* that concentrically cover the whole geography on behalf of the king. These men are tropologically created in two senses. The first tropological sense of this creation is moral: the king's presence can be produced only by men who have a precise set of *noblezas* and *bondades*, the virtues that each law defines and describes.[65] The second tropological sense is rhetorical: those men are the king's voice and body by means of spatial contiguity or metonymy.[66]

Voices

There is a specific dialectics of the dead voice. In the legal text, dead voice is a second-degree metaphor. It comes after the founding metaphor of the living voice. The legislator indicates that after having dealt with living voices, he will now undertake the task of regulating legal writing, that is, dead voice.

Living voices, *vivae voces*, can only be heard as they "flash in a moment of danger."[67] Afterward, it can be argued, they can only be perceived insofar as they become *dead voice*. When this happens, it is not unproblematic: the quicksilver of living voice that figures in the legislation is the vast array of inquisitorial, sacramental (as in the sacrament of confession, or as in oaths taken before testifying), juridical, or otherwise analytical systems of interrogation, which are codified in Titles 16 and 17 of the *Third Partida*.[68] Systems of interrogation in the inquisitorial model are not intended to obtain the truth but rather a truth that is bound to the public matter that set the inquest in motion in the first place. Interrogation is thorough because it has a point, a particular space, as well as defined interlocutors. Inquisitors' manuals, from Bernard Gui (1261–1331) to Nicholas Eymerich (1316–1399) and Fernando de Valdés (1483–1568) explain how prisoners should be prevented from producing confessions and testimonials and that, to that end, they should not have any kind of writing instrument and they should never talk to anybody, either outside their cells or to their inquisitors.[69]

The genealogy of the expression "living voice" is relevant because it cannot fail to invoke the presence of dead voice. Living voice has been identified with oral communication, while dead voice has been frequently considered as the opposite, as written communication.[70] Such opposition is debatable. I would rather argue that living voice and dead voice are involved in a complex mesh of political and legal strategies that ultimately vie for the implementation of dead voice—something that, as we have seen, was subject to debate both in civil and in canon law. This mesh of political strategies can be presented as a dialectical relationship.

This strategic dialectic leads to a productive synthesis of the conditions of possibility of both kinds of voices. This dialectic is marked by a double anxiety. On the one hand, there is a residual fear of losing the living voice as a juridical resource, because living voice is linked to biological life. On the other hand, we can perceive the fear that dead voice may actually be unable to convey the content of the living voice, even while it claims to preserve it

beyond the limits of biological lives. The conservative and productive character of this dialectic resides in the ways in which dead voice can contribute to
the dissemination and archivability of living voice, without living voice's losing its character, and it resides in the way in which living voice can constitute
an epistemological device for the hermeneutics and regime for understanding
dead voice. As we will see, Alfonso's *Partidas* exploit the productiveness of
this strategic dialectics—of which we will now trace a short genealogy.

One of the genealogical lines of the concept of living voice is tightly
connected to the histories of Christianity and Judaism. Moreover, this genealogical line is closely entwined with the development of methods for the
dissemination of the doctrine that include sermons and preaching, public
readings, and commentaries. Finally, there is a clear affinity between living
voice and the inquisitorial method and its development.

We can begin by talking about the first line of Paul of Tarso's concerns
in regard to the reception of his own letters. They certainly came from his
pen, and they did reproduce concepts, ideas, and doctrinal points that he had
already developed through conversations and sermons. On the one hand, he
fears that what he said had vanished right after he closed his mouth, but he
also fears that, once he closed his mouth and the communication could only
continue in writing, the audience to whom the letters were read aloud may
have felt that these written rolls were "heavy" and "strong" (βαρειαι και
ισχυραι; 2 Corinthians 10.10), to the point that they could even terrorize the
audience (μη δοξω ως αν εκφοβειν υμας δια των επιστολων; Jerome
used the verb *terrere* to translate εκφοβειν; 2 Corinthians 10.9). Paul does
not want to produce such written terror. As he said at the beginning of the
letter, in chapter 3, these are not letters written with mere ink on paper or on
clay tablets but rather directly inscribed with the spirit of the living God in
the flesh of the heart.[71]

In his letter to the Galatians, Paul expressed his desire to change his
voice. He wished that such a change would make his audience understand
the profound transformations in the new system of alliances inscribed in the
new Christian law—like, for instance, the substitution of the bodily, fleshly,
ink-like circumcision with a spiritual rebirth through baptism.

Paul does not explain what he understands as voice change. More than
three hundred years later, Jerome of Stridon (347–420), who had already
translated Paul's letters into Latin, wrote a long commentary to the apostle's
epistles. Jerome considers that Paul's voice change is a metaphor and that for
Paul it means the desire to play written texts against living voice in a free

manner, in a constant back and forth in which text and voice productively feed each other's meaning and pragmatic aspects. Jerome thinks that reading those letters is hugely beneficial, and that it would be even better if the reading could be counterpointed with the readers' commentary and instruction:

> *4.20. How I wish I could be with you now and change my voice, because I am confused by you.* Divine Scripture is edifying even when read, but it is much more profitable if it goes from written characters on a page to an audible voice, with the one teaching through an epistle giving instruction to listeners as if he were there in person. The living voice has great power. It resonates from the mouth of its author and is delivered with that characteristic intonation with which it was generated in his heart. The Apostle is aware that speech is more persuasive when addressed to those present, and he longs to turn the epistolary voice, the voice confined within written characters, into actual presence and use live speech (which is more expedient) to lead those who had been seduced into error back to the truth.[72]

Jerome was not the inventor of the expression "living voice" or *vox viva*, but he invested this expression with new strength when he put it in relation to Paul's desire to change his voice. This new strength is the acknowledgment of the relative fixedness of the written text of the letters. It is also an acknowledgment that living voice, which is synchronous with the oral performance of the written object, is not a by-product of the same written object, which can be dismissed as secondary or more fragile. Living voice, on the contrary, is what facilitated the doctrine's and the law's existence in the present, thus preventing the letter from becoming a heavy thing that inspires terror.

The idea of mutual need between the written text and the living voice can be found in other authors, like the Greek physician Galen (129–ca. 215) and the Hispano-Roman rhetorician Quintilian (35–100). They use the concept of living voice to refer to bodies of knowledge that must be transmitted from master to pupil but are hard to convey only in writing. Loveday Alexander thought that this position from such authors revealed a certain skepticism regarding the powers of writing. I would contest the ascription of skepticism, though. In my view, these authors convey only the material insufficiency of writing, or better yet, a certain kind of pedagogical literacy that involves the

necessary collaboration between written text and living voice—a collaboration that can better be explained with the notion of pedagogical interactivity,
a certain polyphony that includes dead and living voices in the transmission
of an art or set of techniques.

Does this polyphonic collaboration between living and dead voice have
any juridical usefulness? The church father and bishop Papias of Hierapolis
(ca. 70–163) took upon himself the task of finding out whether it was possible
to establish a network of individuals who could witness to the accuracy of
the narratives contained in the gospels regarding the life of Christ, particularly about his passion and death. To do so, he set in motion an inquisition
in which he established a series of interrogations that follow patterns similar
to those used by judicial magistrates.

In his *inquisitio*, he determined that there were three kinds of sources.
In the first place, there was a common memory that ran in oral traditions,
which he called "the voice of the ancients," or τος τῶν πρεσβυτέρων
λόγος. There is a second sort of source that cannot be considered oral tradition, because of its specific vivacity, and it is something that arises from the
dialogism that takes place as part of the inquisitorial system itself; he called
this other source "living voice," or ζώση φωνῆ. The third kind of source is
also contingent on the investigation and the result of specific knowledge that
he deemed to be fruitful for the research—he called this third source "surviving voice," or μενούση φωνῆ. Papias became interested in everything, but
those two kinds of voices, the living voice and the surviving voice, seemed to
him more useful than the λόγος (authoritative discourse would be a good
translation in this case) alone, and he put them at the top of his juridical
inquest. He did not doubt the gospels—on the contrary, he took them as the
substance of the juridical and doctrinal body. But he wanted to know how
to reconstruct the network of those who witnessed whether this legal body
was written and transmitted in the correct ways. What he intended to do
was, in the end, reestablish the links of faithfulness between dead voice (the
written law) and both living and surviving voices, which would vouch for the
continuation of legal truth across biological lives.

Again, the dialectics of voice is that of a collaboration, or an exchange,
that tends to preserve something in an interactive manner. As a part of this
dialectical strategy there is a surplus of truthfulness associated with the concept of voice, be it (as we see in Papias) living or surviving.

This strategical dialectic of voice is not absent from Roman law. It occurs in a passage heavily commented on by medieval scholars in Justinian's

Novellae 73. Originally, Justinian compiled laws and edicts from and for the eastern Roman Empire. *Novellae* 73.3 records an Armenian jurisprudential case that acknowledges the possibility that documents submitted for a process lack sufficient credibility because of their material conditions—for instance, cases in which scripts, calligraphies, and *usus scribendi* diverge. In those cases, it would be preferable to pay heed to ζώσης λεγόμενα φωνῆς, that is, to "that that we call living voice."[73]

Medieval glossators to the Latin version of this *Novella* 73.13, and in particular the gloss "cum iureiurando," established a series of limitations to this general precedence of the *vox viva* over the *vox mortua*, or dead voice. Indeed, the glossator (there is no specific glossator attributed, but it could have been Azo of Bologna, the main source for Accursius's *Glossa Ordinaria*) preferred to look at the mutual collaboration between living voice and dead voice as an enmeshed and complex procedure to determine truth and pinpoint forgeries and falsities in general.

Living voice does not point to a mere distinction between orality and writing—although such a distinction may facilitate a working hierarchy. Even though scholars from Jean-Philippe Lévy onward have claimed the existence of a hierarchy of proofs, it would rather seem that living voice and its dialectical correlate dead voice are in a much more horizontal relationship of collaboration.[74] It is by the confluence of both that the sources we are considering build not only the integrity of the juridical voice but also, by this same means, the very constitution of the juridical person in its integrity also.

Also in some Jewish juridical sources there is a question about the perplexities caused by the existence of a living voice that does not correspond to either written law or oral traditions. For Maimonides, living voice has a specific inherent frailty that he addressed. While he was living in Fustat, Egypt, Maimonides wrote, in Hebrew (unlike most of his work, which was written in Arabic), his great juridical contribution, known as *Mishne Torah*. Writing it in Hebrew was a difficult problem to undertake, given the dispersion of the people of Israel. Even in the era of the geonim, the law scholars of the previous generation, Talmudic Aramaic was already a nearly extinct language—and it was the task of the geonim to develop the Mishnaic Hebrew.

Now, reproducing Mishnaic Hebrew already looked like an infraction of the founding principle of the Mishna—its orality. The Mishna is, above anything else, living voice. In the narrative offered by Maimonides at the top of his *Mishne Torah*, he distinguishes oral from written law. Maimonides's thesis is that both sorts of law originate on the same day, at the same time, in the very same godly utterance. In other words, there is a law that was born as written law, and there is another law that was born as oral, spoken law. Each of these legal corpora sports its own legal mark that establishes its materiality: one of them is de jure written in the same way the other one is de jure oral. Writing the oral law seems, therefore, an infraction of the juridical revelation that took place on Mount Sinai—not a minor infraction. Maimonides points to all these considerations at the time he is pressing his pen on top of the writing material he is using, knowing that he is already breaking the law.

Maimonides's first task was to devise the genealogical line that keeps the integrity of the spoken law, or *Torah shebe'al-peh*. Written law had been written by Moses himself and could be consulted at any time in the Torah. But how could one be certain about the exactness of the spoken word, and therefore of the mitzvot, or commandments? The only possible way to establish this exactness was to describe the chain of living voices in charge of authoritatively keeping and disseminating the content of the spoken law. Maimonides could keep track of the different genealogical sequences that secured, in time, the exactness of the legal corpus.

It begins with Moses's transmitting the spoken law to his three pupils, Eleazar, Pinchas, and Joshua. Maimonides needs to stop about 189 (CE), the moment in which Rabbenu HaQadosh, also known as Judah the Prince, compiled in written form what years later would be known as *Mishna*. Here, Maimonides wonders: "Why did Rabbenu Hakadosh make [such an innovation] instead of perpetuating the status quo? Because he saw the students becoming fewer, new difficulties constantly arising, the Roman Empire spreading itself throughout the world and becoming more powerful, and the Jewish people wandering and becoming dispersed to the far ends of the world. [Therefore,] he composed a single text that would be available to everyone, so that it could be studied quickly and would not be forgotten. Throughout his entire life, he and his court taught the *Mishnah* to the masses."[75]

Maimonides introduces two variables to the relationship between the living voices of the oral law and the process of writing of this living voice. On the one hand, it has to do with the danger already perceived by Rabbenu HaQadosh, which can be understood as the anxiety of a double diaspora evoked by David Wacks:[76] not only the Jewish diaspora from Zion but also the diaspora of all the Jews from the places where they first settled and enforced the law after the original diaspora. This double diaspora is Maimonides's own diaspora: not just a Jew in his native al-Andalus but now, also, a Jewish Andalusi in Egypt. This fear in regard to the frailty of the law, a prediction or a preemptive anxiety for Rabbenu HaQadosh, was a vibrant reality for Maimonides.

The second variable is related to Maimonides's ambition to become a universal rabbi: he intends to unify the juridical and theological fragmentation he perceives among Jewish people across the world. Rabbenu HaQadosh was able to attempt this unification for the first time, allowing for the transmission of the spoken law to break the narrow limits of orality, in order to communicate it to the masses. Maimonides found this ambition to be admirable; it is perhaps what inspired his attempt to become a global master; even his *Guide for the Perplexed* was first a serialized work, sent in installments to be read by his pupil in Aleppo, Joseph ben Judah. In this serialized production, the living voice of the master is transmitted in writing as a dead voice that will become new again once pronounced, used, learned, and enforced.

The dialectics of living and dead voice is maybe one of the most productive strategies for the creation and dissemination of juridical language and legal thinking. The titles that precede *Partidas* 3.18 are not only about living voice but, more precisely, about the dialectal productivity of living voice— that is, about how to funnel living voice into the procedural system guaranteed by the archivability and theoretically fixed nature of dead voice.

This dialectics of voice pervades the construction of the *Third Partida*. It sets the rules for the system of relations between *authentic persons*—those in whom the regime of truth is inherent—and other legal subjects at the moment they become legal subjects (for instance, the trial). It is in this dialectical instant that clients of the law negotiate and learn to become juridical persons and to express themselves in the spaces, times, and language established by the legislative code.

Maybe this dynamic can be better perceived in laws like *Partidas* 3.16.26, which regulates the interactions and records that produce the witness deposition. After taking the oath according to the Spanish custom (*Partidas* 3.16.25), the judge must take the witnesses, one by one, to a separate space, away from the rest of the parties involved, with only the company of a learned notary (*algunt escribano entendido*). In that space, what is crucial is the affective environment; indeed, the law regulates how the judge must listen to the witness—very calmly, or *mansamente* (which is an adverb that can also translate as "meekly"), in the sense that the judge's countenance must inspire peace of mind, absolute absence of antagonism. Likewise, the judge must listen to the witness without interrupting him or her while looking straight at his or her face, fully engaged with the witness. It is in these precise and favorable conditions of controlled emotions that the witness can now speak.

Living voice, in this law, cannot be a unidirectional experience. After the witness has finished explaining his truth, the law acknowledges the deep gap that exists between witnessing, deposition, and even confession, on the one hand, and the correct understanding on the part of the judge. Of course, the spoken word comes accompanied by a pragmatic experience that is irreproducible in writing, which no notary could repeat as a verbal discourse. Likewise, such experience is an often agrammatical articulation in which the witness is likely bound to testify in solecisms, imprecisions, syntactic and semantic inaccuracy, and so on, no matter how peaceful and emotionally stable the conditions are in which the deposition takes place. Living voice, because it is alive, is always raw and therefore it needs to be processed, to be edited. But in order to proceed to this edition, the judge must then take the word. The law explains it in a rather theatrical way, using direct speech to allow either the judge or the notary to speak in the first person:

> "And now listen to me, for I wish you to hear if I understand you well," and he should then repeat what the witness stated. If he remembers what he said, the judge should immediately cause it to be written down, or should himself do so, well and faithfully, so that nothing may be either omitted or added, and after all this has been done, he should cause it to be read to the witness, and if the latter thinks that it is correct, he should admit it. Where he sees that there is anything to correct, this should immediately be done, and after everything has been corrected, the judge should cause the testimony to be read to the witness, and if the witness thinks that it is correct he should say so. And he who takes the testimony of the witness, who says that he is familiar with the facts, should ask him how he knows them, making him state in what way he ascertains them, whether by sight, hearing, or belief, and whichever way he mentions, the judge should cause to be recorded.[77]

There is a complex process of grammaticalization going on, a negotiation between the judge, the notary, and the witness, in order to find not only the right meaning (and therefore the truth) but also the right way to put it in its final written form. Dead voice comes only after a process of refinement and purification of the first instances of expression. It is the result of one living voice in close interaction of several living voices that collaborate to achieve the terms in which this negotiation can become an archivable object usable as proof—and as a future act to be retrieved and made new.

The dialectics of voice shows its productivity: the power of the living voice, the *magna vim* Paul and Jerome point to, becomes aptly tamed by those in charge of making procedural sense of it and reducing it to grammaticality, guaranteeing its survival and its legal usability once transformed into authentic dead voice.

Traslado

The act of transcribing a living voice shrouded the particularity of that voice through a system of rhetorical devices. The voice was recorded in shorthand by stenographers, scribes, and scriveners, and only then, if at all, were the resulting documents resolved. The shorthand became the extremely large hand of the law, the *secular arm*—the process became regulated in *Partidas* 3.17 in the title devoted to the inquest, or *pesquisa regia*.[78] This was called, in the Spanish bureaucratic language, the *traslado*, an actual translation from shorthand to legible writing, from wax to paper.[79] Of course, it is a translation from living voice to dead voice, from the agrammatical expression of the particular person being interrogated to the perfectly grammatical, rhetorical, formulaic, and formal expression of the *persona authentica*. Juridical transactions look so much alike because of the *traslado*: it simultaneously multiplies and unifies. In order to read these living voices, the researcher must, above all, clean away the remainders of the *persona authentica* who produced their archival form and material. Its being mainly form keeps the integrity of the archive and prevents the private from mixing with the public, the *personae authenticae* from mixing with those who are not. The archive is an *authentication machine*.

This system of protection could be conceptualized as the process by which the materialities of communication become public. This *becoming public* is a radical transformation of the means that allow for communication between individual, private persons, and the public realm, the *authenticae personae*.

The archives are much more than the space of *commencement* and *commandement* of which Jacques Derrida speaks. The production, location, and administration of these spaces are a dialectical set of experiences, or, put more metaphorically, the production of a battlefield. In thirteenth- and especially fourteenth-century Castile (although the legal code always reads *Spain*), the battlefield included the king, the nobility, and above all, cities as the emerging powers that were simultaneously supportive of the king and antagonistic to the kind of political and administrative organization his kingdom represented. Ultimately, the radical transformation of the jurisdiction promoted by and defined in the *Partidas* was the matter at stake. The *Partidas* built a monarchical central jurisdiction, or better yet, a concentric one.

Concentric jurisdiction explains the complex system of administration created by both the *Second* and the *Third Partidas*: they produced the spaces, the material objects, and the persons that are metonymies of the king. As the spaces under the king's jurisdiction were located further away from the royal chamber, so the officers, archives, and *authenticae personae* grew in number. These authentic persons also produced jurisdictional frontiers and pointed to spaces outside the royal, concentric jurisdiction. They are also the spaces frequently referenced by the apparatuses in the margins of new editions of the *Partidas*, from Muslim spaces in the medieval editions, to spaces of conquest in the early modern editions, to the integrity of the country in different modern editions from 1807 to 1964, to the autonomous regions in present-day editions and *leyes de acompañamiento* (accompanying laws).

The collaborations between dead voice and living voice constitute a central technique for the construction of the juridical person. This collaboration evinces the strategies through which legal language, legal writing, and legal spaces constitute the affective regime in which the juridical person can exist. This logical world of the law is the ecosystem of the juridical person.

CHAPTER TWO

Vernacular Jurisdiction

At the beginning of his *Life of Saint Dominic of Silos*, Gonzalo de Berceo (ca. 1198–ca. 1264), the poet, notary to the abbot, and secular cleric of the Monastery of San Millán de la Cogolla, writes the following lines:[1]

> Quiero fer una prosa en román paladino,
> En qual suele el pueblo fablar a su vecino,
> Ca non so tan letrado por fer otro latino:
> Bien valdrá, como creo, un vaso de bon vino.
> (I will compose a poem in the plain language
> Used by the people for speaking to their neighbors,
> For I am not so learned as to create another text in Latin.
> I believe it will indeed be worth a glass of wine.)[2]

What did he mean by saying that he wasn't literate enough to write another piece in Latin? First of all, he meant that there was already one Latin life of the saint, the one he probably got inspiration from, written by a monk called Grimaldus some time in the late eleventh century. Here, he declares that he does not intend to compete in Latin with an extant and perfectly authoritative life of the saint. Obviously, Berceo was "literate" enough to understand written Latin—and his use of the Latin sources for his own poetic work does not leave any doubt about it. However, reading and writing are certainly not two equivalent tasks at any cognitive level, and to have a reading competence in one language does not mean having a similar ability to write in the same language. Indeed, he also declares something of the sort: even though I may read Latin, I am not "literate" enough to write in this language.

But there is a linguistic literacy he certainly had in Latin: he was able to write, and even forge, documents in Latin, because he worked as a notary for the monastery's abbot, Juan Sánchez.[3] This sentence means, maybe more in depth, that Latin poetic literacy and Latin notarial literacy are two very different things, and they cannot be confused with each other.

The line is quite pregnant, of course, because at the beginning of the thirteenth century, being "literate" and managing Latin constitutes an extremely discontinuous experience: Latin was not only a language but also a constellation of disciplines, each of which had a specialized, technical language. Indeed, juridical Latin differed from poetic Latin, and both from theological Latin and other technical languages that used Latin.

Here is where the previous two lines make more sense. The poet intends to write a narrative—*prosa*, even though it is in a certain kind of mono-rhymed versification known as *cuaderna-vía*.[4] His prose will differ from previous prose in that it will be written in *roman paladino*, that is, in very simple and easily understandable (*paladino*) vernacular language (*roman*, or romance language), the one, he says, in which people speak to one another. In these lines, *paladino* is perhaps more important than *roman*, insofar as the poet advocates a form of expression that may do away with complex explanations and glosses, even though, as Berceo himself declares at the beginning of his *Miracles of the Virgin* (*Milagros de Nuestra Señora*), one needs to understand the anagogical meaning of the stories he tells (or retells).[5] But the point of writing *paladinamente* (clearly) is that it belongs in a domestic space, in a certain community of expression that can work with the language because it is transparent, not only because it is a particular language.

Paladino is a central concept in the writing of the law for Alfonso. At the beginning of his theory on law, he stipulates that "the laws must be complete, carefully written, and thoroughly composed, so that they are reasonable, and that they deal with issues that may be done and are according to nature. And the language to write the laws must be composed of plain and good words, and they must be clear [*paladinas*] so that people can understand them and keep them in their memories. Likewise, they should have neither insufficiency nor excess of meaning, and they must not contradict each other."[6] Alfonso wrote this regulation in the vernacular, quite obviously. It is an expression, if you wish, of *roman paladino*, not only in form but also in theory: he calls for the articulation of a legal idiom that involves an unmatched degree of clarity in the language in which the neighboring legal subjects speak to one another. The law claims that this clarity, this vernacular legal language, is, at the same time, the source of that language's precision, thoroughness, completeness, and carefulness with which it must be presented for the people to understand and retain it.[7]

Now, the challenge of dead voice and perplexing codifications in the Alfonsine era is that they are based on the development and expansion of this sort of vernacular legal language. Can a vernacular codification intend to become universal? What would that desire of vernacular universalization imply?

In his book, *El humanismo medieval y Alfonso X el Sabio*, H. Salvador Martínez makes the case for a "medieval humanism" in the case of Alfonso X.[8] His arguments are manifold, but the central one concerns the cultivation of the vernacular in order to demonstrate the existence of a vernacular humanism that dates to the time of Alfonso. The presence or existence of a humanism on the Iberian Peninsula is one of the central debates concerning more traditional approaches to the Middle Ages from the vantage point of literary history and philology. Because it is somewhat difficult to see a humanistic movement in Latin on the Iberian Peninsula, scholars like Pedro M. Cátedra and Jeremy Lawrance, who were aware of the impact of humanistic intellectual and scholarly trends in late medieval Castile and Aragon, have suggested studying the emergence of a vernacular humanism, or a *romancista* humanism, especially for the fifteenth century.[9] Ángel Gómez Moreno, Ottavio di Camillo, and others have further delved into the question from different perspectives, always dealing with the question of the degree to which Iberian literatures depended on or even emulated Italian humanistic traditions, in a way that, at any rate, turns Iberian humanism into a mediated form of humanism.[10] Martínez's interest is quite original in this respect, because he wants to focus on the *longue durée* of the Alfonsine Era as the springboard for other vernacular humanisms. His book is important in understanding the development of the vernacular in the court of Alfonso X and afterward.

My point is entirely different. I do not intend to resuscitate the question of whether there can be or cannot be a vernacular humanism. What I intend to investigate is how the implementation of an idea of the vernacular constituted a challenge to the general theory and practice of jurisdiction. This is a crucial point to bear in mind as we untangle the strategies that led to the formation of central, or better yet concentric, jurisdiction and examine how this concentric jurisdiction both theorized power and created the means to define the juridical person—as a vernacular juridical person.

Vernacular codification needed to compete with other universal forms of codification and legal scholarship. That includes the grandiose codifications of canon law, in particular after the *constitutiones* (dispositions) of the Fourth Lateran Council (1215) and their consequences. One of the main complexes of codification is the Catalan Dominican canonist Raymond of Penyafort's (ca. 1175–1275) edition of Gregory IX's *Decretales* (1234).[11] These were to be sent to the most active of all centers of legal scholarship and study, such as the University of Bologna and the University of Paris, for the scholars to comment in depth (which they did).[12] By putting the *Decretales* in the hands of those scholars and students, the papal power assured a multifaceted form of dissemination and marginal commentary that would turn the theses of the *Decretales* into mainstream ones at both the historical (*pars historica* of each piece of law) and the regulatory (*pars dispositiva*) levels. Something similar can be said about Raymond of Penyafort's *Summa de casibus pœnitentiae* and the *Summa de matrimonio* (both from around 1230 and normally edited in print as a single book: *Summa de penitentia et matrimonio*), which undertook the task of systematizing and disseminating canon legislation regarding the new developments in the sacraments of penance and marriage.

Those legal codifications define a transpolitical jurisdiction, a universal circulation of sovereign power, and even a practice of *plenitudo potestatis* (the universal jurisdiction of the pope). They also practice their universal (catholic) vocation by using Latin—and by contributing to the universality of juridical Latin.[13]

Even if the *Corpus Iuris Civilis* cannot be properly considered a system of legal codification, it implies specific legal practices in the courts of justice and equally transpolitical marginal commentaries and discussions that happen in that same scholarly, universal language—juridical Latin. When Accursius compiled the *Glossa Ordinaria* and created the *statio* (workshop) and the shop, or *bottega*, to copy it by means of the *pecia* system (creation of copies by quires), he knew that it would become a juridical best seller across Europe (and that he would become, as he did, extremely rich).[14]

It is against the backdrop of those codifications and legal scholarship, and also against the backdrop of the legal and bibliographical industries they set in motion, that the vernacular codification of the *Partidas* emerges. However, the *Partidas* face as well another competing legal tradition, one that is formed by local legal regulations (municipal charters, *fueros*, etc.). Perhaps it is a minor tradition from an industrial and bibliographical perspective, but it is not marginal from the perspective of the formation of jurisdictional domains.[15]

Vernacular Knowledge

The ninth *constitutio*, or canon, of the Fourth Lateran Council regulates how bishops and other ecclesiastical powers must secure the teaching of the doctrine (expressed in the first *constitutio* of the same corpus) in the vernacular of each place.[16] The transpolitical jurisdiction claimed by the Catholic Church thus acknowledged the multilingual character of the world it faced. Cities, parishes, and other population centers were, according to this canon, doubly multilingual. On the one hand, inhabitants of those places spoke many languages; indeed, we can imagine not only the profusion of Romance languages spoken all over both the *Romania continua* (the places where their language derives directly from Latin) and the *submersa* (languages like English or Berber that buttress their grammar with Latin elements) but also the non-Romance languages with which they interacted every day: Arabic, Hebrew, Middle High German, Basque, Britton, and many others.[17] Furthermore, the canon states, the peoples from these places also practiced many different rituals to express their beliefs and their vision of religious life. One of the crucial missions of the Lateran Council was to combat heresy, which this council helped to create by identifying heretical groups and their habits, a task that inquisitors all over Europe would shortly thereafter have the responsibility to carry out.[18] The canon legislator—the pope, through his lawyers—works with this multilingual and multiritual world by trying to find a common denominator among the cultural and linguistic diversity: all people conveyed the same truths in different tongues and were responsible to the same authority even if they were currently practicing different rituals. Vernacular languages and their variants are set at the same level as rituals and their varieties. Both are means of expressing inner thoughts and inner beliefs, and both have the same purpose. Because of this shared purpose, the canon commands the appointment of clerics and bishops who are conversant in these languages and rituals, with the goal of leading the people in general to the Catholic, universal doctrine, common to them all, and expressed in the universal Latin language of the ecclesia, along with its rites.

The church, in other words, recognized this linguistic and ritual diversity only to ensure that the real nonheretical language was Catholic Latin, and the only nonheretical set of rituals were the ones regulated in the canon corpus of law. Legislating and enforcing legislation does not involve doing so in the vernacular, but rather reducing, or reconducting, the vernacular knowledge to the Latin, Catholic world.[19]

Preaching in the vernacular was, for the thirteenth-century Dominicans who perfected the art, a way to inquire into supposedly vernacular religious or spiritual traditions in order to reinterpret them in light of the newly set doctrines and rituals. Likewise, preachers, in their sermons, planted the right themes and quotations in Latin, themes and quotations that came from both the Bible and canon regulations. In many cases, we only know the resulting handbooks for preachers, like those of Etienne de Bourbon (1180–1261), Thomas of Chobham (ca. 1160–between 1233 and 1236), Jean Gobi (ca. 1260–1328), and many others who also occupied important positions in the church hierarchy. But we also have access to individual sermons in the vernacular, such as those studied by Michel Zink, as well as the products of individual preachers—including Pedro Marín (thirteenth century) and Vicente Ferrer (1350–1419)—which Pedro Cátedra has studied in depth and edited.[20]

For all these traditions, the bodies of vernacular knowledge were to be mined in order to consolidate the construction of a Latinate, centralized, transpolitical, and universal (catholic) knowledge. This process of consolidation also involved the production of a clear distinction between official, public, and universal modes of expression (through language, rituals, gestures, etc.), that could be sanctioned as orthodox, and other private, vernacular, particular modes of expression that could adjust themselves to the orthodox ones or be forever suspected of being nonorthodox, even heretical. Inquisitions and official investigations took place in the folding of this diglossic separation between Latin knowledge and vernacular knowledge.

Civil traditions were not completely reluctant to translate their main sources. Translating the legal science taught at the universities of Bologna, Paris, and from 1235 onward, Orléans, into the vernacular was not a complete innovation. One of the most important translations had already been produced in the Occitan territories. These are the same territories the church was concerned about during the thirteenth and fourteenth centuries; there, vernacular rituals seemed to be at odds with Latin and Roman Catholicism.[21] *Lo Codi*, a translation of the Latin *Summa Trecensis* (twelfth century), was designed to instill the new legal science into the judicial practices of judges, attorneys, and legal clients in certain Occitan cities and villages, and it even found its way south of the Pyrenees.[22] *Lo Codi* refers to the major foundational texts of the commentary to Justinian's Code. The translation, therefore, could also be interpreted as a guide to the major Latin treatises, and, as such, it allows its users to locate the original references with the help of the vernacular version as a springboard. The usefulness of this translation, which is dated to the second half of the twelfth century, can also be measured by the multiple times it was, in its turn, translated into French, Castilian, and other languages.[23]

In those cases, vernacular communication (even translation in general) implies a kind of mediation that does not necessarily foster the vernacular product as final. The process of mediation has, if anything, the aftereffect of consolidating the diglossic situation in which Latin remains the dominant, public language, while the vernacular inhabits a private space that facilitates access to the more public.

The concept of vernacularity, almost ironically, did not make it into the *Dictionary of Untranslatables*, nor was it in the original French *Vocabulaire des Philosophies*, edited by Barbara Cassin. Even in this case, one can say that the vernacular has always been kept at home, as part of the strictly private realm, relative, etymologically, to the slaves who were called *verni* or *vernae* because they were raised in the *domus* (the household) and not outside.[24] For a long time, *vernaculus* and *vernacula* referred to the slaves themselves. In his *Liber de Magia*, better known as *Apologia* (II.18.2159), the Latin writer Apuleius (ca. 124–ca. 170) declared that "enim paupertas olim philosophiae vernacula est" (the native character of philosophy used to be poverty): frugal, sober, with little power in itself, and in other ways simple. It is well known that Varro (126–27 BCE) used the adjective to explain how some of the names of aquatic animals came from the local languages (*partim vernacula vocabula*) while others that sound strange were in fact of foreign origin (*peregrina vocabula*).[25]

Toward a Vernacular Jurisdiction

The Latinate, diglossic status quo is, precisely, what Alfonso X intends to counter by means of his legislative techniques. Even though Alfonso's corpus of legislation contains translations and a very complex system of equivalences, it cannot be considered a translation of a similar code.[26] Alfonso did not intend to create a middle ground on which to negotiate a Latin tradition in a multilingual and multicultural (and definitely multiritual) society. In the same sense, he does not intend to make texts necessary for cultural, doctrinal, or political purposes available in the vernacular that had previously only been available in Latin.

I argue that the *Siete Partidas*, which were at the core of Alfonso's project, is such an odd and extraordinary accomplishment because it inaugurates a quite revolutionary idea and practice that I call vernacular jurisdiction. Vernacularity is not only native or domestic; it also refers to the particular and to the private. A vernacular jurisdiction should then fight against its own seemingly confined character: vernacular jurisdiction endeavors to create a universal, central jurisdiction that works from the perspective of the vernacular, that elevates the vernacular to the level of the universal.

Vernacular language should be considered a cognitive instrument rather than a simple mode of communication. Following Alva Noë's theses regarding art in his book *Strange Tools*, I would argue that one needs to consider that a technical language, a disciplinary language, cannot be considered only as a means of communication and dissemination of information; it cannot solely fall under the category of expression. Technical languages need to be considered as forms of investigation, as *strange tools*.[27] Shifting from a Latin technical language to a vernacular implies breaking with the cognitive diglossia that separated professionals of the law from the vast majority of the clients of the law, thus expanding the potential use of such a strange tool. In a society like medieval Iberia's, in which diverse jurisdictions overlapped, the institution of a single power to do justice—as Bradin Cormack defines jurisdiction[28]—and use vernacular languages, as well as a newly minted vernacular juridical language, was nothing short of revolutionary.

I do not, however, limit the concept of vernacular jurisdiction to a "power to do justice" in the romance language. Vernacular jurisdiction is more complex than that. I propose this concept as a means to discuss the way in which the technologies of codification of the *Partidas* include the creation of a moral climate inscribed in the legislation itself, because the technical languages of academic disciplines are modes of research and investigation. In other words, the laws of the *Siete Partidas* include, along with dispositions, regulations, explanations, and so on, a discourse on moral principles that are legally constructed and politically productive. Ultimately, it comes down to the main technical idea that the expression of rules is an insufficient tool for engaging an innovative legislative process, and that both the legislative process and the principles of legislation are better conveyed by the exploitation of what I call perplexing legislation—the inclusion of philosophical ideas and fictional devices in the construction of legislation.

The *Partidas* do that by combining the different senses of the notion of vernacularity: in addition to using a romance language, the legislation exploits a certain tone of domesticity, a certain private regime of affections. What this means is that the *Partidas* are—and this is certain—a very sophisticated legal codification, but also that part of their sophistication resides in the way it communicates the code to its expanding intended audience (composed of *the people*, all of the legal subjects in the kingdom, as defined in *Partidas* 2.10). What I suggest is that the *Partidas* purposely set in place a calculated conceptual weakness that makes the technical language of the law more accessible, more understandable. This conceptual weakness is a powerful device that intends to establish and order legal concepts by making them doubly meaningful: on the one hand, they are technically meaningful, because they are totally or partially translated into Spanish for Spanish legislation; on the other hand, they are morally meaningful as concepts the legal subjects can relate to because of their political and social import.

Legal concepts constitute the process of fortification of the jurisdictional power. I suggest that their moral and political meaningfulness is what puts them closer, via an emotional reach, to the domestic logical world of intelligibility and understandability. It is the combination of these two procedures that can be understood as the formation of a vernacular jurisdiction.

First, I will devote some paragraphs to extricating the challenges faced by any new thesis in jurisdiction and to examining the originality of the *Siete Partidas* in relation to its contemporary discussions about jurisdiction and jurisdictional powers. Later, I will suggest some cases from the *Siete Partidas* in which we can see the poetics of the vernacular jurisdiction at work.

Justice-Saying

A notion like the power to do justice is an insufficient paradigm for the idea of vernacular jurisdiction that I have suggested. That power is rather abstract, while vernacular jurisdictions are part of a project to turn abstract ideas into graspable, visible, or otherwise sensible ideas and notions. Vernacular jurisdictions are part of a poetics of a sensible regime of the law.

The *Third Partida*, the one dealing with questions of procedural law, notarial arts, ownership, and property, among other things, begins by defining justice. It would have been the perfect place to give a highly sophisticated, maybe philosophical account of the concept, maybe even a place to include a discussion of Aristotle's concept of justice as both an ethical virtue and a political-economical issue. Nothing of that is present here. In its place, we can find the poetics of a visual concept, the formation of an image to graphically grasp the order of jurisdiction.

The legislator puts a theological idea of justice (*Partidas* 3, prologue) at the forefront of this *Partida*. Justice is the predicate of God's act of making. Making is, in fact, making justice. God constitutes the paradigm of making justice through three faculties: the knowledge, the will, and the power to do justice. The legislator then turns these three faculties of justice into their human correlates by means of the linguistic operators that are proper to the *fictio legis*: "For *just as* He possessed the knowledge, the desire, and the power to render it when He desired to do so; *in like manner* those whose duty it is to dispense justice for him must possess three qualities. First, they must have the disposition to seek it and *to love it with all their hearts*, bearing in mind the benefits and advantages which this implies. Second, they must know how to render it as is suitable and the circumstances of the case demand, *some with mercy, others with severity*. Third, they must have the courage and the power to accomplish it, when opposed by those who desire to suppress or interfere with it."[29]

I have emphasized the linguistic operators that mark the *fictio legis* (*bien así . . . otrosí*; just as . . . in like manner), which in this case serve as the operators that translate divine legal activity into its human correlate. These operators make one of the manifestations of political theologies visible: they highlight the strategies through which secular and political concepts are conveyed as translations of divine concepts.[30] This *fictio legis* is eminently structural in the sense that it regulates a genealogy of the discourse on justice in general and that all other legal systems need to adapt to this structural concept of justice.

The translation means the inclusion of a set of emotional and affective elements, of political and legal feelings inscribed in the legal poetics of justice. Indeed, the will to do justice is not enough, because the legal subject must express a will to love it in his or her heart, according to the moral gains justice affords; likewise, divine general knowledge is here translated as a particular kind of knowledge that can administer with either pity or harshness according to the particular situation and its moral evaluation. Further, divine power is translated mainly as effort, a concept related to the moral virtue of fortitude. In this translation we can see several moral ideas coming from different sources—from a cluster of them that combines Aristotelian ethics, Catholic morality, and knightly and monarchical concepts of justice that are frequently transmitted in the pedagogical parts of works like *Lancelot en prose* in the early thirteenth century, Ramon Llull's *Libre de l'orde de cavayleria* (1265), and Don Juan Manuel's *Libro del cavallero et del escudero* (1345), among others. The combination of all those elements has only one purpose: the construction of a particular set of feelings and emotions that need to play their role in the triad of will, knowledge, and power to do justice. These feelings, and their complex but simplified poetics, are what constitute the vernacularity of this idea of jurisdiction.

The power to do justice, we begin to see, is insufficient, because it also requires knowledge and will, thus constituting a triad that allows the subject to do justice. These faculties are independent from the administrative responsibility of an individual person. In other words, the faculties to do justice (knowledge, will, and power) are common to every single human being or, better yet, legal subject. The earthly translation of the three faculties to do justice put the latter within reach of each and every legal subject; it is not the property of a single agent. These three faculties to do justice do not regulate jurisdiction; they constitute a common interest in performing justice.

This first idea of justice is particularly important because the legal regulation establishes an individual relationship between the client, or legal subject, and the general concept of justice. In order to fully accomplish this relationship, the *Third Partida* may not be able to provide the readers with will and power, but it can certainly define the terms under which will and power work while providing the third element or faculty: the necessary knowledge to do justice.

Immediately after suggesting this concept of justice and the poetics of justice, the legislator reads the main theses of the previous *Partidas* again (1 and 2) and considers the interpretation of justice. While the *First Partida* was devoted to spiritual justice, "which allows men to gain God's love through their will, and is the first sword governing the world" (*Partidas* 3, prologue), the *Second Partida* talks about the earthly sword. The legislator then proceeds to explain the mission of the *Third Partida*, which is about "the justice that must be done in an orderly way, according to good sense and knowledge, in which everyone may claim their rights in front of the lords or the officers that give judgment on their behalf."

The definition of justice is still not complete. It is presented as a virtue that agrees with the Aristotelian definition of a distributive equity that became foundational and was inscribed in many different sources, from the ancients all the way to the Middle Ages. It became famous in the Ciceronian expression, *sui cuique reddere*, "give each their due."[31] As a virtue, justice never dies; it cannot disappear as long as it remains within the people's hearts and memory, of course, but also, as we will see in Chapter 5, the soul itself. Philosophical ideas of justice are central to this poetics of justice inasmuch as the legislator focuses on their emotional and affective power.

Finally, the legislator offers a visual concept, or a mental image, of justice as a fountain.[32] In philosophical, theological, and legal texts, the fountain of justice is one of the names of God or one of the names of the king. It is the predicate that counts: God is the *fons iustitiae* (source or fountain, or spring of justice) and so is the king. For Alfonso, nevertheless, it is science, and in particular legal science, what constitutes the *fons iustitiae*.[33] Alfonso changes the dynamics of the tradition regarding the metaphor of the source, putting justice at the forefront of the definition, as the subject. There is no subject to be named the fountain of justice, but this, as an emblem, becomes the center of attention for the legislator.

> They compared it [Justice] to a perennial spring, possessing in itself three characteristics. First, *as* the water which issues from the spring pours forth toward the east, *so* justice always looks toward the direction where the true sun, which is God, rises, and hence the Saints in the Scriptures designated Our Lord Jesus Christ as the Sun of Justice. Second, *as* the water of a spring runs perpetually, and men have a greater desire to drink of it because it tastes better and is more healthy than any other; *so* also is justice in itself, for the reason that it is never spoiled or wasted, and those who demand it and have need of it derive greater pleasure from it than anything else. Third, *as* its water is warm in winter and cold in spring, and its excellence counteracts the extremes of the seasons, *so* the rights protected by the administration of justice remove and antagonize the wicked and unjust deeds of men.[34]

One can easily understand the triple power of the emblem, in which we see at work three linguistic operators that are proper to the *fictio legis*. According to the first, the perennial flow of water always runs in the same direction, pointing to the ultimate destination of justice, which is constituted by the divine power and therefore by one, single, centralized jurisdictional spring. According to the second, the water from the fountain of justice will be better for those subjects who look for it—that is, for all those who love justice rather than for those who are persecuted by it. This quality of the water is given in sensuous terms, in terms of flavor and health, thus implicitly convey-ing the idea that even legal subjects, as such, have a metaphoric body that is able to feel and be either healthy or sick. According to the third, the water will adapt itself to counter the wrongs undertaken by men.

The chain of *fictiones legum* governing the ethical and political under-standing of justice is continued in the law that follows the emblem of the fountain of justice. According to the law, there needs to be a regime of affection toward justice and the law. Indeed, justice is not only a legal cate-gory codified and inscribed within the law—which is exactly what the *Parti-das* does all the time, nonetheless—it is also revealed (or better yet, legislated) as a "virtue that glues the world together, making everybody live in peace according to their estate in society, with pleasure, and with abundance of the things they have" (*Partidas* 3.1.2). This new displacement of the regulation of justice gives birth to a new chain of *fictiones legum*, a new series of *as if* that delves into the metaphors of consanguinity, affinity, and political links between clients and justice, because "justice must be loved by everyone, as if it were a father or a mother that provides and maintains them. All people have to obey it as if it were a good Lord to of whom they shall not make a demand. And they have to protect her as if it were their own life, because they cannot live well without it."

This chain of *fictiones* goes directly to the heart of the affective regime of vernacular jurisdictions by underscoring the domestic, familiar, and emo-tional character of the relationship between the legal subject and the concept of justice. The affections, the feelings, the emotions are not only those result-ing from the combination and productive simplification of doctrinal, philo-sophical, or theological corpora. These affections and feelings are, rather, the closest ones, the ones that belong in the private, familiar space of the law client.

The *as if* of the *fictio legis* thus inscribes specific political theories and ideas in the legislative body. Alfonso uses this linguistic and legal-heuristic technique to tattoo the notions of central jurisdiction as central power, the theological orientation of the system of power, and the direct dependence between legislation and justice on the skin of the legislation, while at the same time he creates the affective regime of the law, the idea that it must be part of the ethical, loving, and familiar responses of the clients of the law.

Lawyers and the officers of law and justice, according to a *fictio legis* from *Partidas* 3.2.2, are as if they were knights upholding Justice. This defense of justice is "another kind of open war men engage in at all times." This sort of political statement is also reflected in other parts of the *Third Partida* (3, prologue) as well as in the *Second Partida*, which is devoted to political and administrative law, where the exercise of the law is deemed another sort of knightly practice. In *Partidas* 2.31.8, the legislator considers that "the knowledge of Law [*los derechos*] is another kind of knighthood with which audacity can be broken [*se quebrantan los atrevimientos*] and kingdoms become straight [*se enderezan los reinos*]." In a radical political move, Alfonso presents the kingdom as a set of fluid demarcations with the interior enemy constituted by "domestic treasonous and arrogant ones [*los de dentro torticeros et soberbiosos*]." This, and not a set of physical borderlines, is what extends the capillary reach of his jurisdiction and its domestic character.

The third and last law from *Partidas* 3.1 plays with very well known sources. As always, they are introduced with the clause "as the ancient wise men said" or similar expressions. As we observed in the introduction, the legislator gives us a hint that many ideas, most of them, have been already authorized by saints, ancient wise men, rulers, or the Bible, while withholding the exact reference or the specific name of the author. This interplay between the certainty of a backing authority and silencing the exact source is rhetorically, argumentatively very important, because of the way in which Alfonso's workshop used it to work the sources. They cut and combine the sources in a way that transforms the denotative and connotative aspects of the original text in its original place.

A perfect example of this are the legal precepts of justice conveyed in *Partidas* 3.1.3, which the legislator lists as being three: "first, that every man should live honorably, so far as he himself is concerned; second, that he should not do wrong or injury to another; third, that he should give to each one that to which he is entitled."[35] This is in principle a simple translation of Justinian's *Institutiones* 1.1.3: "Iuris praecepta sunt haec honeste vivere, alterum non laedere, ius suum cuique tribuere."

The first precept has been expanded from "living honorably" to "living honorably so far as he himself is concerned." Alfonso is here reading the margins of the *Institutiones*, an Accursian gloss to "honeste" that reads "scilicet quantum ad se."[36] In other words, the workshop mixed the text from the *Institutiones* with the medieval gloss. This does not mean too much insofar as we cannot know what kind of manuscripts of the *Corpus Iuris Civilis* the Alfonsine workshop was working with. We know that this gloss existed and that it does not seem to be pre-Accursian, because there does not seem to be any pre-Accursian gloss to *Institutiones* 1.1.3.

Accursian glosses to this part of the *Institutiones* are interesting because they were intended to formulate theoretical issues. For instance, an Accursian gloss to the three precepts of justice indicates that the third one (to grant each their own right) cannot be understood from the perspective of the action, only from the perspective of the affect ("'ius suum cuique tribuens' intellige quantum ad affectionem, quia ad actum non potest"). Affect, therefore, here means passion, rather than action. This small gloss therefore implies an important operation in which granting all people their own right is of an affective nature, involving feelings and emotions that, nevertheless, neither the Justinian text nor the Accursian gloss develops fully.

The Accursian gloss indeed provides the reader, as well, an ethical analysis of this precept. The gloss to *Suum* ("ius suum cuique tribuere," or "granting each their own right") indicates this ethical opening: it does not suffice, the gloss says, to not damage the other. To grant each their own right also means to help the other; in other words, whereas the precept may be understandable from the perspective of affect, it does not exclude ulterior action ("non sufficit abstinere a malo, nisi fiat quod bonus est").

Alfonso is working not only with the central text but also with the glosses. This detail is important because of the way in which Alfonso's legal workshop worked with those texts. The three legal precepts are obviously embedded in Alfonso's text, but they are embedded along with one bit of one gloss that opens up a major question: the affective and ethical one.

Alfonso develops this question further because of the context in which he includes these three legal precepts. They cannot be read against or in company with their sources but rather in the new context in which they have been included. They need to be interpreted not as the result of a certain tradition but as the product of a new idea of justice wherein these precepts acquire a new meaning.

This new meaning is profoundly ethical and suggests the affective character of justice. Alfonso has given those two features force of law. Both elements are inscribed in the Accursian margins, which were supposed to serve law students' full understanding of what is at stake in the text; even the *Institutiones* were originally composed as a handbook for law students. Alfonso does not make distinctions among the different readers and clients of the law. All of them have access to the same kind of legal statement.

In that sense, the legal text expresses a deep desire for individual readers to approach the *Partidas* from all social, political, and professional distinctions. From the beginning of the legal code, when the legislator stated the virtues of the law (and the laws), he expressed this desire by putting an enormous load of responsibility on the readers themselves:

> Whence it is proper that whoever desires to read the laws of this, our book, should reflect upon them very carefully, and should scrutinize them in such a way as to understand them: for if he should comprehend them thoroughly, he will observe all that we have said, and he will be benefited in two ways: first, he will become more learned, and second, he will obtain much profit from them. In like manner, as wise men have said, he who reads the Scriptures and does not understand them is like one who rejects them. And, moreover, such a person resembles one who dreams something and when he awakes does not find it true.[37]

The law may refer to two different meanings of *leer* (to read): one that simply means to read the text that has been written on the page, and the other that used to mean, in the Middle Ages, to interpret. This is why the legislator insists that such hypothetical readers must actually delve with care into the meaning of the laws. The last words from the law probably come from Psalms 75.6 of the Vulgate: "turbati sunt omnes insipientes corde dormierunt somnum suum et nihil invenerunt omnes viri divitiarum manibus suis."[38] The loci offered by Gregorio López Madera in his glosses to the *Partidas* from 1555 are parallels rather than sources, but this does not matter. Indeed, it is all the more interesting that he offers parallels; in this case López Madera volunteers a text from a gloss (*si ex cautione*) to the *Codex Iustiniani*, which reads, "sileant qui scripta tantum discurrunt et propter frigiditatem stomachi in eis contenta non digerunt" (keep their silence all those who are interpreting the writings while their stomachs, because of their coldness, cannot properly digest what they read). Whether it is a source or a parallel, what matters is that it points to a specific way of establishing a relationship with the law that is individual, private, a relationship that has to do with the attention one pays to the text, even with physiopsychological issues—like the coldness of stomach—of clear Aristotelian lineage.[39]

It is in this privacy, in this individuality of the reader, that the first precept of the law, which was reformulated with the help of the marginal gloss and then inscribed in a deeply affective context of the law, also carries a different sense. This precept is that every man should live honorably, so far as he himself is concerned. In the new context, this is a requirement that finally puts the technologies of the self and the hermeneutics of the subject into political and legal service.[40] Elevated as a legal statement, this precept requires legal subjects to analyze themselves, because that analysis is necessary to refashioning themselves according to the new legality.[41] This is the same requirement that appeared in the general prologue of the *Siete Partidas*, when the law was compared to a mirror in which the king must look at himself, analyze himself according to the laws, and instead of modifying the laws, modify himself—and then submit that modification to the rest of the legal subjects in the kingdom.[42]

This very same law we are now examining, *Partidas* 3.1, makes a displacement that I find especially important. It establishes that laws and rights are *contained within*. In other words, laws and rights (including, of course, obligations) are not means that serve the purpose of achieving justice. Justice already encompasses both laws and rights.

This displacement is important because it demonstrates that justice is not an abstract virtue—a moral virtue in the Aristotelian ethical theory. Justice is visible, empirically perceptible, and concrete by dint of the concrete laws and the concrete rights it contains. They *do* justice. This displacement implies, as well, that sovereignty and jurisdiction are empirically observable through laws and rights—that is, through a justice that can be read because it has been written in the form of laws and rights.

Circulation of Power in the Vernacular Jurisdiction

In previous publications, I have underscored the centrality of jurisdiction in the definition of power. I proposed that the study of discourses on jurisdiction would give us a different approach to understanding the concept and practices of sovereignty.[43] Jurisdiction, unlike perhaps sovereignty, is a sensible form of the circulation of power. In other words, it can be perceived, it can be made visible. The acts by which jurisdiction is regulated, delegated, and enforced are part of an empirical form of the circulation of power. Unlike the abstract concept of power, jurisdiction works in certain ways that are channeled through the judicial system and its procedures. This is why the displacement made to help us define justice as a set of laws and rights is important: it consolidates jurisdiction, law, legal science, rights and obligations, and justice.

Whereas I do not think it is necessary to establish any sort of hierarchy of concepts in the definition and pursuit of power, I still think that empirical expressions of power have a preferred juridical manifestation. Even expressions of power, based on what Foucault called *illegalisms*, have a preferred juridical character; indeed, illegalisms require the acknowledgment of a specific legality and its limits in order to be able to establish modes of dissent and action taking place beyond the reach of such legality.[44]

Power is unpredictably metamorphic, but perhaps the transformative movement, the metabolism that underlies power, is the ability of different agents to claim rights. This claim is not, so to speak, an empty claim but rather one that intends to have those rights included in the economies of jurisdiction.

Because the features of the concept of jurisdiction are fluid, this form of the manifestation and circulation of power—jurisdiction—was the object of a profound debate during the Middle Ages. The semantic terms of this debate have been explored by Pietro Costa from the vantage point of structural linguistics and semiology—two disciplines that, I would argue, are in a relation of affinity with the disciplines of both law and legal history.[45] By paying special attention to conceptions of jurisdiction, legal scholars like Jesús Vallejo have endeavored to understand the complexities of the hierarchy of concepts underpinning the right to produce norms and statutory laws.

I would like to focus on the poetics of the concept itself—that is, the different building blocks used by medieval legal scholars (and analyzed by Costa and Vallejo) that elicit the political transactions underlying the practices of power surrounding jurisdiction. Such a poetics, *the making of the concept*, is relevant because it can help us understand the question I posed before—how to productively manage legal diglossia, which is a main concern for any discussion of a vernacular jurisdiction.

I have already defined the domestic, private, and even intimate terms in which the vernacular legislation works. In order to link it to the question of jurisdiction, and in order to complete my definition of vernacular jurisdiction, I am going to reuse elements from the classical definition of "jurisdiction," which was coined in the thirteenth century by Azo (fl. 1150–1230) in his *Summa Codicis* and then commented on and expanded by glossators and commentators during the thirteenth and fourteenth centuries, including Accursius (ca. 1182–1263), Cino da Pistoia (1270–ca. 1336), and Bartolus of Saxoferrato (1313–1357). The definition of "jurisdiction" was conceived in the context of glosses of the civil law, but, as Jesús Vallejo has shown, also became part of the debates regarding jurisdiction in canon law among *Decretals* scholars.[46]

The center of Azo's concept of jurisdiction is the *potestas iuris dicendi*, which I would translate and expand as the "power to establish laws and rights from both the perspective of legislation and the perspective of legal science."[47] *Ius*, indeed, is a complex concept that involves both the body of laws (*laws, lois, legge, leyes*, etc.) and the science of the disciplinary world in which those laws are in force (*the law, droit, diritto, derecho*, etc.), a concept that can also be collapsed with that of justice: an Accursian gloss (*Institutiones* 1.1.3, gloss *suum*) defines *ius* as the art or technique of being good and equitable (*ars boni et aequi*). This is why my translation insists on including all those elements as essential to the concept of jurisdiction: they all, in collaboration across disciplines, constitute the substance and the form of jurisdiction. They all, in collaboration, constitute the observable character of sovereignty.

This specific power is closely related to discussions about *merum imperium*, which normally translates as "absolute power."[48] It works at the ordinary level (*iurisdictio ordinaria*)—that is, the level at which the sovereign is the very jurisdictional source. It also works at the level of the delegation of power by the sovereign or by officers to the specific individuals who can hold this jurisdictional power (*iurisdictio delegata*). We immediately see that we are at the level of sovereign power but definitely not at that of the exception, not at the level of the sovereign as the individual who can decide on the exception—in the Schmittean sense that has been at the center of the discussions of sovereignty tackled by Giorgio Agamben in his *Homo Sacer*.

If anything, here, we are dealing with a sovereign who is the master of the norm.

Potestas iuris dicendi is an expression with many working parts. I understand this *potestas iuris dicendi* to be articulated through the use of the vernacular and certain vernacular institutions (including Arabic and Jewish ones, and therefore not only from the *ius commune* tradition and mythology) with the purpose of subjectivizing the people. This "people" is the people described by Alfonso in his own *Second Partida*—as we will have the opportunity to see more closely in Chapter 4. His concept of people does not necessarily coincide with the concept of *populus* used in the Latin legal tradition, a slippage toward a general idea of people from the Roman expression *populus romanus*.[49] The subjectivization of the people is the process whereby citizens and natural persons become subjects of the law, that is *personae fictae*, or juridical persons, as we will see immediately below—because these processes entail the articulation of philosophical *corpora* and fictional devices, thus embracing perplexity.

The *potestas iuris dicendi*, or jurisdiction, works across an incoherent territory in order to make it cohere by using the linguistic and disciplinary creativity of the law. Indeed, the indexes of legal terms indicate that jurisdiction is one of the elements of territorial coherence—even though some legal scholars from the thirteenth and fourteenth centuries advocated a *iurisdictio divisa* or even a *iurisdictio divisa per territoria*.[50] This vernacular jurisdiction has a double purpose: on the one hand, a self-referential purpose of establishing the *potestas* itself in time and space; on the other hand, the purpose of controlling uprisings, by "removing disagreements among the people" (*Partidas* 2.1.1) and by using the *iuris dicendi* "against those who are arrogant and unjust [*tortizeros*]" (*Partidas* 2.1.3; *Partidas* 3, prologue). In this second sense, vernacular jurisdiction also seeks to control plebeian experiences and expressions of revolt that take place among citizens and in the vernacular language.[51] This seems especially important because of the ways in which this *potestas iuris dicendi* establishes its mode of exercising absolute sovereignty —by creating norms ("*condere legem est meri imperii*," as Gregorio López himself reminds the reader in his gloss d to the *Partidas* 2.1.1). *Condere legem*—that is, producing laws by embracing philosophy and a whole array of fictional devices—is a way to control and limit both the exception and the local uses of the vernacular founded upon the *illegalisms* lurking in the spaces of legal misunderstanding created by legal diglossia.

Using only the Azonian definition, the briefest one, the powers that constitute a poetics of justice include the following: establishing the topology, geography, and chronology of *potestas*; describing what is public, and establishing the identities of public persons as well as the regime of delegating jurisdictional powers (the power to *coerce*) across different "authentic persons" (*Partidas* 3.18, prologue); formulating the vernacular diction of the law, as well as its necessity, from the vantage point of political and social creativity; and creating the regimes of equity and their expression in the vernacular, highlighting their genealogy and etymologies, and detaching them from the limits of the *ius commune*.

Alfonso's regulations and investments in vernacular jurisdictions are not independent from the Latinate recognition of multilingualism and multiritual spaces by the Lateran Council canons. It is clear that these canons are, in turn, a way of configuring jurisdictional spaces and models of collaboration between the ecclesiastical body and the secular arm, between canon and civil legislation. The same *constitutio* mentioned before, canon 9, forbids, precisely, jurisdictional multiplications: "Prohibemus autem omnino ne una eademque ciuitas siue diocesis diuersos pontifices habeat, tanquam unum corpus diuersa capita, quasi monstrum." (We prohibit one single city or diocese's having several figures of power, because it would be like a monster that has one single body and several heads.) Alfonsine vernacular jurisdiction is nothing other than an attempt to tame the monster of many different legal systems working in relative independence from one another, thus dissolving the concept of monarchical sovereignty based on a centralized jurisdiction.

One of the consequences of the Lateran Council is the cultural research it indirectly undertook in treatises for preaching, confessional models, systems of interrogation, and many other procedures for registering living voices (as we saw in Chapter 1).[52] The council's views on jurisdiction also foster a catholic sort of jurisdiction that was later challenged, and readapted, in Alfonso's *Siete Partidas*. This document, boldly, also includes canon legislation enunciated by the king in the *First Partida* and many different discussions about witnessing, interrogation, and inquisitions in the *Third Partida*, among other interesting challenges advancing civil, monarchical, and vernacular jurisdiction.

Setting the terms of a vernacular jurisdiction in motion involves combining law, philosophy, and fictional devices. In other words, embracing the dialectics of perplexity is a way to advance vernacular jurisdiction—the legal set of decisions that involve the rupture of legal diglossia and the capillarization of coherence across a territory, a new theory and practice of power that redefines *merum et mixtum imperium*, localizing it in a single political and legal space, thus avoiding the creation of a many-headed monster.

Love Against the Monster

There are many doors to Alfonsine ideas of sovereignty and jurisdiction. Legal scholars have delved into technical traces of jurisdiction in order to link them to their Latinate institutions, discussions, and practices. However, the *Siete Partidas* constitutes a challenge to these technical analyses insofar as it uses many different building blocks that have been purposely separated from their sources—both textual and technical. The second reason why the *Partidas* challenges this sort of analysis results from the specific techniques of codification worked out in the *Partidas*.

Indeed, the *Second Partida* is an entire treatise on jurisdiction. It is based on the centrality of the monarch and the fact that even said monarch—as well as all other subjects, the *people*—is bound by the law. If there is a centrality of monarchical jurisdiction, it is only because there is an empire of law—a rule of law, as it were—that subsumes all other jurisdictional sources, either claimed or real. The *Second Partida* focuses specifically on the king because of his being the origin of the self-fashioning and modification according to the law, as expressed in the metaphor of the mirror in the prologue of the *Partidas*. This modification has a capillary character and must continue down to every single member of the people—every single legal subject. While the first eleven titles of the *Second Partida* are devoted to this kind of king, the rest (Titles 12–31) explore the rest of the subjects according to their status, the work they do, the specific powers they receive from the jurisdictional source, and the mission they have to fulfill. These titles on the other subjects of the kingdom begin with Titles 10 and 12, which give access to the universe of legal subjects, beginning with the definition of the people as the gathering of all legal subjects regardless of their political or economic status.

How do the techniques of codification and law-writing interfere with the way in which Alfonso talks about jurisdiction and sovereignty? What are the techniques by which sovereignty and jurisdiction can be put forth in the vernacular terms we are exploring? In other words, how is princely sovereignty made present in a private, domestic sense but with general political and public consequences? How can the monster of multiple jurisdictions and sovereign dissolution be tamed?

The answer is *love*. It is in *Partidas* 2.10.2. Right after defining the people in the previous law (*Partidas* 2.10.1), Alfonso stipulates how the people must be loved—and he uses the passive voice—by the king. This passive voice is all the more important because we are in the terrain of affect, in the territory of passion. Kingly love is a passion, something that befalls the people.

This passion of love on the part of the king is, of course, a legal expression. This love fosters jurisdictional relationships by conferring the status of legal subject on the people. The love that befalls the people is the very process of subjectivization. Love descends upon the people, thus creating the juridical persons.

Love seems to be a very transparent political-theological strategy. Political theologies are not a scheme to be projected onto something but rather are a labyrinthine and rhizomatic set of strategies. This is what makes political theology unpredictable and all the more effective—it always breaks the horizon of expectations. This particular strategy seems transparent, and it is most probably because it is a very conscious one at that.

The king's love blooms in three branches: mercy (*merced*), pity (*piedad*), and compassion (*misericordia*). These three manifestations of love help the legislator characterize the king as soul (*alma*) and life (*vida*) of the people. In this sense, we begin to see the poetic—that is, creative—character of the king's jurisdiction. Indeed, he is the one granting understanding and feeling, because both originated in the soul, according not only to Christian doctrine but also to Aristotelian philosophy and its commentaries in the Mediterranean basin. Likewise, the king is the one granting life, which is a continuation of the soul, since the soul is the warmth of life. Because the king is soul and life—that is, the origins of being—there is creation, there are people. The manifestation of pity characterizes the king as the head of a body that feels pain when one of its members or organs hurts; the law also characterizes this manifestation of pity from the perspective of the metaphor of the king as father who suffers when he is in need of punishing his children. This sense of pity is the one that creates those subjects, the hurting member or the unruly child; instead of amputating them, or instead of expelling them from the household, the king assumes them as constitutive parts of both the body and the home. Finally, the manifestation of compassion (*misericordia*) is the one by which pardon is granted.

Thus Alfonso X fully deploys the visibility of the political-theological strategy by quoting and commenting Psalms 84 and 118 (Vulgate). In Psalms 84.11, the verse quoted in *Partidas* 2.10.2," *misericordia et veritas obviaverunt sibi; iustitia et pax osculatae sunt*," or in Alfonso's translation, "la verdad et la misericordia se fallan en uno, et la paz et la justicia se besan" ([when] truth and mercy are together, peace and justice kiss each other). It is not all, because the legislator includes this citation as a clause subordinate to a larger sentence regarding the well-being of the kingdom: indeed, the kingdom is well maintained when truth and mercy find each other, and when peace and justice kiss each other. This is a "peace kiss"—in the typology established by Yannick Carré.[53] The *Bible with Ordinary Gloss* gives a small number of marginal glosses to this passage, but the most important one is Nicolas of Lyra's gloss, which comes after Alfonso's *Partidas*.[54] In all of these glosses, they always read the kiss typologically, as a figure of salvation. This kiss is nothing other than the act of Christ's salvation and his exaltation as the savior. In other words, the kiss also recognizes the universal sovereignty of Christ. The kiss is the final mark of the political-theological strategy. It condenses the moment of love in this encounter between justice and peace facilitated by the active love that the king professes to the people. It is, in effect, a kiss of sovereignty.

After treating the three manifestations of love, the legislator goes on with two more series of three affective manifestations. First, the king must honor the people; and second, he must protect the people. Honor comes in three ways: first, by keeping all subjects in their own social and political place according to their lineage, their virtues, or the service they performed; second, by verbally praising the subject's good deeds; and third, by publicly reasoning that mutual praise for good deeds is a way to foster horizontal solidarity. Protection also comes in three movements: first, from the king himself, by not engaging in damaging his own people; second, from social turmoil or internal danger, containing the haughty and the wrongdoers; and third, from external danger.

These ways of honoring and protecting, which come after the expressions of love, are also strategies for consolidating a centralized idea of sovereignty and jurisdiction that works as if by way of capillarity. While the demonstrations of love are actions from the king, the others are actually strategies to foster horizontal solidarity—albeit, of course, directed by the king.

Most important, the ways of honoring and protecting all appeal to private, domestic, vernacular emotions. There is a very beautiful passage in which Martin Heidegger reads Friedrich Nietzsche's definition of the will to power as affect, passion, and feeling. Nietzsche does not develop the differences between the three, but that does not mean, says Heidegger, that he thought they were synonymous. Heidegger demonstrates the contrary: affects seize us in an unreflective mode, whereas passions—and Heidegger gives the main example of hate, later expanded also to love, the one that interests us—are part of a reflection, a "resolute openness," a certain kind of emotion, that "gives vision and premeditation." Passion, as he characterizes hate and love, "is that through which and in which we take hold of ourselves and achieve lucid mastery over the beings around us and within us."[55]

This conceptualization allows us to understand the regulation of love within the vernacular jurisdiction as a strategy of premeditation, as the foundation of a collective passion that involves the configuration of a "lucid mastery," of a "resolute openness." Neither the lucid mastery nor the resolute openness can be Heideggerean anymore, since they are ethical and political—

two fields of thought he was not considering in his readings of Nietzsche. I am using those terms in order to locate them elsewhere, to use them beyond the purpose for which they were intended.

As we will see in the chapter about friendship, this strategy pervades the whole *Siete Partidas* and constitutes one of the main central concepts—the invented concept of *naturality* as the buttress of love—that serves as the foundation of all the relationships taking place among legal subjects. The vernacular jurisdiction is, in the end, a poetics of the spaces, relationships, and languages that take place among legal subjects. It is, indeed, a poetics of the legal subject. As such, it defines the entire universe in which the *Partidas* operates, by defining, as well, this universe in terms of a vernacular one. By this vernacularity, we understand the private, domestic, and familiar languages and emotions that are used in the public constitution of the legal subject.

Conclusion: Legal Thinking

Legal thinking is what vernacular jurisdiction fosters. In the vernacular jurisdiction, the law speaks the language of the clients of the law. If they are required to become juridical persons and legal subjects, drinking by their own will from the fountain of justice, they don't need to cross beyond the boundaries of their own vernacular language, thus ridding them of the diglossic situation in which the law expresses itself in a hieratic, technical language while the clients of the law speak in their vernacular.

In the vernacular jurisdiction, the law deploys emotional and ethical strategies that foster closeness. It articulates affects, passions, and feelings as part of the legal codification techniques. The inscription of these emotional and ethical strategies unfolds, as well, political and theological discourses, instead of leaving them implicit or unexplained. On the contrary, part of the very strategy is its opening up before the clients of the law. It can be considered a logical unfolding, a logical disclosure, since those theological and political concepts are part of the everyday culture of the clients of the law, who are constantly exposed to predication, within and outside of the church. The law capitalizes this other vernacular cultural formation as part of the strategies that foster closeness.

In the vernacular jurisdiction, narratives support legal regulations. The narratives constitute the basis of complicated conceptual maps, like the very concept of justice, for which the tropologies of the fountain of justice are crucial. These narratives point to cases and to case-thinking, using exempla or arguments coming from many different narrative sources, including the Bible and historical texts. It does not suffice to stipulate, for instance, that the oldest male sibling is the one that must inherit the kingdom, as established in *Partidas* 2.15.2, one of the laws with the longest glosses in the 1555 edition of the *Partidas*. In addition to that, the legislator must prove it by putting it within a legal case that demonstrates it narratively; for this purpose, the legislator tells the history of Isaac and Jacob in Genesis 27. However, the narrative importance of this story is that it is the story of Jacob tricking his disabled father and taking over his older brother's primogeniture. The real point is that the legal recognition of primogeniture by means of the blessing cannot be retracted and it is legally binding—even if, as in this case, it is nothing else but trickery. Case-thinking, the narrative of the case, does not only represent cases in the same way the marginal glosses to both *Corpora Iuris* do. Both glosses also establish the one and definitive precedent that generates jurisprudence by embodying it not in hypothetical characters (like the typical Titius, Seius, and Caius found in the *Corpus Iuris Civilis*, the glossators and postglossators, all the way to Leibniz and beyond) but on characters whose presence in culture is pervasive, like, obviously, biblical characters.

In the vernacular jurisdiction, narrative can be interpreted not as the contrary of dialectical thinking—contrary to what Giles of Rome claimed—but as a way to better understand the law and its consequences while considering personal experiences. Examples of this form of legal rationality include liminal experiences, like the tragedy of the knight who knows he is dying in the middle of the battlefield and yet intends to write a last will. The legislator claims the knight may write it with his own blood on the top of his shield, or on the earth with his finger, or even in sand, for no matter how he does it, it will be valid (*Partidas* 6.1.4). The *Partidas* is full of those sorts of liminal experiences, now narrated within the law. In Chapter 5, we will consider some of them, since they are in close relation to the deployment of legal and political love. All of them create the sensation that every single experience may indeed become a juridical experience.

The vernacular jurisdiction reveals its own way to think about life and law. This is legal thinking—nothing other than the ways in which the clients of the law are required to think about life and experiences according to legal regulations. For this purpose, the legislation offers its clients, all of them, these crucial supports from the vernacular jurisdiction: an understandable language, affective relations, cultural references, and a system of rationality based on narrative. Furthermore, legal thinking in the vernacular jurisdiction is based on the underlying idea that every single piece of human experience is a legal experience and that the right way to examine the world is to examine it juridically—as the time and place of an extended jurisdiction that expresses itself in terms of closeness.

CHAPTER THREE

Revenant Manuscripts

"Paradoxically, the most living voice is that of the deceased." With these words, Jean-Claude Schmitt addresses the way in which medieval scribes who were in charge of reporting the apparition of a ghost tended to offer the latter's discourse through use of direct speech techniques, whereas the voice of the living who entered into contact with the deceased were reported by way of indirect speech. As Schmitt points out, the ghost is very often an "image of voice." The scholar makes specific reference here to the life of Rabanus Maurus, in which is related the story of the greedy monk, Adelhardus (or Edelhardus): to take revenge on him, God sends against him an impetuous assembly of ghosts, who surround him screaming in unison an image of voice ("vocis imagine consonantes").[1] This image of voice, or maybe voice image, is an "authoritative voice, and it must be conveyed in the most faithful way possible"—according to its own form and to its own language—even if it means that the scribe, a literate notary, must change from Latin to the vernacular language, although this happens only in a number of exceptional cases, as in some of the manuscripts containing the *procès-verbal* regarding the ghost of Gui of Corvo.[2]

When Jean Gobi, the prior of the Dominican monastery of Alès in southern France, was asked to come to the merchant Gui of Corvo's house, he already knew that he might have to encounter a ghost—Corvo's ghost himself. Gobi came accompanied by three monks from his own monastery to act as witnesses, one of whom, Jean Bonafous, was a reader in philosophy, and with them also came more than one hundred other people, including the prominent secular powers of the city of Alès. What Gobi intended to do was maybe nothing other than an inquisition. He undertook an investigation into an issue that had gathered much attention in the city for over a week: in effect, the late Gui de Corvo was still speaking his mind in his own household.

The record of the conversation between the Dominican and the ghost, in particular the interrogation of the ghost, is a faithful reproduction of the inquest. Under the circumstances of the "particular purgatory" in which he now lives and compelled by the presence of the *corpus Christi* in the hands of the *priour*, the ghost, with the voice of the dead, always tells the truth.

The particularity of this truth, once the prior has established that he is dealing with a good spirit and not with a demonic vision (or audition, rather, even if there is an invisible presence that can be somehow felt), is that it does not need any of the attributes of the living voice: ears, mouth, tongue. This truth exists beyond the physical life of the individual who was once the merchant Gui of Corvo. He left behind a sin, and this sin, this trace, this mark, stays alive even if he is dead. There is a ghost because there is some unfinished legal business, even if it is related to religious law.

In this chapter, I will talk about one particular kind of legal thinking that involves what I will call ghost, or revenant, manuscripts. These manuscripts are witnesses to unfinished legal business, and as witnesses, they are summoned, interrogated, doubted. I call ghost or revenant manuscripts the legal manuscripts that keep coming back to renew the force of law they once had. They are crucial to fostering and keeping legal thinking alive, both in the documentary world they belong to and in the imaginary, in the artistic, and literary logical worlds in which they may become fictional devices.

Ghost, or revenant, manuscripts are indicators of a broader unfinished business: the ways in which the particular lives of individual, anonymous people cross paths with legal institutions and how this path-crossing changes the lives of the individuals. It is very often because they crossed paths that we, the historians, know that these individuals existed. What we know about those legal subjects has, nonetheless, a phantasmal character. Through those manuscripts, the legal subjects have become lives in template.

They are lives in template because what we know about these legal subjects is the result of legal interactions that have their own regulated format. *Partidas* 3.18, like many if not all notarial arts, is a compilation of forms, models, and templates that try to cover all kinds of document writing that a legal subject might need in her or his interactions with the legal world, both private and public. The names on these forms, models, and templates may have once been those of a human being, but now they appear there, on those templates, as shadows of the natural person they were. Their own activity on those forms is exemplary: they scream that those names and the remainders of their lives can be erased and replaced with other names that fit the same kind of bill: a sale, a trade, a privilege.

These exemplary structures are essential for conducting business in accordance with the law. They are equally essential to testifying that the biological persons holding a given name can become a legal subject. These templates, forms, and models are the structures that perform the mutation between biological person and legal subject or juridical person, the latter frequently called *persona ficta*. Those models constitute the paperwork that evinces the constant transformation that operates in the base of history. For, indeed, history tells the stories of legal subjects, of those whose existence and experience have been preserved in the archives by means of such paperwork.

Thanks to microhistorians, we are used to reexperiencing the exceptional lives of exceptional characters: Lucrecia by Kagan, Menocchio by Ginzburg, Martin Guerre by Davis.[3] Most of the time, however, ghost manuscripts are unexceptional; the individuals who exist in them are regular people, so much so that sometimes their names disappear forever in order to be—as I will show later—*fulanized*, that is, turned into a so-and-so or a John Doe.

Unfinished business, paperwork, templates, and even ghost, or revenant, manuscripts are some of the names of dead voice and its consequences. Dead voice has many different forms, but the most pervasive of them is the one legislated as such—*voz muerta*, in its dialectical relation with living voice—in Alfonso X's *Siete Partidas* (3.18). Dead voice is everything that results from the system of production of documents and documentation that regulates public and private affairs, at different levels of perceptibility, which include verbal, aural, visual, and material or tactile. Dead voice encompasses both the content of the document and the affects and emotions caused by the presence of the law when it becomes intelligible as law, that is, caused by the aesthetic regime of the legal object.

Dead voice produces revenant manuscripts. They are documents that wander in the realm of the living for centuries, much beyond the biological lives of those involved in the procedures that first gave birth to the legal writing. The biological lives may have ended, but the legal institution of dead voice maintains alive the legal subject.

Dead voice works by means of a *fictio legis* that modifies the temporalities of legal written acts: documents representing acts from the past repeat those acts as if they were taking place in the very moment when we read the paperwork concerning the laws to be enforced. The thirteenth-century intellectual

Siger of Brabant proposed, as one of his six emblematic *impossibilia*, or impossible things, that "the war on Troy is happening right now."[4] It may be impossible from the perspective of a medieval specialist in logic, a dialectician, and that, actually, was his contention. However, some fictions, and in particular the *fictio legis* of dead voice, could, in a sense, perform this sort of miraculous time bending. As we saw in Chapter 2, lawyers like those from Sinibaldo de' Fieschi all the way to Baldo da Ubaldis considered the power of written documents to be nothing short of a miracle, or something that went against nature and against the *ius gentium*, precisely because the synchronizing power of the document (the past act is happening right now), by means of the fictional device that governs dead voice, permits the documents to last beyond the biological lives of those narrated by them in the first place. When Yan Thomas studied the medieval limits to the Roman *fictio legis*, he may have demonstrated that nature should constitute one of the barriers to the heuristics of the *fictio legis*, but dead voice is just one of the ways in which Alfonso's legislation crosses that line.

Dead voice is what makes it that biological lives, turned into juridical lives, can be historically active and actively projected onto the present and the future of other juridical lives, *personae fictae*. Dead voice turns them into pieces of parchment or paper and ink, into portable objects and archivable materials. These are the revenants whose presence and periodical reactivation actually change things from the past, even from pasts that are hundreds of years removed from the present. This historical activity of revenant manuscripts is unsettling for those who enter into contact with them precisely because these manuscripts provoke refractions in the lives of those who participate in the transaction.

How do revenant manuscripts come back? We can identify three different ways for those ghosts to return. They all occur outside the archive, the official space that keeps documents inside, thus kidnapping the ghosts so that they cannot frighten regular people unless the very legal institution is the one that exhibits them.

The archive is the institution that locks up the documents. It is a definitive repository of juridical lives. The ecosystem of dead voice, instead, is the action on the paths and roads outside the institution, and all the places, even the imaginary places, where the development of a plot depends on the activity of a document, or a series of them.

Consider, for example, the manuscript that contains a piece of dead voice that haunts successive generations of subjects each time it is made present with the purpose of changing the development of an event. This is the first way to consider the coming back, or return, of documents. Persons, corporations, fraternities, and other collectives presented privileges, charters, and other documents to kings during their visits or during the *cortes* summoned in different places.[5] Those manuscripts often came from a past generation during which things happened in a different way.[6] From there, they were retrieved and exhibited to the king or the *cortes* with the purpose of changing royal policies. In order to understand this first manifestation of the revenant manuscript, it would be necessary to study the legislation regarding the materiality and the durability of the manuscript, as well as the legislation concerning the procedures for copying and registering the document and the laws concerning the time and duration of a juridical transaction.

The second kind of manifestation of the ghost manuscript explores the "more philosophical" world of poetry.[7] "Poetry" has two different senses here. In the first place, it refers to imaginative creativity that uses words. Second, it refers to the specific literary institution of poetry. Likewise, there are two different poetic returns of the manuscript. In both cases, the manuscript is made present by declaring the absence of the manuscript: the original is not simply exhibited but also described with the help of another manuscript. The first kind of description is often inscribed in copies of the original, or copies of the copies, either as part of the document or as a note on the back of the copy itself—a dorsal note. The second type of description is a description of fictional action, which is instrumental in some poetic accounts. Let's consider, for instance, the chirograph in which Theophilus signs the sale of his soul to the devil in some miracle tales between late antiquity and the late Middle Ages, or the letter in Shakespeare's *King Lear*.[8] Both kinds of ways for the ghost manuscript to come back are related to a poetics of the law—and also to an aesthetics of the law.

The third manifestation of the revenant manuscript is the series of notes created for notaries and other notarial officers. As agents of jurisdiction, notaries used those notes to conduct all private and public affairs among particulars throughout the jurisdictional spaces, both by ordering the production of a document (*iussio*) and by producing the document itself (*redactio*).[9] These books of notes contain all sorts of juridical *lives in template*. These templates stand for pieces of juridical life that intend to assist individuals to undertake different kinds of juridical transactions. Notaries compiled these notes but were less interested in the private details contained in the original documents than in the possibility of universalizing or generalizing the use of each piece.

For this reason, they frequently erased the proper names or the real location of the actual transaction as they *redacted* the documents and replaced the particular details with general ones, *fulano* (like Jane Doe, or so-and-so) instead of the proper name of the persons mentioned in the original document. This is the process I call *fulanization*, a process whereby the *persona ficta* becomes at the same time spectralized (a ghost *fulano* in the place of the real individual on top of a piece of dead voice) and universalized (a document that can be used across jurisdictional space and time.) These fulanized notes show us the backstage of the fictional part in the expression *persona ficta*. The vessel for this other kind of return of the revenant manuscript is the notary, or more exactly, the different kinds of notarial officers who have different tasks in the juridical and judicial arenas.

The relevance of these three forms of documentary return can hardly be overstated. On the one hand, they regulate the ways in which dead voice can be used. On the other hand, these manners in which revenant manuscripts come back normalize the uses of written legal documents. Documents, and the production of documents, have been totally naturalized for us; they are commonplace. Yet, this naturalization is, ultimately, the process of normalization of the ways in which history becomes active in the present and in the future. In effect, these documents are dead history alive: they repeat, by means of dead voice, what was active in the past and that, by dint of the *fictio legis* underwriting dead voice, can become active again as if they were new. This normalization is a juridical effect and a key element of the construction of vernacular jurisdictions. Furthermore, it has a cultural effect in the perception of how to manage the spectralities of the past—its images, its fragmentary remnants—as part of political negotiations.

Such normalization would not be possible without the participation of the disciplines that study documents, books, and manuscripts—that is, codicology, paleography, and diplomatics. Therefore, I would argue it is fitting to say that codicology, paleography, and diplomatics are crucial legal operations. They are not ancillary disciplines at the service of history (*vernaculae*, so to speak; "domestic slaves") or even at the service of philology. Instead, they are some of the central disciplines that buttress the legal discipline itself and constitute its autonomy.

Because they are useful in predicting the future, codicology, paleography, and diplomatics are epistemological devices that are key to the formation of vernacular jurisdictions. This future is, indeed, that of the duration of the legal act, the time of legal procedures. Furthermore, it is also the material future, a future in which all those legal objects come back to claim their ability to be enforced, grounding their enforceability in the codicological, paleographical, and diplomatic descriptions that are integral parts of their legal language. In this sense, none of these three disciplines are exclusively the quantitative sciences that we study in history and philology departments, sciences that reclaim their neutrality. These are heavily politicized disciplines that play a crucial role in the ways in which the past becomes present.[10]

First Revenant: Legislation

Legislators have always been afraid of the dead and the absent body. A dead witness (or an absent witness) makes forgery possible. Because the physical presence of the witness is no more or not available, documents become necessary. In his *Novellae* 73, the emperor Justinian posits that the comparison of manuscripts to determine whether a document is a forgery or not has been prohibited. It is tremendously difficult, he says, to decide whether one person has been the author of two manuscripts that are many years apart: younger writers and older writers differ from each other, because the latter sometimes are tremulous; similar are the effects of fatigue (*languor*). And yet we insist, says Emperor Justinian, in focusing on the change of paper and ink, when these are open to multiple explanations. He complains about how all those problems are real headaches.[11]

At any rate, the dead and absent witnesses face the lawyer as if, or perhaps, with forgery. "Forgery" (*falsitas*) is defined as *imitatio veritatis*, or an attempt to imitate truth, the truth of living voice.[12] Those words resonate with the very issue underlying dead voice: that dead voice is the result of a series of imitations, or fictional devices, working both at the level of the production of the document and at the level of the temporalities of the document. This is why the dead body and absent body, as well as the return of the dead voice as part of an unfinished legal case, elicited specific legislation in the Iberian Peninsula. Such legislation fostered the consolidation of the legal operations that constituted the disciplines of codicology, diplomatics, and paleography.

Ferdinand III (r. 1217–1252), Alfonso's father, promulgated the *Liber Iudiciorum* or, in Spanish, *Fuero Juzgo* in 1241. The declaration was the probable consequence of his newly acquired vast territorial power—which covered

Castile (1217), León (1230), Galicia (1231), and very large parts of al-Andalus—achieved either by conquest or by pacts and agreements of vassalage (1228–1248). Aquilino Iglesia Ferreirós considers the promulgation of the *Liber Iudiciorum* from 1241 onward as the generalization of what had been a specific institution for Córdoba.[13] Indeed, the conquest of Córdoba in 1236 was most probably the key point for the translation of the *Liber Iudiciorum* or *Forum Iudiciorum* into Spanish and the enforcement of the *Fuero Juzgo*.

This code is a compilation of Iberian (Hispanic) Visigothic statutes and jurisprudence that had begun to be promulgated around 642 by Chindasuinth, not unlike the Justinian compilations that were promulgated by Justinian I for the Eastern Empire from the spring of 529 onward. The *Liber Iudiciorum* was the imperial expression of Iberian Roman Germanic law and therefore seemed an appropriate fit for the new juridical situation lived by Ferdinand, which easily dovetailed with the vague ideas and practices of the *Imperium Totius Hispaniae* embraced by Alfonso VII (emperor, r. 1116–1157) by influence of the latter's mother, Queen Urraca (r. 1109–1126), and father, the other emperor, Alfonso VI (r. 1065–1109).

Fuero Juzgo 2.4 is devoted to witnesses and witnessing. Law 3 regulates the case "in which the witness declares one thing orally while a different thing is said in writing."[14] In this law, the legislator considers the possibility that the oral deposition of a witness is countered by a document or letter in which the same witness said something different. The legislation gives preference to the written document, unless the witness asserts that he was not the one who wrote said document. In that case, the one who first showed the document must prove that the witness did, in fact, write the document. If he cannot prove it, then it is for the judge to begin a *pesquisa*, which is the Castilian term for the Latin *inquisitio*, or "inquisition," an inquest. The word *inquisitio* does not appear in the Latin version, since the procedure was not yet regulated, but Ferdinand's translation is post–Lateran IV Council and therefore is already in a dialogue with the new procedures and regulations.[15] Unlike *Novellae* 73, the inquest must compare scripts and the *usus scribendi* from other letters and documents given by the same witness whose testimonies are being questioned. The process of comparing and evaluating scripts and writing habits is one of the crucial elements of paleography, codicology, and diplomatics, and they are here inscribed in the law as integral legal resources.

Regardless of the fact that written proofs may be presented, they are counterpoints to living voice. They are a method of verifying that the witness is telling the truth, or that the truths said in living voice are equivalent to those expressed by means of dead voice. As Law 5 of *Fuero Juzgo* 2.4 establishes, the witness must testify in person, not by letters (something that the *Partidas* 3.16.31 will reaffirm as a rule). The consequences of the contradiction between the bodily deposition and the written document are measured in bodily materiality depending on the social condition of the person to whom the case pertains: if it is a nobleman, he must pay a fine that will hurt his economic body; if it is a person of *menor guisa* (lesser condition), then it will be his physical body that suffers the pain of one hundred lashes.

These laws on witnessing underscore the materiality of biological life and put it at the center of the procedural system. Even though dead voice may have an important role, the living one is what matters for all sorts of juridical and judicial transactions. The ultimate law regulating it is *Fuero Juzgo* 2.4, in which nobody may witness on behalf of a dead person.

In *Fuero Juzgo*, the whole system is built to preserve the direct relationship between dead voice and living beings to link them by an unbreakable chain of mutual truth-telling in which dead voice and living bodies that belong to the same juridical person tell the truth to each other in an autonomous way. Title 5 of *Fuero Juzgo* 2 is entitled "De scripturis valituris et infirmandis ac defunctorum voluntatibus conscribendis" (Concerning valid and invalid writings and how last wills should be composed).[16] While the Latin original has seventeen laws, the Castilian includes twenty. All twenty laws were there to control the "dead" in dead voice, or, in other words, to subject the production of documents to living beings and to their biological duration. The insistence on how to verify whether a document, especially a will, is produced is telling of this anxiety about the preeminence of the living body: *Fuero Juzgo* 2.5.15 stipulates that, as concerns wills,

each man must write his testament by his own hand . . . and then . . . he must write at the bottom of the letter that he confirms everything by his own hand. And then, if the inheritors and their sons have had this letter after thirty years [of having been written], they must show it to the bishop of their land, or to the judge within six months [of the death of the will's author], and the bishop or the judge must then collect three other writings written by the hand of the man who wrote the original will: and then they must check and match the script, to see whether they look alike, and if they do, then the will can be confirmed [as valid].[17]

Similar anxiety may be found in other laws, including *Fuero Juzgo* 2.5.16, in which the legislator empathetically says, "We do not want to withdraw our support of the lesser people," and then he proceeds to give a rule on how to compare and certify a series of documents among those who are mostly illiterate. This legislation is all about the biological markers that not only index the document and make it valid but also curb the possibility of an uncontrolled ghost haunting future lives.

One can see how these documents addressed by the *Fuero Juzgo* insist on the close relationship between the document itself and the person who first wrote them and on a system to evaluate whether the manuscript is a holograph or not. The bishop or the judge is the ultimate paleographer; it is the bishop or judge who is in charge, as well, of deciding the validity of the document with no other intermediation. They execute the diplomatic, codicological, and paleographic exam on the one hand and the sentence regarding its enforceability on the other. In order to do so, they do not create any other authentic person (which we discussed in Chapter 1) different either from themselves or from the author of the document.

Alfonso X went in a different direction. He disembodied the document, so to speak, in order to focus on the document itself, in its form and its personhood, and created a series of other officials and authentic persons who could work with documents in very different ways according to their needs. The system, as we saw in Chapter 2, was much more flexible but also much more complex.

Although it is perfectly possible—even more, it is quite likely—that Ferdinand III was already involved in a series of legislative changes that would move away from the *Fuero Juzgo* and toward a more Romanistic codification, the project would come to fruition only during the kingdom of Alfonso X, with the progressive establishment of the *Fuero Real* first in Aguilar de Campoo in 1255 and then to other cities and polities. At the beginning of the *Fuero Real*, the king addresses the question of the lawlessness of the different places where the *Fuero* was given and expresses his desire to give it so that it may be kept forever and, in a way, legally unify the kingdom. This declaration also amounts to saying that, at least according to this legislator's voice, the *Fuero Juzgo* had also been superseded by local customs, charters, and *fueros* and that the legal situation had perhaps not become the one intended by Ferdinand. The new codifications—as we know, *Fuero Real* from 1255, *Espéculo* from around 1256, and *Siete Partidas* from about 1270—are attempts to break with this situation of jurisdictional multiplicity.

It is the *Third Partida* that was instrumental in designing a codicological, diplomatic, and paleographic discourse internal to the law and inscribed in the legislation. Codicology, diplomatics, and paleography thus become legal and thinking operations: operations that have the purpose of controlling the future and all the possible ways in which juridical manuscripts return to play a role in the present; they are also operations that control the ways in which these manuscripts need to be perceived.

This legislation establishes two kinds of procedures. On the one hand, the law expresses its interest in the types of materials with which a document can be composed. On the other hand, the laws regulate the knowledge and skills necessary for the notaries and other officers who are the custodians of the integrity of dead voice as they become legal philologists. I use "legal philologists" to refer to their expertise in textual material analysis and their ability to examine documents codicologically, diplomatically, and paleographically.

Partidas 3.18.5 is the law that makes the difference between those documents that must be written on leather parchment (*pergamino de cuero*) and those other documents that are to be written on cloth parchment (*pergamino de paño*). The first type of parchment is made out of animal skin, whereas the second one, more fibrous and fragile, is a certain variety of paper produced mostly by recycling linen shirts, a paper very common in Arabic manuscripts and also called Ceuta paper or Toledo paper.[18] The laws legislate the materiality of written communication while at the same time controlling the procedures for copying and dissemination of those documents and the other materials that complete the document in its entirety: seals, signatures, color codes, and so on.[19] To begin with, the document is not just text, script, or hands confirming hands. The document is a multimedia object that includes many elements that, coming from very different spaces of craftsmanship, from different labors, also configure a composite thing. The composite thing is subject to different kinds of loss. Indeed, it can definitely lose text, but it is easier to lose a seal, or a cord, or even a fragment of paper, whereas it is perhaps more difficult to lose a piece of leather parchment.

Dead voice is much more complex than the representation of writing considered as the signs that reproduce oral utterances. Dead voice is much more complex, too, than the mere relationship between individual persons and their hand, their *usus scribendi*, or their will. Dead voice is, in this sense, a site of different media that becomes, at a certain point, independent from the very ability of individuals to create their own documents. Dead voice de-links the document from the individual, liberating it from the biological life of that individual and creating a regime of existence that is proper to the document itself.

For Alfonso, the creativity involved in the regime of dead voice's existence goes beyond the mere verification of the document. Legislating dead voice is also about taking into account the productive elements surrounding the fragility of the manuscript. Such fragility is constituted by marks and features that make visible whether the document has been heavily used or not, whether it has been restored or not, whether it has been modified or not, because the fragilized document cannot come back devoid of its age, of its creases and wrinkles, of its loss of color.

Privileges, a type of document regulated in *Partidas* 3.18.2–3 and that had to last for generations and be kept in archives, cartularies, or other similar collective repositories, show more durable material conditions than those other documents that are given to individuals for more concrete reasons, reasons that have their own time and that last for only a small number of years. Other laws from *Partidas* 3.18.121 are devoted to the materiality of the written object in order to address the kind of private writings that individuals kept in their own "notebooks" (*quadernos*), including lists, or budgets, or other fragmentary notes; the law is interested in these materials in order to exclude them from the procedures, precisely because they are too close to the individual body, to the biological life. These notebooks are devoid of the other material elements that form dead voice as an integral complex site of communication, and they are juridically unreadable. These notebooks can never return as revenant manuscripts because they are not acts; they exist only as a memento of something else (*por remembrança*)—they are far from being part of the collective memory of legal power that is the responsibility of the sensitive soul of the kingdom (*Partidas* 2.13).

The laws from *Partidas* 3.19 to 3.21 are devoted to regulating the tasks and skills of notarial officers, who are in charge of the production of documents and of examining existing manuscripts. These officers are the actual legal philologists and, as regulated by *Partidas* 3.18.111, they must be able to identify the external characteristics of a document as well as the materials with which it was produced; they must also be able to date the script and, in some cases, identify the places where cancellations or erasures may have occurred, determining when they occurred and whether those cancellations or erasures are sufficient to validate or invalidate the document.[20]

Before the aging document, the clients of the law—those who need the documents for their own purposes, those who can either confirm or abolish them—can make difficult decisions with the help and participation of those notarial officers. Here is the case of one of those documents presented to Alfonso at the beginning of his rule. It is a document of confirmation now preserved in the Archive of the Burgos Cathedral, dated and signed May 1254 (Alfonso began reigning in June 1252):

> Don Alfonso, by God's grace king of Castile, Toledo, Leon, Galicia, Seville, Cordoba, Murcia, Jaen, to all the people in my kingdom who see this letter, health and greetings. Let it be known that the inhabitants of Villalbilla came to see me in Toledo, and they showed me a privilege given to them by the emperor, and they asked me, by mercy, that I confirm it. And I, who had other more urgent things to do, could not confirm it. I however command that you keep their privilege as it was first given to them during the time of King Alfonso, my great grandfather, and the time of King Ferdinand, until his death. And this, temporarily, be like that, until I come up there to their land; then, I will look at it, and I will be informed on how they were given this privilege, and then I will decide as I find fitting.[21]

This temporary confirmation declares both a psychological and a material reality. The people from Villalbilla, which today is in the province of Madrid, had traveled for over sixty-eight miles to get to Toledo in the hopes that their 1135 privilege, which had been signed by the Emperor Alfonso VII and apparently confirmed by Ferdinand III, would be confirmed as well by the new king. The king, occupied in more pressing concerns and unwilling to be hurried in this matter, decided that the document would keep its legal force until he could travel himself to Villalbilla. The document not only concerned a legal transaction but also evinced an aesthetic issue: the document was insufficiently examined because of the king's having been engaged in other business and the rush with which the inhabitants of Villalbilla came to show the king their privilege, a privilege that had been alive for almost one and a half centuries across the political body of four kings and, very likely, several generations of Vubilleros. This insufficient examination of the document, returning from the past, provoked the temporary confirmation of the document. The document could not be described until the king himself completed a visual inspection of the document, so that he could match the description and reading. Only from that moment onward would the confirmation (or lack thereof) be possible.

From here, we will be talking about an aesthetics of dead voice—a legal aesthetics, really—that we will explore in depth in Chapter 5 of this book. It is because of this aesthetics that we can tackle the reactions experienced by the physical and juridical bodies in front of the materiality of the legal object—the object transporting the law across spaces and times—during the moment of juridical exchange.

This aesthetics is not only a private reaction that works at the level of the individual, feeling, or the heartbeat, it is also a reaction that conditions ulterior legal operations. The insufficient examination of the document is one of them. It causes juridical uncertainty, a lack that also includes the very terminology: since (says the king) I was not able to confirm the privilege, we must do *as if* the document had legal force until, once examined, the confirmation becomes possible or not. Here, the *fictio legis* acquires a specific value by means of its expression about the document that does not pertain to the moment of legislation but rather to the moment of jurisprudence in the civil, juridical exchange. The extension of the fictional device to the jurisprudential archive is one of those elements that expresses the particular negotiations that take place at the level of vernacular jurisdiction.

The document's spectrality is inscribed in the document itself. Signed by Alfonso VII in 1135, it had been validated by four successive kings, but the only remaining trace of that validation is the living voice of the Vubilleros, who told the king about it. While the copies of the document had been successfully passing through space and time for generations, the only element that helped control the uncertainty of dead voice was the surviving voice of the Vubilleros, which is represented as a living voice.

During the same years, the first months of 1255, Alfonso was constantly confronted with urgent requests for confirmations of all sorts of documents by collectivities who were afraid of seeing their documents—and therefore their privileges, rights, and others—fall into some sort of legal limbo where they had neither applicability nor the lack thereof; they were simply waiting, but in the wait they risked becoming irrelevant. Often, these confirmations were requested en masse, and the king was presented with fourteen or twenty documents at once, so that he could confirm them all at the same time.[22] Each time a document was seen, the document was the object of description: the confirmation letter also reproduced the aesthetic moment, insofar as this being seen allowed the king to proceed toward the confirmation of the document and to the identification of the same document for future exhibition: future instances of the revenant manuscript.

In less busy circumstances, only a little bit after the first incident, Alfonso seems to have been able to evaluate the privilege granted to Villalbilla by the emperor. It was January of 1255, only eight months after the first encounter between the Vubilleros and the monarch. The document, it turned out, was not a simple privilege but, rather, a much more important kind of document from the perspective of the royal jurisdiction. It contains *fueros especiales*: a special charter, that is, a local juridical regime that had been approved exclusively for them. After looking at it, Alfonso gave an external description of the manuscript—the document did not have a seal—and the king also added to the document the assertion that, according to the Vubilleros, the privilege had always been confirmed for them. Alfonso's confirmation was, in its turn, reproduced by ulterior confirmations by Sancho IV in 1286, Alfonso XI in 1332, and Peter I in 1353—that is, at the very beginning of their kingdoms, which is a clear index of the historical urgency of the Vubilleros' eagerness to resuscitate the dead voice given by the emperor, as if it were granted now for the first time.[23]

Alfonso did not intervene in the document granted by his great grandfather. This is relevant because of the jurisdictional issues that surround the *fueros especiales*. He accepted the historical record, but by refusing an aesthetic participation in its materiality, the king also refused to index it with a symbolic mark of his jurisdictional authority. Adding such a mark would have been like questioning his own drive to foster a central jurisdiction, because it would have accepted exceptional jurisdictional rights from a particular territory in his kingdom.

Alfonso, nevertheless, was eager to intervene in the accruing legal aesthetics of other documents by restoring them. In the same month, on January 22, 1255, Alfonso was presented with a privilege granted by his father, Ferdinand III, slightly less than ten years before. In this document, the king sanctioned the sale of some properties. A lead seal from Ferdinand still hangs on the document. Alfonso instilled new life into this document by adding, "so that it stands firmer, my own lead seal."[24] This modification of the manuscript and its legal aesthetics is a juridical operation insofar as it helps to determine and condition the very document's future: the addition of the seal makes the act stand more firmly, heavily, as well as making it more visible by giving it the weight of two royal generations. The document, with its new seal, would also be more difficult to forge, thus controlling the royal anxiety, which was expressed in the preambular pieces at the inception of the manuscripts of the *Espéculo* and the first edition of the *First Partida*, that people in his kingdom might erase parts of the legal writings in order to write something else on top of them.[25] The modification was a physical restoration of the document: by renewing its material elements, the new ones gave the document a new life, a future that began right then; the dead voice was as if it were a new act.

Revenant manuscripts and their legal aesthetics did not exclusively affect kings. Legal aesthetics in vernacular language, as part of a growing vernacular jurisdiction, touched everybody. It is by means of these ghost manuscripts that we can see juridical persons on parade, since they are indeed juridical persons and not people in flesh and bones. Even when flesh and bones are mentioned, these are juridical flesh and bones coming back from different bands of the social spectrum.[26] What seems more relevant in this vernacular construction and the vernacular expansion of the juridical person is the creation of a juridical vernacular language fostered by Alfonso X, which was really generalized and developed by and for him, that envelops the existence of all the citizens in an early realization of what Ángel Rama famously called *la ciudad letrada,* or "the lettered city."[27] The language of the law in the vernacular, even if it was only an army of false friends, was still the biggest cultural event of the Iberian thirteenth century.

Although many examples could be provided from a large corpus of documents, I will only give one. In 1354, before the notary Nuño Pérez, the Franciscan friar Fray Antonio de Belver produced a "privilege written on leather parchment and sealed with a lead seal, hanging on red and yellow silken cords, from Pope Boniface, as it was apparent."[28] The original document, Fray Antonio assured Nuño, was fragile and could easily be destroyed "by fire, or in a fireplace, or by water, or any other accident" (por fuego, o por leña, o por agua, o por otra ocasión). For this reason, he asked for a copy "or two, or more." In many of the letters asking for copies of the documents (*letras de traslado*), the interested parties show their anxiety about being able to keep and preserve their copies, and therefore, they ask for as many copies as possible, spectral letters with which to inundate spaces and times around them. A costly enterprise indeed, because according to *Partidas* 3.19.14–15, each copy represents material and intellectual labor that must be paid at a recommended price of between one and four *sueldos* of good currency, excluding gold and silver coinages. The same *Partida* also recommends, however, making several copies of certain documents, so that one can be kept on the subject's body—as if dressed in the document—while the others can be kept at a friend's house, a church, or any other place of safe deposit.

Antonio de Belver's request became a negotiation. We cannot know whether there was tension between the positions of the notary and that of the friar. Nuño does not seem to review the original document, neither the content nor the quality of the Latin in which it was written. Nevertheless, Nuño is what the *Partidas* call, we have seen, an authentic person. A second verification on the part of the bishop became necessary, and this verification agreed with two laws, *Partidas* 3.18.111–112: "la petiçion . . . era buena e justa, et . . . el dicho privilejo non era rroto, nin corruto, nin cançellado, nin emmendado, nin era sospechoso en todo nin en parte del" (the request was good, and fair, and the privilege was not torn, it was not corrupted, it did not have emendations, it did not have cancellations, and it was not suspect as a whole or in any of its parts).

The *letras de traslado* (letters that contain the reasons why a document was copied) are excellent narrative machines, even in those cases in which their brevity makes us think of yet other formulaic conventions already catalogued in diplomatic handbooks. As narrative machines, the letters accompany, describe, and envelope the original manuscript and thus become an essential part of the legal aesthetics of the manuscript as well. They show the negotiations that took place around a certain document, whether the latter was a privilege that needed to be confirmed or reenforced or another kind of document that somebody wished to have copied. They are positive letters, insofar as they always show that the document has been confirmed and that the document has been examined and then copied; they never show a failed transaction, only successful ones. These letters foreground the negotiations around the manuscript and the efficacy of the verification procedures as well as the expansion of the domain of sincerity, both historical and diplomatic.[29] Spread throughout the jurisdictional chronotopes, the letters transmit those negotiations and debates, the people who participated in them, and the sincerity that is the backbone of the forms of the archive and of the varieties of juridical transactions, both public and private. The letters also account for the way in which the very system works, and as such, they are also sources of social and political tranquility.

The narratives contained in them have different degrees of complexity, but most of them have something in common: the way in which they describe the original documents. This description makes present what was past, investing the copy with the same value as the original, but without the original.

Tuesday, May 2nd, 1307. This day, Corroçano of Briviesca came
into the presence of Pedro Bonifaz, the king's mayor in Burgos. The
former produced a letter, written on leather parchment, and signed
with the sign of Juan Pérez, presenting himself as the notary of the
city of Carrión. The letter had a wax seal hanging on a black silken
cord. The seal was shaped as an escutcheon, divided in four fourths,
with wolves; around the escutcheon, there was written "Gonzalo
Gómez's S." The letter was healthy, it did not have erasures, it was
not torn, corrupted, or doubtful in any way. [30]

The *letra de traslado* does not say anything about the content of the
original document. It does not address the language, either. It reads the original in order to assess its completeness. It also makes sure that it is adequately
transmitting the external circumstances that led to the request of the copy
and who is who in the negotiation. Finally, and more important, the *letra de
traslado* envelopes the copy of the original and translates in words, and by
means of philological legal description, something that cannot be transported
by any other means: the very materiality and the legal aesthetics of the
original.

The copy is description. It eliminates from the realm of the visible and
the tangible the aesthetic elements that constitute the codification of the
language of authenticity contained in the original. Such language of authenticity is the original object having been written on a certain kind of parchment or paper, the kind of seal and its external aspect and materials, and
whether the seal hangs from one or many cords and their color. The original
letter is the body of a juridical subject that cannot be actually reproduced,
that cannot be subject to any sort of market, and that cannot be disposed
of. All that is outside the material characteristics of the copy. The letter
accompanying the copy is the body of knowledge, the security that somebody
else has seen the original documentary body, that has been in contact with
it, indexed by it; the *letra de traslado* may describe the original, and by doing
it—by becoming a narrative of the original—also creates the language in
which to refer to a certain document, to a certain ghost that is not there and
whose effects are nevertheless active because it can be described according to
a certain legal philology. This paratext that is the *letra de traslado* has the goal
of securing that the legal aesthetics, even though imperceptible to the senses,
may be realized by linguistic means; it is a mental image of the original, or

in the language of medieval aesthetics, a *phantasma*.[31] The description contained in the paratext that we call *letra de traslado* pinpoints the contact zone where another *fictio legis* becomes real: the copy must be considered as if it were the original before, after, and during the legal procedures, whichever they are.

Neither diplomatics nor codicology nor paleography are simply descriptive sciences exterior to the manuscript. By the same token, diplomatics is also not something that allows us to understand the juridical act once we are in front of it. Codicology, diplomatics, and paleography are inscribed in the legal manuscript; they are some of the manuscript's legal operations. There is, on the one hand, a verbal inscription, a certain anxiety in the description of the manuscript presented in front of the king, coming back to him from remote generations, or in front of whoever is in need of the document, or a copy of it, or two, or many. On the other hand, there is this written description—the one that accompanies the copy, the one that stands for the original—which creates a language and a style in which to refer to the irreproducible one that needs to be kept in some archive.

Second Revenant: Poetry

Juridical manuscripts, and documents in particular, have a life beyond their physical appearance, even when it is a physical presence that is doubtful, weak, torn, almost transparent, a hand holding up a shred of paper, or nothing at all. Juridical manuscripts also have a literary life that is essential for the understanding of their spectral regime of existence.

Our common conception of literature cannot be adequately applied to the Middle Ages.[32] Medieval literature is very often a laboratory of legal aesthetic. Poetry is not only about artistry with words, because many Aristotelian commentators—commentators that include al-Fārābī (c. 872/257–c. 950/339) Averroes, and the Christian translators Herman the German (fl. 1240–1256; d. 1270), William of Moerbeke (ca. 1215–1286), and Dominicus Gundissalvus / Gundissalinus (1115–ca. 1190)—put it in the same epistemological group with dialectics and rhetoric, as a logical artifact. Narratives and fictions are heuristic and epistemological devices that were widely theorized in legal science and scholarship, as we know already. An exemplum is also a legal concept, sometimes meaning "precedent" and sometimes "document copy." Using all those practices and theories, authors (named and anonymous alike) explored the cognitive effects of the presence of the juridical object.[33] Acts, documents, seals, and contracts are like fetishes that travel across literary texts. In those literary texts, dead voice becomes one of their strangest characters, whose presence and movements are marked by exchanges, secret lives, lies, forgery, and forgetfulness that change the lives of the other juridico-literary characters not only in their temporal lives but also in their afterlives.

The *casus*—case, but also "fall"—of Theophilus is perhaps paradigmatic of how dead voice becomes a character. The story is very well known. It is about a church administrator (*economus, vidâme*, etc.) who, according to a very emotional sermon pronounced in Amiens (Picardie, France) in 1260, "estoit du tout devenus hom au diable, dont dex nous gart" (entirely became a devil's vassal, God save us!).[34] The stained glass windows of Laon's Cathedral, created around 1205–1225, tell the story of Theophilus, too. In one of these windows, Theophilus kneels in front of a greenish, horned devil who is taking his hands, while *li gius* (the Jew), as the French poet and cleric Gautier de Coincy (1178–1236) calls the human antagonist in his *Miracle*, raises a document aloft. Similar images—which evoke a thirteenth-century iconographic workshop with special interest in the miracle of Theophilus—can be found among the windows of Sainte-Chapelle in Paris (among other churches), now preserved and exhibited at the Musée du Moyen Âge, Thermes de Cluny in Paris; likewise, the image of Theophilus as the devil's vassal with the Jew showing the document can be seen on the tympanum that gives access to Notre Dame de Paris in the North transept. In all of them, the hands in the hands of the devil are underscored by the prominence of the signature on the contract accounting for the sale that has just taken place.

The miracle of Theophilus has a very long genealogy, but in the thirteenth century, it was linked to the emergence of what Alain Boureau has called the heretic Satan.[35] The images in Notre Dame de Laon, Notre Dame de Paris, and Sainte-Chapelle are also sermon sites, places where the preacher can point to the characters involved in the story and how, in fact, the signed contract is transformed from the triumphal element of the victory over sin, the victory of the past—as we will see immediately—to the ultimate expression of the new truth represented by the doctrines of Lateran Council IV. As Aden Kumler has shown, the images produced after this council are marked with the idea of translating truth.

In the very different sources of this miracle story in Greek, Latin, German, French, and Spanish, the document is the real main character in the narrative, because the miracle cannot be acknowledged until the document has been destroyed or has vanished forever. Authors and rewriters of the story of Theophilus have indicated that the real antagonist of the narrative is precisely the revenant manuscript, the document that can come back, even in spite of the miraculous intervention of the Virgin.

In most versions, the document, the contract, is a chirograph, an eminently private document that sports two symmetric versions which are separated but can be reunited by the *divise*, usually a word (the word "chirograph," for instance) or an alphabetic series (A B C). The alphabetic series from the two symmetric parts must be matched in order to recognize the document's validity.

The production of the chirograph also invokes a more fundamental miracle, a universal one in this case. In his *Epistle to the Colossians*, Paul explains that by replacing circumcision with the new alliance represented by baptism, Christ has definitively taken the contract of sin—a chirograph signed between the malign and mankind—from the devil's hands: "[13] And you, being dead in your sins and the uncircumcision of your flesh, hath he quickened together with him, having forgiven you all trespasses; [14] Blotting out the *handwriting of ordinances* [χειρογραφον τοις δογμασιν; chirografum decretis] that was against us, which was contrary to us, and took it out of the way, nailing it to his cross."[36]

Recovering the document was not enough: it was necessary to nail it to the cross, to crucify it, and to exhibit it forever on the very same instrument of salvation by sacrifice, now without Christ's body, after his resurrection. On visual representations of this moment, including seventeenth-century emblems, the chirograph is indeed nailed to the cross, while on both sides one can see the melancholic, utterly lost figures of Adam and the devil, the first signatories.[37]

Likewise, the chirograph signed by Theophilus that led to his soullessness—which is represented by the loss of his shadow—cannot simply be invalidated, even, in this case, by the Virgin. The document needs to be recovered. In Gautier de Coincy's version, the devil "en enfer ses lettres emporte" (brings his letter to hell), and when the church administrator seeks the Virgin's help, he is most explicit about what needs to be done:

jamais nul jor n'iere asseür
devant que je ne raie l'écrit,
qui ma mort devise et décrit.

(I won't feel safe for a single day
until I can scratch the writing
that my death marks and describes.)[38]

The Virgin, nevertheless, does not destroy the letter. She puts it on Theophilus's chest. In the Castilian version by the monk and notary Gonzalo de Berceo, Theophilus asks the Virgin to retrieve the document, but the Virgin responds that she does not want her son to go back to hell, where he had already been to recover the chirograph Paul said had been signed by humankind.[39] Despite this reluctance, the letter that he had asked the Virgin for on Thursday is delivered back to him by the Virgin herself—with a certain violence—on Saturday, so that on Sunday, during mass, the preacher can show and describe the letter in his sermon. The letter, after having been shown and described, can thus be burned at the stake *coram populo*, a cycle that reproduces that of the death, resurrection, glorification, and recuperation of the original chirograph for the redemption of humankind.

On the windows of Cathedral of Laon, the last moment—the retrieval of the document now presented to the bishop before its destruction—shows that the document has become a completely different sort of manuscript, one on which there is nothing written. Rather, it represents an image: that of a big fish, the original image of Christ and the paleo-Christians, the first men fishmongers.

Literature—poetry—is full of revenant manuscripts and documents, because literature itself is one of them. In the Middle Ages, the aesthetic of literary manuscripts is not different from legal aesthetics. Both explore similar effects by means of dialectics and fiction—philosophy and fiction—and have a clear series of theses to present about the power of legal bonds and transactions: effects that are directed to the emotions, to the affects, to the reverential fear and other that mix bodily and cognitive responses.

Third Revenant: *Fulano*

Title 18 of the *Third Partida* is devoted to the regulation of dead voice. In order to regulate it, the legislator does two different things. First, he gives a typology of possible documents. Although the legislator is not systematic, he is always very precise, and in this typology he tends to include elements regarding the materiality of the document: the kind of content, the things a document does, and the time a document lasts. In some cases, the legislator privileges one part over the other. For instance, addressing the *privilegio rodado*, the legislator includes a full description of the material aspect and components of the *privilegio* (*Partidas* 3.18.2–3). In other cases, as, for instance, when he addresses the typology of the letter for selling properties of the church, the same legislator seems less concerned with those material or aesthetic elements and much more with the effects of such letters (*Partidas* 3.18.63). Also, in many cases, aside from describing the object itself, the legislator gives a series of examples of those manuscripts. Here, "example" has its full juridical sense of both "copy" and "precedent." In other words, these manuscripts generate a sort of jurisprudence that can be used to homogenize the way in which juridical business takes place across the vernacular jurisdiction.

Any notarial system always makes a corpus of documentary models available. In thirteenth-century notarial arts from Bologna and from Paris, the lion's share of the texts is devoted to the reproduction of models for notarial writing. In a different sense—because it is not notarial art but rather the law—*Partidas* 3.18, the title about dead voice, is a collection of models and forms useful for notarial writing. Notaries from the fourteenth and fifteenth century often created their own books of notes, of which we still have many copies preserved from al-Andalus, Castile, Aragon, and Galicia.[40] After the *Third Partida*, the most important is probably the *Notas del Relator*, which was compiled by Fernán Díaz de Toledo around 1450 and printed from 1493 onward to become a best seller.[41]

I would like to raise the question of how notarial forms play with the dialectical relation between closeness and disembodiment. Here, closeness is the sensation that the document is making a statement about somebody—or about something that seems to be part of everyday life. Closeness is also the sensation that it is about someone whom I, the reader, might know. Conversely, disembodiment is the certainty that, in the end, this closeness does not seem to refer to anybody in particular and that all the events and cases from the document are, in fact, hypostatized ideas or a typology of political, social, and otherwise juridical problems.

The dialectics between closeness and disembodiment exploits the spectral nature of the juridical manuscript. As we have seen, *Partidas* 3.18 preserves, almost embalms, by means of the miniarchive it legislates, a collection of documents that seem to have had force of law, sometimes from the Castilian chancery (although originally in Latin), and that have been translated for the occasion; other documents have been translated and copied from other notarial formularies originally in Latin; and, finally, other documents have been invented specifically to be part of this legal title, because of a series of new necessities.

This archival spectrality is an operation related to jurisprudence. As jurisprudence, however, it is unique, insofar as what we see in notarial formularies is the way in which a concrete case has become a formal model. Jurisprudence, as we know it, is all about the concrete case and its particular details, all of which need to be described with great precision in order to become a precedent in content that can be enforced again so that the case can constitute a mandatory piece in legal science and its applicability. As such, the sentences from the jurisprudential archive can be repeated because they are able to solve prior legal cases, according to the principle of *stare decisis et non quieta movere* (to stand by decisions and not to change what has already been settled). The jurisprudential archive produces a sensation of integrity: every case has a precedent, and judges and magistrates, as well as other lawyers in their arguments, can always find the lineage of one given case and the sentences produced in such a case by means of a retrieval system able to collate narratives, arguments, and events.

Spectrality, on the other hand, might suggest erasing some concrete details from the juridical case in order to make room to the model. Its goal is no other than recycling a system of formulas that belong both to the domain of language and to the domain of juridical procedure. Concerning language, the spectral notarial formulary makes sure that legal operations remain untouched, particularly in all those operations that Yan Thomas categorized as the "artifices of truth." The artifices of truth are those discursive strategies that turn the results of a conceptual fabrication in juridical thought into a juridical reality. In relation to juridical procedure, these models make sure that all juridical persons who enter into a given legal transaction describe things in the same way, following the same order, with the same rhetoric. These things are, in fact, complex parts of the procedure that can end up changing the lives of those involved in the trial or other judicial process.

This operation of spectrality can, in fact, have many different consequences: for instance, it can affect the ways in which real estate may be sold as a piece unattached to the personal history of the individuals who make the transaction—the seller and the buyer; their memories disappear forever from the surface of the document, so their feelings can never become archival concepts that can disturb the possible futures of this transaction. Let us imagine a seller who does not want to sell, and let us also imagine that this unwillingness, and the violence the sale inflicts on his feelings, are to be represented in the document. As another example, consider some inquisitions, like the one undertaken in 1280 by Alfonso X and his son, the *infante* Sancho, in which a precise one hundred witnesses from the city of Frías were interrogated using the very same questionnaire and the same formulas for each one of them. Although the law is eager to do productive things using feelings, emotions, and affects in its own interest (as we will see more clearly in the next two chapters), legislators also prefer to give the sensation that juridical acts are free of emotion, dispassionate.

With the purpose of spectralizing juridical objects, notarial formularies erase some important elements from the actual documents: dates are done away with, and personal names, as well as toponyms, also disappear. Here is one example:

> Let all those who see this letter know how I, John Doe, and I, John Doe, the sons of John Doe, inhabitant of Some Place, us, and each of us, with no restriction or pressure whatsoever, and without having been forced by anybody, but rather on our own and free will, we declare and certify, by this letter that: you, John Doe, son of John Doe, inhabitant of Some Place, have or had been accused regarding the death of John Doe, our brother, during a riot and quarrel that occurred. However, we, all the aforementioned, and each of us, have been assured and certified by means of good, credible, and trustworthy men, that you, said John Doe were there, and that our brother was responsible for his aforementioned death, whereas you were and are without guilt, and it was said John Doe who instigated the quarrel.[42]

The text presents a model for dismissing the accusations against somebody concerning the death of a relative. The form is in itself an intriguing, thick plot. The individuals from the original have completely disappeared, their names have been replaced with the Spanish form of the Arabic indefinite *fulān*. The whole scene seems spectral: the juridical persons get confused with one another, the place is not there anymore, and the dates have vanished. What remains is the raw account of urban violence among relatives and friends. What remains is the possibility of a quarrel, of a sudden death in the middle of a fight, and accusations being made. What remains is the pervasive possibility of this narrative's being repeated ad infinitum, so much so that a model becomes necessary, so that new names can be filled into the blanks of the plot formula. What remains is, ultimately, the possibility of blaming the victim and the possibility of a pardon. Everything is presented in the same way, with the same description of the events, and those involved in the events address urban powers, juridical powers, the king, and God in the same way. The form establishes in a metonymical regime the order of fidelities of the many John Does that are there.

Repertories of formulas are pure form. They are there to be detached from the codex that contains them so they can be filled out with particular data from a future case. They are also a way to posit that should a certain document reappear before us, it must return in a certain fashion, with certain aesthetic values, within a given regime of perceptibility, and while relinquishing any particular or idiosyncratic characteristics. Every juridical transaction must adjust itself to narrative and descriptive features that are contained in the formulary. The formulary dictates an aesthetics of the continent, to which the juridical persons must accommodate themselves.

The Unsaid

After Aristophanes recovers from his hiccups—an undesirable effect of too much drink—he tries to "unsay what I had said" (καί μει ἔστω ἄρρητα τὰ εἰρημένα: ἄρρητα, "unsay"; εἰρημένα "what has been said") using a polyptoton that makes much more sense in Greek than in English. According to Socrates in *Phaedrus*, this would be possible only in the realm of the oral, while words, once gone through the pharmacy of the written word, can never be unsaid. Walter Ong had a similar perspective when he talked about how written texts, as opposed to oral utterances, keep saying the same thing over and over again.[43]

Alfonso X didn't seem to think the same way—at least not always, at least not systematically, at least not in particular cases. He was anxious about the fact that once uttered the word can never be unsaid and also that it can, as it were, rebound multiplied against the walls of culture (*Partidas* 2.4.1). On the one hand, he was interested in how living voices perform their testimonies in many different ways that need to be not only listened to but also recorded, reread, and corrected, so that they can be stabilized in one single performance ("performance" is the right word because they are always doing something very specific, they are an act). On the other hand, Alfonso was clearly concerned with the fact that written texts actually never say the same thing—they can and do change all the time—and the spectral lives of dead voices are very complex devices that are extraordinarily hard to arrest in a certain way that can "remain permanently, firmly, and stably."[44] In the economy of history, documents are not what remain from previous eras. They are, according to the legal fiction governing dead voice, always contemporary. They become new by dint of their own spectrality, by their ability to be active across generations.

Dead generations are contemporary, as Marx said, because they exert a nightmarish weight on the brains of living generations.[45] Throughout the centuries, dead generations have presented themselves dressed in leather parchment, or in linen parchment, or in other writing material. Sometimes they come dressed for a party, and sometimes in rags, but they are always accompanied by the way in which they enforce the law, a force of law that has been able to keep its spectral being for centuries in very concrete circumstances. Voice may die, but since it can be unburied from particular archives, from personal archives, from local and institutional archives, this voice is never completely dead, and it keeps haunting both legal professionals and the clients of the law.

Revenant manuscripts are scary, and it is necessary to conceptualize this fear in two different domains. The first is the representation of the feelings provoked by its presence. The other is the theorization of those feelings within legal codification. One of my tasks is, precisely, to explore the ways in which the Law conceptualizes emotions and affections as well as feelings. We already know how Roman law shows its interest and codifies the *vices of the will*, creating, for instance, specific laws about *quod metus causa gestum erit* (that is, about all those things that we do because of fear).

In vernacular legislations, feelings and emotions are not in a diglossic regime but, rather, have become part of public expression in a language that resembles everyday language. It is by that that legal thinking occurs.

CHAPTER FOUR

Legislating Friendship

Al gouernamiento de las gentes pertenescen las leyes que ayuntan los
coraçones de los omes por amor: es esto es, derecho e razón: ca destas
dos sale la justicia cumplida, que faze a los omes biuir cada vno como
conuiene. E los que ansi biuen, non han porque se desamar, mas
porque se quere querer bien. Porende las leyes que son derechas,
fazen ayuntar la voluntad del vn ome con el otro desta guisa, por
amistad.

—Partidas 1.1.7

Therefore let this law [*lex*] be established [*sanciatur*] in friendship: neither
ask dishonourable things, nor do them, if asked."[1] This is the only *law* Cicero
accepts for friendship, and it is the center of what has been called his *lex
amicitiae*, or friendship law. Cicero's friendship law has, however, a strictly
political character; it belongs in the realm of moral philosophy, not in the
realm of legislation. Despite the fact that he wrote it, it remains an "unwritten
law," part of Cicero's conception of friendship as a civil duty, which he also
elaborates on in his *De amicitia*.

Aristotle addresses friendship in *Nicomachean Ethics*, book 8. Right at
the beginning, he states, "when there are friends, there is no need of justice
[δικαιοσύνης]." Indeed, he says, "friendship keeps the city united, and
legislators [νομοθέται] devote more of their effort to it than to justice
itself."[2] For Aristotle, love of friendship is similar to "concord," or "oneness
of mind, or thought," which are the meanings offered by the different dic-
tionaries for the concept of ὁμόνοια used by Aristotle. By means of this

concord, by means of friendship, cities are eager to expel hatred and enmity (ἔχθρα).

The affinity between law and friendship seems strange or tenuous at first. While friendship cannot be legislated, it can supersede legislation or make justice simply unnecessary. Alternatively, it is governed by the law of virtue. For Aristotle, friendship, which is either virtue or comes accompanied by a virtue, is what is most necessary for life (ἔτι δ' ἀναγκαιότατον εἰς τὸν βίον). For Cicero, this life is civil life in particular, the republican kind of community that reproduces itself by means of links including friendship. This law of virtue, ethical and civil, is also central for Averroes, who produced a middle commentary to *Nicomachean Ethics*, whose Arabic version is not extant, although we have Hebrew and Latin versions. The Latin version of Averroes's *Middle Commentary*, translated from Arabic by Herman the German, also underscores the centrality of this affinity between friendship and the law and translates νομοθέται as *legislatores*; in Averroes's commentary, as in Aristotle's text, the legislators rest when friendship is present, because they know that justice will be preserved by means of love (*dilectio* is the Latin noun used in the *Commentary* in Latin).[3]

Aristotle's *Nicomachean Ethics*, Averroes's *Middle Commentary*, and Cicero's *Laelius de amicitia* are the main sources of Alfonso's legislation concerning friendship. To the best of my knowledge, there is no other legislation of friendship—or at least none that could have inspired Alfonso's own take. Alfonso, however, understood this affinity between law and friendship in a completely different way, and he took it in a direction that is worth exploring.

In exploring this legislation, we look at how Alfonso's legal workshop understood and practiced the techniques of dead voice as perplexing legislation. An examination of this legislation of friendship will allow us to delve into the legislative techniques implemented by Alfonso's workshop to obtain political advantages from a redefinition of the legal discipline and its autonomy, even when it involved the incorporation of external disciplines like philosophical corpora and fictional devices.

This exploration of the legislation of friendship will also allow us to further investigate one of the main elements we have already conceptualized as central to the technologies of legal codification implemented in the *Siete Partidas*, namely, the constitution of a legal science that is supported by an economy of affects, passions, feelings, and in particular, love as the Alfonsine workshop used the concept. This affective turn in the technique of legislation has political and social consequences that will be addressed in this chapter.

Finally, it can be argued that legislating and generally regulating friendship is one of the ways to consolidate central jurisdiction and sovereign power under the premises of the constitution of a more horizontal, delocalized, and capillary circulation of power. As we will see, legislating and regulating friendship is a way to remove agency and power from the relationship among anonymous friends in order to turn them into juridical subjects; friendship itself, as a kind of relationship, is removed from the private sphere to be made a relationship under specific jurisdiction.

I can offer a more contemporary model of the regulation of friendship. Modern concepts of friendship and their regulations on the part of some social-media companies also utilize affect relations to more easily target consumers commercially and ideologically. They seek to build and grow communities and networks of consumers that share stories about themselves, their lives, their private interests, and customs in a sort of never ending auto-ethnography. These "social media" businesses foster a growing desire among redefined, regulated friends to submit themselves to a voluntary servitude of sorts to the capitalist market. In these cases, the documents regulating the contractual terms between the company and its customers (who are not friends of the company but rather friends among themselves) establish a series of friendship norms, the concept of friend, and the acts of befriending and de-friending that form part of the larger "expository society" recently studied by Bernard Harcourt in *Exposed*. In his book, Harcourt critically thinks about the challenges that result from the continuous system of digital oversharing and the consequences it has for the definition of the *persona* and of a new social model—Harcourt's expository society—after the punitive society and the disciplinary society.[4]

The mediation (and perhaps regulation) of friendship by contemporary companies recalls the necessities of legislating friendship in the medieval vernacular jurisdictions studied in this chapter. This is because friendship also constitutes one of the areas of surveillance (based on desire and obedience) of the *persona ficta*. In the legislation of friendship, the corporation and the king play the similar role of a third friend, as the object of identification of the friends—in Freudian terms—since both the corporation and the king have actual access to the things desired by the friends considered to be subjects of the law.

Legislating friendship involves different kinds of challenges. In the first place, the concept of friendship needs to be emptied of its conventional significance in order for it to be defined in legal terms and yet maintain its ethical underpinnings and productive features. Legislating friendship requires, at a deeper level, the formation of a politically significant juridical concept that must be part of a genealogy of morals, part of a society dominated and consolidated by means of love and its related feelings (loyalty, guilt, faithfulness, etc.). The bond of friendship is the result of a feeling that is of necessity mutual and dual. In facing the possibility of regulation through the theories and practices of jurisdictional power and its balance—the main purpose of Alfonso's legislation—friendship appears to be extracted from the realm of the individual and from its dual and mutual features so it can be projected as a much broader category of personal links encompassing the whole society, the entire political body. From this legal perspective, friendship is a synecdoche for the concept of a juridically based political peace as it was often obliquely understood in Roman and German law (although neither created a specific series of norms or statutes governing friendship).[5]

In this sense, legislating friendship is tantamount to conveying that affects, passions, feelings, and the whole world of emotions may be defined and decided by the law and that there is a legal ontology of friendship. Looking at this legal challenge to friendship, we can better understand the infinite ramifications of the concept and practices of friendship itself and how it underwent—and continues to undergo—a process of mercantilization that ultimately led to a capitalistic commodification of emotions.

In summary, this means that "friend" may become one of the names of the juridical person, the artificial person, the *persona ficta*. In other words, if the legislator wants—and this is strictly an act of will, the creation of an institution, and not a spontaneous effect—to legislate friendship, such legislator has to turn the friend into a juridical person. This transformation is bound to have a perverse aftereffect. As Michel Foucault put it in his seminar of November 21, 1973, the promise of the humanities (and the legal humanities) is that if we scratch the juridical *persona*, we will end up finding "man" himself, but a "man," Foucault continues, who is nothing other than the "disciplinary individual."[6] The friend as a juridical person may appear as a disciplinary individual, but only because such is the legislative effect of a sovereign power. In this situation, even as the juridical person is subjected to the expression of feelings that consolidate social bonds, he recognizes the presence of the sovereign power: the king, the company.

There is a modern philosophical discussion of friendship undertaken by male philosophers from Emmanuel Lévinas and Jacques Derrida to Giorgio Agamben—in a tradition of androphilia, as it were, which was central to

Western philosophy and the ethics of friendship. It includes, of course, Aristotle and Cicero, Alfonso's main sources. In this tradition, friendship has been analyzed as a future relationship in which the distance from the friend is, in a certain way, infinite, since the friend cannot be identified as a subject. In his book on friendship (part historical, part philosophical), in which he advocates an ethical performance of friendship, Franco Masciandaro reads and interprets Levinas, Agamben, and Derrida to focus on the "infinity of the Other," the "dis-subjectivization at the very heart of the most intimate perception of self," or the "friendship to come."[7] The intellectual apex of Masciandaro's book is his suggestion that literary studies are a productive way to philosophize friendship, likening the ethics of friendship to the ethics of reading. Friendship and reading constitute forms of interconnection with a stranger, with, according to Levinas, the infinity of the Other.

In a different, and more politically active, theoretical position, Brazilian philosopher Marilena Chauí considers that friendship (*amizade*) is the way out of voluntary servitude.[8] Martin Hägglund, in his recent book *This Life*, also criticizes the question of the infinity of the other: to care about the other, this other needs to be a finite being: "It is because I am finite that I am in need and that it can matter to me how I am treated."[9] This finitude is what approaches friends politically, what makes them dependent from each other.

The Alfonsine concept of legal friendship, however, forces us to go in a completely, even radically or diametrically, different directions. Legal friendship, or legislated friendship, needs to be able to identify the friend, to identify friendship. The friend must become a subject of the law, in the sense used by Foucault in his seminar on *La Société punitive*, and therefore a subject of both disciplinary and sovereign power.[10] If anything, friendship is also part of the regimes of voluntary servitude.

From the perspective of the transformation of the friend into *persona ficta*, it is possible to argue that in order for the legislation of friendship to operate that way, this legislation—and friendship itself—must be invested with the legitimate authority to perform a social heuristic. Indeed, through this legitimacy, juridical friendship identifies the spectrum of social relations in which subjects of the law are discovered and created. Friendship bridges the infinite distance between subjects of the law, narrowing down the possibility of pinpointing the friend as one of such legal subjects. Or, in other words, the legislation of friendship permits one to give the name "friend" to one of the manifestations of the juridical person. However, all this happens within a legislation that uses the language and vocabulary of philosophy as well as the devices and hermeneutical techniques proper to fiction.

Creating the friend and friendship as legal subjects is one of the ways in which to horizontally extend—by means of sets of emotions that are purported to be and often de facto are subject to legislation—the circulation of royal, central power across a space that can be pacified by means of this affective and emotional legislation. This is one of the strategies used to expand vernacular jurisdictions.

Legislating friendship is also a challenge to the codification of the law itself. For the legislator to legislate intimate experiences, affects, emotions, and feelings, and relocate them to the horizon of political and juridical concepts, such a legislator must resort to fields of inquiry, bodies of knowledge, and sciences that exist outside and independent of legal epistemologies. Otherwise, fictional devices, or philosophy, in this case, must be summoned to legislation's inner world in order to do their work. This is a crucial departure from the ways in which judicial procedures often invoke the participation of other disciplines—forensic disciplines, at least for the duration of the trial—including, for instance, neuroscience, medicine, or even literature. Although they may be essential for the procedures, the trial, or even the verdict, they are not inscribed in the legislation itself.[11]

Friendship and the Laws of the *Fourth Partida*

The general challenges of legislating friendship have a counterpoint in the complexity of placing such legislation within the legal code. The *Partidas* are exceedingly complex, among other reasons, because they need to constitute a framework of concepts and institutions that very often must be crafted from scratch, a system that involves the creation of the very words designating legal concepts and institutions. In other words, Title 27 of the *Fourth Partida*, in which Alfonso legislates friendship, is not a title one can read in isolation, even though it has been commonly read in isolation from the rest of the *Partida* and from the *Partidas* in general in order to link it to its external sources in a traditional philological manner. Although isolating it may be useful, interesting, or otherwise essential for understanding the individual title, this title distills a long chain of conceptual creativity and crafted fictions that need to be linked to the constitutional horizon created by the *Partidas*, that is, from the vantage point of concepts and institutions that anchor legal hermeneutics. As Alfonso puts it in the first titles of the *First Partida*, laws are not to be memorized literally ("decorar las letras dellas") but to be interpreted; to be interpreted, they need to build the framework that secures their autonomy, even when they resort to external bodies of knowledge or otherwise embrace the creative character of perplexity.[12]

Despite the assiduous commentaries made by Alonso de Villadiego Vascuñana y Montoya, an early modern commentator on the *Liber Iudiciorum*—the Visigoth legal code compiled and put in force in 1241 by Ferdinand III, according to whom "Amicus plus valet quam aurum in capsa, & est alter ego"—nothing of the sort can be found in either the *Liber Iudiciorum* or the Spanish translation known as *Fuero Juzgo*.[13] This important descendant of German law, which informs many legal undertakings throughout the thirteenth century, including the *Siete Partidas*, does not include any legislation on friendship at all. It only mentions the word "friend" when it considers the presence of witnesses for plaintiffs or defendants in a trial and in other less relevant parts of the code.[14] In other words, legislating friendship does not seem to have interested any legislator before Alfonso in the *Fourth Partida*.

Roman law, similarly, does not pay special attention to friendship as an object of legislation. Some of the glossators gathered by Francesco Accursio for his *Magna Glossa* (ca. 1250) give a definition of "friend" (*amicus*) that turns out to be sourced from Isidore of Seville's etymology of the word (*Etym.* 10.4): "Amicvs quasi animi custos," or "the friend is like the custodian [*custos*] of the soul [*animus*]."[15] A different glossator resorts to a negative statement to establish an ethics of friendship, as "non est amicitia inter latrones et fraudatores, sed inter istos est fraus et dolus" (there is no friendship among thieves and liars, rather, among them there is only fraud and evil).[16] Whenever Roman law concerns itself with friendship, it is in order to solve issues regarding the accuracy of the deposition, the adequacy of the witness statement, or other issues regarding truth-telling in other stages of the judicial process.[17] Friendship is seen in a more negative light, as it may taint the truth-telling procedures necessary for the administration of justice by compromising confidence in the witness's veracity.

The fact that Alfonso's legislation of friendship is at the very center of the *Siete Partidas* is definitely not related to any previous legislation, nor is looking to Muslim or Jewish legislation on friendship more helpful in locating antecedents (or at least I have not been able to locate any such sources). Legislating friendship is, rather, an act of this particular legislator's will, an act with a particular legal and political purpose. Of course, the content of this legislation, and the need to discuss friendship, does not exist in a void; it seems to be closely related to the interest in friendship developed by thirteenth- and fourteenth-century European political writers and preachers (who invoked and retransmitted tales from older, often Oriental and orientalized sources), sometimes in translations of Arabic sources collected in frame-tale narratives.[18] Likewise, it is related to the affinity between law and friendship found in the Aristotelian and Ciceronian sources mentioned at the beginning of this chapter.

In the following sections, I will focus on how legislation on friendship and its philosophical articulation within the law allows us to enumerate and analyze the fictional devices that Alfonso set in motion in this part of his legal code. In other words, I will explore how the poetics of a vernacular jurisdiction works from the vantage point of an adoption of perplexity. Although I will also refer to other parts of the *Siete Partidas*, I do not intend to be exhaustive or to catalog cases of this or that fictional device or philosophical discussion.

Inceptive Tropes, Inchoate Narratives

Seven laws governing friendship comprise the twenty-seventh and last chapter of the *Fourth Partida*. To understand the importance of these laws, one needs to consider the *Fourth Partida* as a whole, because the legislation of friendship is the culmination of a series of narratives and fictional devices connected by a juridical reading of a philosophical and political corpus. To closely examine the laws concerning friendship, one needs to begin from afar.

As Alfonso says in the prologue to this *Fourth Partida*, this is the *Partida* that stands in the middle of the seven parts. It focuses on the importance of marriage, the primary alliance from which degrees of consanguinity and affinity are established and measured. According to Alfonso, "what people can see is easier to learn than what has to be learned by the ear" (a quote that could fuel a case for the preferred mode of disseminating the *Partidas*), and so these two types of relationships are represented, both in manuscript and edited versions of the *Partidas*, in diagram form: as an *arbor consanguinitatis* and an *arbor affinitatis*.

These two illustrations, normally reproduced on facing pages, consolidate this *Partida*. The 1555 edition shows them in folios 17v (consanguinity) and 18r (affinity): in two different architectural structures. The table, or tree, devoted to consanguinity shows four generations of the married couple's ancestors and descendants, each branching in horizontal rows. The structure representing the tree of affinity, in contrast, is organized around the married couple as a central column from which spread the four degrees of affinity around them. Both trees "are in agreement with canon and civil law" and indeed permit the reader to quickly grasp the norms regarding marriage and its limitations as prescribed by the Lateran Council (canons 50–52).

Marriage is, doubtlessly, at the very center of the *Fourth Partida*: Alfonso explains how it was not only the first of the seven sacraments, but it was also the first to be instituted, as God himself created it in Paradise. This is the sacrament without which "the other six sacraments could not be kept and honored."[19] This is the first way in which this *Partida* is put at the center of the other seven.

This centrality is also a way to establish cohesive links between canon and civil law, between religious regulations and secular life, as enunciated by a secular power, the legislator king. This enunciation speaks to how religious regulations and civil norms serve common purposes, not only by means of the civil reading of a biblical passage established in the *Fourth Partida* as the epitome of juridical or statutory precedents, but also through the articulation of a discourse on nature, for, as the prologue to the *Fourth Partida* says, marriage allows humankind to keep its natural, sinless status (as marriage was created before mankind created sin).

The beginning of the *Fourth Partida* also affirms its own centrality among the seven through two tropes. The first makes use of the corporeal tropes frequently employed in medieval society. This regulation has been put "in the middle of the seven parts of this book in the same way in which the heart has been put in the middle of the body, where the man's spirit resides, from where life is brought to the rest of the organs and limbs." The second is an astronomical trope: the center of the *Partidas* is equivalent to the fourth heaven, where God put the sun, which "illuminates everything"—in particular "the seven stars that we call planets"—and that, "as told by his [God's] law," shines on "all the stars."[20]

Since Alfonso used these metaphors in the text of the law, these metaphors also *are* the law. In other words, they are inscribed within the law as the law itself. They, in turn, call upon cultural systems of interpretation that include philosophical and biblical sources. Indeed, we do not need to resort to Aristotle's *Parva naturalia* to understand why the heart and the warmth of life are interconnected; even Ḥayy ibn Yaqẓān, Ibn Tufail's protagonist and *autodidactus philosophus* par excellence, was able to find this out on his own by dissecting his doe mother.[21] Nor do we need to resort to Saint Paul's 2 Corinthians 3.3, where the epistle is written on the heart itself ("in cordibus nostris," "εν ταις καρδιαις"), not with ink ("atramento," "μελανι"), but with the living spirit of God ("Spiritu Dei vivi," "πνευματι θεου ζωντος"); not on stone or on clay tablets, but on the tablets of the fleshly heart ("non in tabulis lapideis sed in tabulis cordis carnalibus," "ουκ εν πλαξιν λιθιναις αλλ εν πλαξιν καρδιας σαρκιναις").

These two tropes are part of a prologue. Cornelia Vismann, in discussing the role played by the prologue, or the preamble, in laws, considers them to be barriers to the law that do not close the path to the law itself but rather establish the point where the law begins and demarcate its autonomy.[22] Drawing upon this distinction, I see this barrier as the border where the legal discipline separates itself from other disciplines, a line demarcating the autonomy of the law. Her metaphor for the preamble helps further explain this demarcation of disciplines. Vismann argues that the preamble, which has an "annunciatory function," is like the furrow drawn with the plow in order to establish the point where the future city will be raised. A preamble, in this sense, would be a promise of what *will be*. Building on Derrida's "Before the Law," Vismann comments on how the preamble, a "parasite of law," constitutes a legitimizing narrative, reveals the anxieties of the persona ficta called legislator, and asserts that "law and preamble are said to be subject to the law of hospitality, according to which the host depends on the guest."[23] Before going on to consider Kafka's "Before the Law" as none other than a preamble without a law, Vismann concludes, "in technical terms, preambles occupy the domain of narration, the space of literature."[24]

My perspective on the legal preamble is quite different, although it partakes of some of the perplexities expressed by both Derrida and Vismann. Alfonso's preambles can be confused with literature, but they exist outside of the material conditions of the literary institution as we know it.[25] They face the challenge of creating not only a narrative but also a whole vernacular vocabulary. This means that Alfonso is endeavoring to establish not only the limits or the borders of his narrative system but also the constitutional concepts that serve as the main characters of the whole system. Far from being parasites of the Law and lacking juridical value, Alfonso's preambles describe the legal city from the perspective of the particular furrow plowed with this narrative. Those preambles also establish their difference and their complementarity with the other preambles and parts of the legal code and explain what they intend to add to, and how to look at, the legal construction from the perspective of the concepts they put forth. In this sense, the preamble has a constitutional character: it develops a theory of power and creates a logical world that agrees with the concepts legally generated in the preamble.

The preamble's constitutional character lies in its ability to create a theory, a vision of the location and name of sovereign power in all its manifestations. Each of these manifestations is both a logical world and a possible world. The preamble sets up the concepts and actions that are constitutive of each of these possible worlds and that conform, in heterocosmic constellation, to the general theory of power articulated in the preamble.[26]

The corporeal and astronomical tropes used as constitutional elements by Alfonso are the *Fourth Partida*'s centers of gravity, and the *Fourth Partida* is both the sun and heart of the *Partidas* as a whole. What kind of legislation would use these two metaphors as constitutional limits for understanding a part of the law? The answer is simple: one that is trying to connect two philosophical realms of inquiry—the macrocosm and the microcosm—from the perspective of natural knowledge. Interconnecting these realms is not only one of the well-known tropes of literary tradition, as Francisco Rico has demonstrated,[27] but once it becomes part of the legal system, this connection becomes much more than a trope: it establishes the jurisdictional purview of the legal code and implies, from a naturalistic perspective, the breadth of legal inquiry in all philosophical orders.

Furthermore, these two tropes constitute a figural regime.[28] In a figural or typological regime, which is a reading and a writing technique, everything is a figure of something else that ultimately constitutes its fulfillment. In this sense, the *Fourth Partida* is none other than the fulfillment of the promise figured by the two tropes—sun and heart—and the role they occupy in the universe and within the living (mainly human) being.

There is a third level to the metaphors: heart and sun, purveyors of blood and light, are crucial from a legislative perspective because they create the concept of dissemination, that of the blood that uses every vessel in the circulatory system, even the capillaries, to arrive at the far reaches of the body parts: parts in which the physical and the mystical inhere in tropological and anagogic terms.[29] Considered another way, light vibrates in all planes, as John (1 John 1.5) puts it, fulfilling the figural announcements from Psalms 18.18 and other biblical loci that "God is light" ("Deus lux est," "ο θεος φως εστιν"). This means of dissemination is also its centrality: the center of the body politic, for instance, or the star that gives off light generated by itself, as in the metaphors of papal power in which pontifical authority is considered direct sunlight, while royal power is considered to be the reflection of solar light from the surface of the moon to the temporal and secular system of powers.[30] These metaphors neatly secure this theory of power and the capillary dissemination of such power, the arrival of its direct light to every corner of the jurisdiction.

These tropes directly point to the legal need to colonize feeling and thinking. Alfonso's metaphors are, therefore, much more than a couple of pretty tropes that lend variety to the cold, dry text of the legislation. On the contrary, they constitute the affective regime of legal writing and of legal creativity. The sun and the heart are not simply objects; they contain the spirit ("el coraçon es puesto en medio del cuerpo, do es el espiritu del ome, onde va la vida") and they enlighten ("el sol que alumbra todas las cosas, e es puesto en medio delos siete cielos"). In other words, they are metaphors of thought; the heart is also the memory and the repository of truth, and the soul is the *anima* with which humans both perceive and think.[31]

This is an essential part of Alfonso's legal aesthetics derived from Aristotelian aesthetics. The *Second Partida*, which is devoted to administration and society, stipulates in one of its titles that the people (that is, the whole population, without exception) are the "sensitive soul" of the kingdom, that is, those in charge of perceiving and politically interpreting what they perceive. As I will demonstrate in Chapter 5, Alfonso's reading of philosophy—in this case Aristotelian treatises and commentaries on aesthetics (including *De anima* and *De sensu et sensibile*)—gives the legislator the foundational ideas from which he can reframe society as a knowing subject with political responsibilities, in particular, that of perceiving and thinking about the political consequences of legal life.

We are already in the middle of a sea of perplexity in which tropes become crucial for understanding a piece of legislation. If they are crucial it is because of their explicit philosophical underpinnings based on philosophical scholarship and research. The philosophical and rhetorical (even poetic) presentation of legal concepts is the result of a very transparent plan, since Alfonso not only defines his structural designs but also gives us the whole intellectual system that supports it.

That the laws governing friendship appear near the end of the *Fourth Partida* where the latter deals with all sorts of alliances of consanguinity and of affinity establishes and theorizes the affective regime of the *Partidas* as diverging from a center. Friendship is located in that part of the *Partidas* because in a certain way it constitutes the purest way to present a relationship of affinity as if it were a relationship of consanguinity; friends are, in fact, like brothers. Friends are linked by a totally disinterested feeling of love, a love that is stronger than any other, as Alfonso affirms in the *Fourth Partida*, 24. Here the plot thickens, because this raises another important thesis of the *Partidas*: social and political bonds are, in short, expressions of love. Again, the law puts an affect at the radiant center of its rationality and as a constitutional horizon.

This affective regime is a key for dead voice, that is, for the writing and codification of a legal system that cannot be easily altered. Affects try to guarantee the closeness of the law to the subject of the law. This regime is not beyond the subject's reach but is instead part of the constitution of the *persona ficta*: its building blocks. As such, this regime buttresses the construction of a vernacular jurisdiction, a familiar, domestic language that can contribute to the dissemination and remembrance of the code itself and that establishes, for those persons, the ways in which central power comes to them as the sole or principal jurisdictional power that can claim rights.

Philosophy, History, Stories: The Pervasiveness of Vernacular Jurisdictions

In order to legislate friendship, Alfonso mobilizes two different philosophical corpora, extracting them from their natural environment of ethics and politics to reinsert them within legal science. The first is Aristotle's *Nicomachean Ethics*: in particular, books 8 and 9, along with Averroes's *Middle Commentary*, which is probably Alfonso's actual primary source. The other is Cicero's *Laelius de amicitia*, a dialogue through which Cicero presents his understanding of friendship as a civil duty.[32] These two philosophical corpora allow Alfonso to actually enumerate his arguments about friendship and to theorize friendship in legal terms. Alfonso's laws define friendship, disentangling it from what cannot be called friendship while explaining how it is preserved and how it is broken.

In his sixth law, Alfonso suspends the statement of rules in order to tell a story, that of two friends, Orestes and Pylades. Orestes and Pylades are arrested by a king whom Alfonso does not name for charges only defined as *maleficios*, or "wrong-doings." The king sentences Orestes to death and absolves Pylades. In the morning, one of the king's officers calls for Orestes to send him to the gallows. Before Orestes can say anything, his friend screams, "I am Orestes!" while Orestes insists, "No, no, it's me," and so on, each claiming that he is Orestes. The king is fascinated by this proof of pure friendship: the friend ready to sacrifice his life for his friend. He interrupts the execution, pardons Orestes, and asks the two men to adopt him as their third friend.[33]

The story is well known; it has been proverbial for centuries. In one sense, it is a story about male heroic friendship and nothing else, just another line in the catalog under the subject heading "friendship as androphilia." But it is more than that: it is a story about monarchical power. In it, friendship is why the sentence (not the law) is suspended and sovereignty reconsidered, reordered, as it were. Friendship, in this sense, may seem exceptional, as it can elicit a change in a judicial resolution without a new trial. It looks like a sovereign decision.

The problem, however, is more complex. The unmentioned reason why Orestes and Pylades are friends is that Orestes has avenged wrongs committed against Orestes's father, Agamemnon. With the help of Pylades, he killed his mother, Clytemnestra, and her lover, Aegisthus, in revenge for their assassination of Orestes's father, Agamemnon, king of Argos. In this friendship, there is something missing: the paternal figure, a third, more elevated object of love, represented by Agamemnon, the object, in Freudian terms, of identification for the son.[34] In medieval spiritual readings of the philosophy of friendship, such as Aelred of Rievaulx's *De amicitia spiritualis*, this third point, or father identification, is none other than God. In the case of Orestes and Pylades, only the king himself can claim to fulfill this role, thus restoring order and hierarchy to friendship. In short, if friendship is politically productive, it is because it suggests, as its final term of identification, the love of the king and all that the king has access to: namely, jurisdiction. This is really what underwrites legislation on friendship: a final demonstration of royal power, because he is the one who has access to the object of desire.

The interest in exploiting perplexity led to the practice of inscribing political theories in the legislation itself. In this particular case, it is a powerful political theory. Despite the legislator's claim, echoing Aristotle or Averroes's commentary, that a society based on friendship and love would not need a system of justice, such a society would still require a monarchical father to run the system. Since the monarchical father also holds jurisdictional power (*señorío*), or the *potestas iuris dicendi*, in combination with the power to give or to take life, including the power to change the first verdict given by the monarch himself, this means that any horizontal alliance with political purview needs to be validated by the king.

It is easy to put forth a historical interpretation of the use of this particular narrative in law. Since Alfonso inherited the kingdom in 1252 from his father, Ferdinand III, he had the responsibility to repopulate enormous expanses of land conquered from taifas in al-Andalus, including Seville, Murcia, Requena, Puerto de Santa María, and others. Repopulating those spaces was a challenge, as we know thanks to the documents transmitting the different *repartimientos*, or division of the territories. One of the strategies adopted by Alfonso was to distribute the lands among knights, both noble and nonnoble, to thus create a network of horizontal alliances that would be under the king's jurisdiction.[35] Under these circumstances, friendship secured monarchical jurisdictional power over those new territories.

What does Orestes and Pylades's narrative have? Is it to allow the legislator to build a political theory within legal discourse? As we have said, the *Fourth Partida* begins with two powerful tropes, two similitudes granting the legislator the possibility of establishing a poetic or rhetorical constitutional horizon for this part of the law. Understanding the law is not simply the ability to read it, of course, but also the ability to locate the terms according to which it must be interpreted. The foundational tropes of the *Fourth Partida* suggest that the existence of the whole legal system elaborated in the *Partidas* springs from this particular section of the legal code, and not from the other six, although the *First Partida*, which legislates ecclesiastical and religious life, might appear at first glance a more likely location for the whole legal system to be sketched out. These tropes are here not to embellish the codification but rather to establish a series of concepts about the law itself. These tropes are not outside the law; they *are* the law, even though the perplexed historian may have the tendency to amputate those metaphors from the legal body.

Furthermore, we have also seen another kind of narrative, that of Orestes and Pylades. It is difficult to understand how the legislation could survive without it, so perfectly ingrained it is within the law. The narrative is politically crucial, because without it, the laws would not have anything to say about the monarchical system, while with it, the monarchical system becomes the center of gravity of this last title of the *Fourth Partida* and, according to the foundational tropes, of the whole *Siete Partidas*. But the process whereby the story became part of the law is quite transparent, quite sincere. The legislator attributes the story to some unnamed ancient histories from which the legislator has taken it. It is difficult to know from which, but it is quite plausible that the legislator borrowed it from Cicero's *Laelius de amicitia*, where the Roman philosopher, orator, lawyer, and politician refers to it: when the Romans, says Cicero, go to the theater and watch the moment of perfect friendship between the two heroes, they burst into a standing ovation. Cicero then makes a comment in which he wonders how they would react to this manifestation of fictional friendship if it were a real one. The king, projected onto the fictional king projected onto the real and royal legislation, provides quite a good example of how to react in a productive manner.

Allegations and Concordances

It is unlikely that any of the possible readers of the *Siete Partidas* would go to the neighborhood library or to his or her own copy of Cicero, or Aristotle, or whatever other textual source to check it against the law. Sources are not here to be fact-checked by readers, not even to be known or recognized by readers; they are, exclusively, building materials. What is interesting is something else: the illusion (another building material) that there is a frontier that separates the legal text from the texts that have been summoned from outside the law in order to be part of it, legal immigrant concepts. In this operation, the legal text delineates the borders where the law is in contact with the cultural world outside the law to show how this extralegal world can become part of the legislation.

Legal writing resorts to two different techniques to define these borders: *allegationes* (henceforth, "allegations"; not to be confused with accusations, under which a defendant faces trial prior to conviction or exoneration) and *concordantiae* (henceforth, "concordances"). Allegations allow for the internal cohesiveness of the law by including cases and circumstances already mentioned in the legal code, and they help support the legal discussion in question through internal legal cross-references. Allegations are also essential to the compiling, normally in the margins of the legal texts, of the legal rule, which can be defined both as the norm in consideration of the exceptions and as the confluence of norm and exceptions as a whole.[36] Concordances are pieces of textual evidence that frequently appear as external cross-references with the same purpose of contributing to specific arguments in legal discussions. The difference between allegations and concordances is very slight, and sometimes one piece of evidence can be both an allegation and a concordance. Both techniques are, in fact, important resources drawn from narrative. They include, as part of the actual legislation, what can be called invisible narratives that expand the whole system of interpretation represented by the law.

Law, indeed, can be interpreted only under one condition: only the law can be and become a reference for the interpretation of the law. Since the law cannot travel outside itself in search of interpretive elements and principles, the only alternative is to include those external elements in the law. Allegations and concordances allow legislators and legal scholars to do exactly that. Although no reader of the *Partidas* is likely to resort to the Ciceronian or Aristotelian source to check the law, the legislator can, selectively, incorporate the relevant parts as elements of the legal system, thus allowing narrative, philosophical thought, and interpretation to happen while building the autonomy of the discipline.

The story of Orestes and Pylades is one such concordance. The legislator introduces this story when he is legislating that friends should be willing to risk life and property for their friends; then he says, "What is found in ancient histories of two friends, one named Orestes and the other Pylades, agrees [*acuerda*] with this" (*Partidas* 4.27.6). This agreement is what makes it possible to match the rule and the story, so that they inter-interpret each other.

Allegations and concordances play a very active role in the codification of the law. In addition to their political and legal uses, these invisible narratives also have the aesthetic effect of creating legal memory, memory being one of the internal senses of the sensitive soul, according not only to Aristotelian aesthetics but also to the *Partidas* (2.10.11), as we will see more closely in Chapter 5.

As we have seen, the *Fourth Partida* itself begins with a biblical concordance (the invention of the sacrament of marriage in Paradise) in order to establish the legal genealogy of marriage and to interconnect civil regulations with canon or religious regulations. The case of biblical concordances and allegations is broader, however, since the legislator expressed from the beginning that one of his sources was going to be "the sayings of the saints" (*Partidas* 1.1.6), by which he means the Bible. For instance, the regulation in *Partidas* 1.4.64, on how clerics must keep churches and their contents clean and use them only for the purpose for which they were first devised, prompts the legislator to tell the story of Balthazar's dinner in Daniel 5 which recounts the king's profanation of sacred objects. This story is not purely religious but also clearly political; his profanation led to the destruction of Balthazar's kingdom at the hands of his enemies.[37]

Allegations and concordances come in many different shapes. A full digital catalog of them would give us a clear picture of their legal and political
consequences, including those invisible narratives in the legislative process.[38]
Every one of them has a double purpose: incorporating political practices on
the one hand, and establishing a link between legislation and nature on the
other. For instance, *Partidas* 2.9.1, which is devoted to the selection of counselors, refers to the *Secretum Secretorum* in order to establish the proper social
and economic status of the king's counselors, while *Partidas* 2.10.1, which
also draws from the *Secretum*, simultaneously lays out a better way to organize
the kingdom's officials and their correspondence to the different aspects of
nature, both at the level of the human body and at the level of the non-
human.

Cases and Extreme Cases

The case fuels legal philosophy. *Causae*, according to lawyers, or *casus* in the
Scholastic idiom, are the stuff of legal thinking. Casuistry, as Yan Thomas
put it in his study of the institution of nature, is an operation of thought:[39]
the path or method through which logical structures and individual narratives
can elicit general reflections on legal issues, or, in other words, where logical
thinking and narratives about individual problems constitute a philosophical
poetics of the law.

Yan Thomas's research into the limit case of the *droit savant* focuses on
the creation of the fiction of the *persona* devised to provide communities with
a "constant juridical identity," abstracted and separated from the lives and
deaths of the individuals who constitute the community.[40] The limit case can
be formulated this way: is the community still a community if all of its
members but one are dead? Is Theseus's ship still Theseus's ship if every
single one of its parts has been removed to be replaced, and nothing remains
of the original materials with which the ship was built? And, more important,
are these cases—which are profoundly narrative themselves—relatable to
other cases by means of analogy or commentary, as "fictions matricielles"[41]
upon which the law and its economy of glosses and allegations can be practiced? How does the limit case become part of the legislative process and
juridical practice?

The questions about the limit case and its consequences within legal
philosophy reach far beyond the concept of the exception. The limit case

constitutes the "intrigue matricielle," or the "micro-récit,"[42] that allows the theorist to rethink legal concepts that, in the end, constitute the theory of the *persona ficta*: the juridical person.

Indeed, the complexities and limits of the construction of the juridical person is Alfonso's main interest. "In all the seven parts of this book of ours, we have talked about the persons of humans, and about their actions, as well as about the other things that pertain to them" (*Partidas* 7.33, prologue).[43] In other words, the legislator is not interested in men or women as natural entities but instead in their juridical personas, in the many different masks they can wear, in the many different ways in which they are subjects of the law. The legal thinking found in the *Partidas*, which is not scholarship (unlike the cases assembled and studied by Thomas) but rather legislation, takes as its object what is also its subject: the modifications, transformations, and actions of the juridical person, everything pertaining to the complex modeling of the person.

The legislator makes an important specification about limit cases and exceptions in relation to legal thinking and interpretation: "Laws must be made only about things that happen frequently. For this reason, the ancient wise men did not care about legislating something that happened only a few times, as they thought they could be judged based on other cases according to a law already written" (*Partidas* 7.34.36). This rule, however, does not prevent the lawmaker from delving into the limit case. On the contrary, the *Partidas* constantly explores the limit case as fodder for legal thinking. Thinking about friendship is not just about establishing friendship as the goal of a well-regulated society that understands the "third friend" to be the *person* of the king; it is also about the limit case determining that one's life may be effaced in exchange for a friend's life. What's more, limit cases are invoked in legislation at an astonishing rate in Alfonso's codification. Cases that have occurred only a handful of times, or never at all, are deemed necessary, because there is no rule, precedent, analogy, or jurisprudence considered sufficient for judging them. There is no possible legal precedent for giving up one's life for a friend's life.

Alfonso's legislation of the limit case even demonstrates a certain degree of anxiety about how the exceptional may happen, so that he can also predict it by means of legislation. He wants to explore the places where legislation may be on the verge of fracturing. It may be implausible to think that a slave would be called by the master very often to perform a service at the very same moment in which the slave's wife needs her husband to have sexual intercourse with her:

a duty within the sacrament of marriage.[44] *Partidas* 4.5.2, however, turns this limit case into a legal decision: the slave must obey the master unless he can see that failing to go with his wife will result in her having sex with somebody else. Likewise, for the legislator it does not suffice to provide an explanation for impotence, whether such individuals were born impotent or something else caused it. If the latter is the case, he wants to cover all the limit cases, so that nothing is governed by happenstance or by singular decision in the face of the exception: they may have had their genitalia torn off while jumping over a palisade, or had them ripped off by a bear or a wild boar, or even had them cut off by a man (*Partidas* 4.8.4). All those cases must be inscribed in what was intended to be a totalizing law.

This totalizing legislation is not only about choosing between sex or duty, or even about impotence but, more importantly, about inchoate narratives. These narratives, according to Alfonso, need to be taken into account for one to think about and live according to the law. A man who is a heretic or who converted to Islam or to Judaism cannot accuse his wife of adultery, since he has "committed spiritual adultery" (*Partidas* 4.9.8) or "spiritual fornication" (*Partidas* 4.10.3). Or, if during terrible hardship a man feels desperate, can he sell his son? Does he have the right to eat his son (*Partidas* 4.16.2–3), as Ugolino della Gherardesca was asked to do by his own children?[45] The limit case may also spring from a philosophical-scientific consideration, as in *Partidas* 4.22.4–5, where the *corpus Hipocraticum* is the basis for separating the normal from the liminal and the monstrous in terms of gestation and labor. It would be easy to gather limit cases by the dozens. But what do these cases do?

They explore the political limits of love. They serve to think about how love—the central constitutional concept of power and power circulation in the *Partidas*—works. These cases are ways to foster the idea that legal life, legal interpretation, legislation, and its moral and political representations are governed by love. Limit cases, in short, explore the constitutional value of love. This is not only what the *Fourth Partida* foregrounds but also what—at the center of the seven codes—it irradiates across the other *Partidas*, like light, like blood, those two foundational tropes of the *Fourth Partida*.

This is the very nature of legal thinking. These limit cases show that all experiences are subject to legal questioning. Legal thinking is something that, even in the most extreme case, has consequences for the construction (*fictio*) of the juridical person (*persona ficta*) as a repository of the constitutional affect of love. The juridical character of everything, even the most extreme limit case, must be thought about through vernacular jurisdiction.

Embracing perplexity implies the combination of legal interdisciplinarity and affective power—the power of desire. The first-level reading of the incorporation of the story of Orestes and Pylades into the legislation of the *Partidas* on friendship indeed shows the articulation of a political goal: centralizing power by identifying the king as the all-encompassing third vertex of any relationship based on friendship. There is a teleology of this kingly friendship. But this is only a first-level interpretation. The concordance opens up the law in a much more crucial way: it provides us an extreme case, and not just any sort of extreme case, but a particular one: the extreme case of affects and feelings.

Why is this so important? Because the lawmaker is invested in gaining disciplinary territory in the surveillance of affects and feelings. In the end, the people are the sensitive soul of the kingdom, as we have seen. Love is the central political foundation that buttresses the legal building. Legislating friendship is not only a way to underscore the political productivity of friendship and not only a way to incorporate the concept of friendship into the constitutional vocabulary, but it is also a way to allow the very practice of power to extend jurisdiction and the *potestas iuris dicendi* into the most private spaces, the cloisters of the soul: feelings and affects. In this way, jurisdiction takes on the characteristics of disciplinary power. The extreme case does not merely situate us in the geometry of concordance (the lines that cross spaces and create typological figures). Instead, it inserts us into the moment in which the law itself seems about to crack and fall apart; even there, at the limit, the law works by means of an unforgettable narrative. There, what was supposed to be the exception becomes the extreme, but still in the interior world of the law. By operating in this way, vernacular jurisdictions create a new way of legal thinking, in which, by means of affect and interdisciplinarity, by embracing perplexity, the universe of *juridical persons* may be conveyed to demonstrate that every single movement in real life is, in fact, a movement in legal life; that personal experiences are, indeed, experiences of the juridical person.

Love-Reading: *Fictio legis* and the Fiction of Naturality

On a number of occasions, I have mentioned that love is at the center of the constitutional discourse of the *Partidas*. The laws concerning friendship state that love is the greatest possible bond between humans (*Partidas* 4.27, prologue). I have also said that love is the central political concept of the *Partidas*. How does love become such a powerful structuring concept? From the very beginning of the *Partidas*, the legislator rules both that "the laws that concern the government of people are those that gather men's hearts by means of love, which is *derecho* and reason" (1.1.7; see the first note of this chapter) and that laws benefit humankind insofar as they "gather men by means of love, which entails that each wants the rightful thing for one another" (1.1.10).

As a corollary to the political discourse about love, Alfonso arrives at two different conclusions about the virtues implicated in legal codification: first, it promotes peace and prosperity (1.1.10); second, "rightful laws help one man to join will with another by means of friendship" (1.1.7). Political love is the basis of social peace, and the highest possible level of social peace is the expression of mutual friendship: a friendship that, as we have seen, names the king as the third of three friends.

We know from the marks left on the manuscripts that contemporary readers of the *Partidas* were interested in the discourse of love. They were sometimes concerned by the fact that this was essentially a political, secular love. Meinardo Ungut and Stanislao Polono—the Sevillan printers of the 1491 edition, which was prepared by Alonso de Montalvo—decided, either with the participation of Montalvo or not (we don't know), to enhance the seven laws on friendship with two more spiritual chapters on friendship from the Castilian translation of the *Viridiarium Consolationis* by the Dominican friar Jacopo de Benevento (fl. ca. 1360), an addition that lasted for several editions and printings, including the one by Tomas Junta in Venice in 1526, until it was excluded in Gregorio López's edition in 1555. This intervention constitutes a challenge to the integrity of the laws on friendship insofar as it introduces a theological reading of the profoundly secular legislation coming from a corpus oriented toward use by preachers.[46]

The manuscripts of the *Partidas* have been heavily used and oftentimes are "heavily soiled."[47] Anonymous readers marked up these manuscripts. Even those readers who were clearly lawyers and who were primarily interested in more technical questions regarding procedural law, wills, or criminal law sometimes marked up the title on friendship. Readers of the *Partidas* would have been exposed to the complex philosophies and narratives that, ultimately, made this law so original. In other words, they curbed their perplexity by underlining the places where the law entered into close contact and collaborated with philosophy and fictional devices.

In his now-classic study on reader annotations on medieval literary manuscripts, with special attention to the so-called *Libro de Buen Amor*

(1330–1343), John Dagenais wondered about the most frequent types of reader interventions in manuscripts, and he formulated an ethics of reading based on a series of ethical readings by readers who were interested in practical ethics, in self-help topics, or in otherwise inspiring textual snippets: an ethics that Dagenais beautifully calls florilecture.[48] I would like to reformulate his thesis ever so slightly: the ethics of reading and ethical readings are part of the same intellectual movement—the Augustinian drive to find out what connects the intellectual life of reading and practical or active life.[49] This movement, in other words, endeavors to think about the public character of individual study.

To be sure, there are many manuscript versions of the *Partidas* that have no annotations in the section articulating the laws on friendship.[50] Other manuscripts, instead, as well as many copies of the printed editions, have been marked up in many different ways: with braces, *maniculae*, and marginal notes.[51] These marks are the expressions of individual readers who were interested in the corollaries about love, like the words in *Partidas* 4.27.1 that state that friendship puts human wills in agreement with one another, and that love conquers all.[52]

Some notes mark and summarize important passages. One is the interdiction that friends spread rumors behind each other's backs, since a rumor is an experience of the juridical person that may lead to an inquest (3.17). Another appears in the *Partidas* 4.27.7, in which the legislator explains how treason destroys friendship and therefore also breaks the link of "naturality" that unifies the friends in the first place.[53]

This "naturality," underlined by one reader, is in fact the key concept in the theorization of love, as well as the most important fictional device exploited in legal heuristics: the *fictio legis*. The concept of naturality as a *fictio legis* is the central legal operation that turns love into the central constitutional concept of the *Partidas*, radiating from the *Fourth Partida* to the others. This *fiction of naturality* is, indeed, the ultimate moment of perplexity-embracing, because the fictional device also entails a philosophy of love and a natural philosophy.

The *fictio legis* is a legal operation that changes something into something else by means of a family of idioms germane to the expression "as if." In his two fundamental studies on the *fictio legis*, Yan Thomas has explored ways to express *fictiones legum* in Latin (*sicut, veluti, ac sic*, and so on), and he provides a catalog of common expressions and *fictiones legum* from Roman law as well as a detailed study of how medieval lawyers established important barriers to the activity of the *fictio legis* based on natural principles.

Thomas's theses need to be underscored here. First, he defines the *fictio legis* as an operation that "cross-dresses" facts: "Fiction is a procedure that . . . belongs to legal pragmatics. It entails, in the first place, cross-dressing facts, making them out to be something they are not; and deriving, from this falsification and this false supposition, the consequences of the law that will align with the truth they have deceitfully manufactured, as if this truth existed *sous les dehors qu'on lui prête*."[54]

The *fictio*, according to Thomas, may be defined by its relationship with falsity. This is also the central point made by medieval lawyers theorizing *fictio*: that it assumes as truth something that is not true. Therefore, contrary to presuppositions that are based on truth (even if that truth is uncertain), the relationship between *fictio* and lying seems to be essential. As Thomas puts it in his elegant and conceptually rich style, "[The *fictio*] assumes the radicalism of a rebellious decision on the order of being and not being. . . . With fiction, we are in the presence of the mystery that is the most radically foreign to common thinking: it does not offer juridical thought, but rather, and more precisely, legal technique, the *ars iuris*."[55] Contrary to the perspectives adopted by other legal scholars, Thomas does not see the *fictio legis* as an economical way to preserve the law. *Fictio legis*, from his perspective, cannot be explained in terms of preservation, but it can in terms of creation. Thomas is looking at the artifice and at the artifact. He is interested in the ways in which the *fictio* radically transforms the relationship between the law and nature. "The Roman *fictio*," says Thomas, "helps us ask ourselves about the relationship that fundamentally links the law and fiction, juridical positivity and construction, in short, about the radical disconnect between institutionality and the world of natural things."[56] The *fictio* establishes a way to constitute the law apart from fact, creating a crisis in a principle that says "in facto ius oritur" (the law springs from the fact).[57]

Alfonso employed the same fictional operation with correlative Spanish expressions: *bien así como si*, or *semejante a*, and others that are equivalent to the English expression *as if*. This set of expressions, however, is only the external appearance of the *fictio legis*. The operation itself is much better explained by way of an example that allows us to cap our argument about perplexity, law, philosophy, and narrative: "Naturality is an obligation that humans are under to each other to love and cherish each other for some just reason. The difference between nature and naturality is this: nature is a virtue by means of which everything is in the place determined by God. Naturality is something that resembles nature and that helps to be and maintain everything that descends from nature."[58]

This law gives birth to a concept: *naturality*. The birth, however, does not take place only in the simple definition at the beginning. The real birth occurs because a *fictio legis* is in charge of begetting the concept. According to the law, *naturality* resembles nature, but it is not nature. *Naturality* acts as if it were natural, but it is not. Naturality is a legal institution that permits the order of things designed by God through nature to stay in place. But the definition of naturality as an *as if* of nature means that naturality is the bond of love among humans. It is a double definition, in fact, because naturality, which seems to be defined by nature, also defines nature in the same legislative movement: nature is none other than the loving impulse to friendship that binds everything together. In its turn, nature is translated into legal terms as a narrative about love in which humans redefine themselves in terms of naturality—or, if you prefer, in terms of mutual love.

Naturality and love are the two final institutional centers of foundations of the *Partidas* and radiate from the *Fourth Partida* to the other six. Both are profoundly linked to philosophy and fiction, to the philosophy of love, to the philosophy of nature, and to the fictional devices used in the complex process of legal creativity. They are at the center of this gesture of creating a vernacular jurisdiction, the creation of a *potestas iuris dicenci* in which the different elements are speaking the language and the emotions of the clients of the law. Philosophy and narrative are two crucial disciplines in the development of a legal science able to incorporate political theories and affective regimes.

Legal disciplines and legal interpretation claim to be literal. They need to work perfectly autonomously, within a logic and a semiotics of their own. In modern constitutional legal systems, the ultimate frontier of legal interpretation is the constitution itself. Interpreting the law is essentially being able to understand its literality. Sometimes we hear about the letter of the law and the spirit of the law, which is a Paulinian formulation.[59] The spirit of the law is a very specific spirit: in legal science, the spirit of the law is the rationale for the law itself, its own science. This was the claim made by associate justice of the United States Supreme Court Antonin Scalia and the lexicographer Bryan Garner. The conservative justice and the creative lexicographer joined forces to keep the possibility of interdisciplinary legal hermeneutics at bay.[60]

But the codification of the law, then and today, is made of words. And words come to signify out of feelings, affections, doubt, and perplexity. They are troubling ways of truth-telling, and fictional devices, friendship, and love constitute the affective regime of vernacular jurisdictions. According to the philosophical threads included in the legal codification as part of the law, love and friendship are affects that are consubstantial to the sensitive soul, to the people. Since nature cannot be translated into words, the legislator decided to create one fiction, naturality—something that resembles nature—in order to configure a concept of love that could consolidate the whole codification. The affective regime also entails, like Aristotle's *Problemmata*, fictional devices like stories, paradigms, examples, and others (even those that I have called invisible narratives) as the best means to learn and to understand. They do this, in part, for the same reason trees and diagrams do, because they permit the legal scholar or the juridical person (part of the sensitive soul of the kingdom) to create a phantasm, a mental image, something understandable rather than something to learn literally.

Legislating friendship is, in the end of the central *partida*, a way to rearticulate the meaning of a sovereign power that builds itself in collaboration with disciplinary power. Friendship is always a case of the extreme that involves psychology, politics, ethics, and narrative. It is the ultimate case for the construction of a constitutional value of love in the vernacular jurisdiction.

It is, also, the ultimate product of dead voice as a perplexing legislation; in order to create an unusual legislation on friendship it is necessary to stir conventional modalities and techniques of law-writing by including philosophical works and fictional devices that are part of the legislation itself and that, in the end, also upset conventional views about the autonomy of legal science itself.

CHAPTER FIVE

Sensitive Souls

Toward a Constitutional Aesthetics

Codifying the law involves both the creation of vernacular jurisdictions and legal thinking, but these tasks are asymmetrical. Creating a vernacular jurisdiction implies the production of a location for the *potestas iuris dicendi* by means of a language in which the "proper meaning of legal words" and "the common use of speaking" look remarkably similar, thus blurring the original distinction made by the glossator of the *Corpus Iuris Civilis*, according to which "verba legis debent intelligi secundum propriam significationem, non secundum communem usum loquendi" (legal words must be understood according to their proper meaning, and not according to the common use of speaking).[1] Vernacular jurisdictions are the responsibility of the legislator insofar as he is the one giving birth to them by means of the law.

Legal thinking, on the other hand, is an unpredictable form of power circulation in which the clients of the law actually own the language made available across the vernacular jurisdiction and through the vernacular codification of the law. In that sense, legal thinking is the client of the law's mutual responsibility. In a certain way, following the concept of Andreas Philippopoulos-Mihalopoulos, it is the result of the desire to be part of the lawscape by enjoying the right to use legal language in both legal and non-legal circumstances as a general language of exchange. Legal thinking is, in fact, a strategy of the lawscape itself, or, still following Philippopoulos-Mihalopoulos, a constraint of the space of justice, in which all legal mechanisms, affects, and language are visible.[2]

In my view, the real challenge faced by vernacular jurisdictions is in fostering legal thinking, engaging the people in the process of accepting the legal language of jurisdictional power in a way that the language becomes normalized, usual, new, seductive, and yet common and comfortable at the same time. The challenge is persuading the clients of the law that there is no outside the law. In other words, the challenge is the very creation of the lawscape and the space of justice.

I will argue that part of this challenge in fostering legal thinking is connected to what we have called perplexed legislation. Legislating with philosophy and fiction is a way to foster legal thinking. (Whether it is successful or not is another story.) With philosophy and fictional devices, the legislator creates the people's responsibilities.

In order to do so, the legislator locates some of these responsibilities in the aesthetic realm—that is, the realm of external and internal senses. The external senses cover the perceptions while the internal senses constitute the different operations of thought, including fantasy, imagination, consideration, common sense, and memory. It is important to notice that the division in five internal senses that include these operations of the soul does not come from Aristotle, but rather from the Arabic commentators of Aristotle in Persia and al-Andalus. In other words, here we have a direct glimpse to the Arabic philosophical sources used in the Alfonsine workshop.[3]

In other words, perplexed legislation establishes its foundations in an aesthetic and affective standpoint; that is, they revolve around the philosophy and politics of affects and sensibility. Here, the main question is how (and why) legal codification became interested in aesthetics and affects. I will propose the concept of constitutional aesthetics as a way to understand how the legislator inscribed aesthetics (and in particular Aristotelian-based aesthetics) as an element of his theory of power. Constitutional aesthetics is the best characteristic of dead voice: the technique of perplexing law-writing in the vernacular jurisdiction.

Why constitutional aesthetics? How and why would legal codification become interested in aesthetics and affects? What kind of aesthetics is it? What are the theories of power conveyed by constitutional aesthetics? These questions will allow us to address some rather intriguing parts of the legal codification and will open doors to a quite original way of creating a politics of the soul: a reading of the human soul in legal terms that entails political performance and political activity.

In order to answer these questions even partially, I will focus on *Partidas* 2.12–13. In these two titles of the *Second Partida*, Alfonso begins to legislate the responsibilities and obligations of the people toward the king as the personification of the kingdom; that is, the juridical person in whom the jurisdiction of the kingdom is concentrated. First, I will explain the role played by these two titles in the *Partidas*. The *Partidas* also very precisely conceptualizes the concept of *people*, which I will explain. I will suggest a reading of these two titles from the vantage point they set up by invoking Aristotelian aesthetics and psychology. Finally, I will concentrate on one particular issue raised by Alfonso—the inner sense he calls *remembrança*, or "memory" and how this concept of memory is closely connected to dead voice. In order to more fully show the governmental implications of memory that appear in the middle of this legislation, I will finally discuss a manuscript from the Archivo Histórico Nacional that transmits a royal inquisition, or inquest (*pesquisa regia*). This analysis will allow us to see the collaboration between the people and the kingdom on legal and political matters.

We the People

Titles 12–13 function as the two hinges of the *Second Partida* by permitting the lawgiver to shift subjects in his long path toward the creation of a body of constitutional legislation dealing with the theory and practice of sovereign power, in particular with the legislation concerning *imperium*. Whereas in Roman law the concept of *imperium* seems to be unrelated to jurisdiction, in medieval law, glossators like Jacobus de Arena thought that "est merum imperium iurisdictio severioris" (jurisdiction is the highest form of absolute sovereignty), a kind of jurisdiction that agrees with Ulpian's definition of *imperium* in *Digestus* 2.1.3: "gladii potestatem ad animadvertendum in facinorosos homines" (the power to use the sword against the criminal).[4] This power to hold the sword and to act against criminals is exactly the one claimed by Alfonso for the emperor in *Partidas* 2.1.1, which is clearly linked to jurisdiction. The emperor has the power to codify the law and to control seditious individuals (*soberbios*) and criminals (*tortiçeros*), a power that he will affirm in successive laws as they relate to the emperor and the king, always insisting that the best weapon against the *facinorosos*, or *tortiçeros*, is the production of the law (*Partidas* 2.1, and *Partidas* 3, prologue).[5] Finally, it is noted that the power held by emperors is the same power that kings hold in their kingdoms (*Partidas* 2.1.5).

In this way, the legislator examines, one by one, the many social and political agents who partake of the concept of monarchical power so that he can detail lexical precisions, definitions, obligations, and rights. In other words, he analyzes from a legal standpoint the terms in which jurisdictional delegation and *modica coercitio* (an attribute of jurisdiction that delegates forms of coercion) must work.[6] The first eleven titles deal with the emperor and the king, different projections of monarchical power, and *merum imperium*, whose differences are based on jurisdiction. These titles show a growing interest in the figure of the king, perhaps because, as some scholars have suggested, by the time the *Second Partida* was completed, Alfonso was not hoping to become the Holy Roman Emperor, a circumstance that perhaps was still on the king's horizon of expectations when he began composing the *Partidas*.[7]

After these first eleven titles, the legislator shifts from the emperor/king as a subject of the law to the people in general. Throughout the *Second Partida*, Alfonso legislates in-depth social strata and orders (*ordines*), as well as officers and other groups, both in times of peace and times of war, finishing with a title, the thirty-first, devoted to education and the university. With this new subject (everyone who is not the king but who is part of political society) in the legislative mind, the lawgiver delves into how the people must understand, consider, and love each of the social divisions. The people, as we saw in Chapter 2, is the patient, the object of royal love, which encompasses the people's regime of affects. These titles create the entire universe of legal responsibilities for the people.

Titles 12 and 13 lay the foundations of the legal responsibilities of the people. To do so, the laws give a theory and practice of those responsibilities stemming from the legal and political interpretation of an Aristotelian body of philosophy. The first legislative step in the process of creating the legal responsibilities of the people is, indeed, defining what "people" means. His definition specifies what needs to be understood by the noun "people," since the legislator is changing the common meaning of the word, the "communem usum loquendi," and replacing it with the "propriam significationem" as noted earlier: "Some think that the word people means the common people, as, for instance, artisans or peasants. But it is not so. For in ancient times, in Babylon, Troy, and Rome, which were very important places, all these matters were regulated according to reason, giving each thing its proper name. People are called the union of all men in common, those of superior, middle, and inferior condition. For all of them are necessary, and none can be excepted, for the reason that they are obliged to help one another in order to live well and be protected and supported."[8]

This people, as I argue, is the collective definition of the *personae fictae*, the whole set of juridical persons within the kingdom. Legislations preceding the *Partidas*, like the *Fuero Juzgo*, the *Fuero Real*, and the *Espéculo*, all refer increasingly frequently to the people or to the "people in general," but only the *Partidas* actually defines the people and their legal purview, thus creating a legal concept that explicitly fosters a new sense of legal and political solidarity within the kingdom. As we saw in Chapter 4, this is the kind of solidarity that *Partidas* 4.24 expressed in terms of love *and* in terms of how and why to love. The paths of this political love from the king toward the people came to include concepts that reveal the following (as we also saw in Chapter 4): "grace" (*merced*), as the king is "soul" and "life" to the people; pity (*piedad*), insofar as the king is head in relation to the people considered limbs; and mercy (*misericordia*) to forgive the people (*Partidas* 2.10.2).

Immediately afterward, the legislator explains why the people must be loved by the king (see Chapter 3) and then articulates what we called an invisible narrative consisting of concordances and allegations based on the counsel of Aristotle to Alexander the Great, since this counsel appears in the widespread governing art called *Secretum Secretorum*, thus legislating openly about what used to be a technique of government based on secrecy.[9] The lawgiver identifies a number of political tropes from this textual tradition that allow the king to establish a new metaphor for the political perception of the kingdom: a figural promise that he will fulfill in the remaining titles of this *Partida*, according to the processes I explained in previous chapters.[10] One of these tropes partakes of the theories of nature as an institution, deviating from the corporeal idea of the state: while the kingdom is an orchard (*huerta*), the people are like the trees (*Partidas* 2.10.3). In this approach to the people and the kingdom as an institution of nature, the legislator creates a social-tropological system that immediately acts as a mnemonic space with actors and functions linked to it: "The king's officers, those who have to judge and have the mission of helping to maintain justice, are like the peasants. Noblemen and knights are like soldiers who must keep justice. Laws and *fueros* and rights, they are like fences protecting justice. Judges and justices are like the walls and hedges that protect it, so that nobody can get in and damage it."[11]

The trope helps the reader to understand social and political functions within the walled estate and the walled state. In this walled territory, justice is pure labor, and the officers of the king, those delegated instruments of jurisdiction, are laborers, *peasants*. Instead of creating a wall with military force, however, the legislation identifies the administration of justice and the law as the real set of walls that keeps the estate/state safe from foreign threat. This metaphor neatly corresponds to Philippopoulos-Mihalopoulos's metaphor of the lawscape.[12] Within the lawscaped orchard, the noblemen and knights are responsible for keeping legal order. They are the most important administrators of punitive order. This is an entire reorganization, by means of a managed-nature trope, of the organization of medieval society as we commonly understand it:[13] peasants are not peasants but instead instruments of central power, while the military forces are in their turn conditioned not by the "knightly code" of chivalry but instead by positive legislation and a specific concept of justice.[14]

While the people receive this attention from the vantage point of the monarch, the code also needs to redefine the people itself. The code also analyzes the role of the people within the kingdom and in relation to the monarch. In order to do so, the people need to be theorized from the point of view of the anthropological and tropological system in which the body and soul constitute human identity.[15] But instead of speaking about the materiality of the body—which is already inscribed in the institutional-natural metaphor of the garden—the legislator focuses directly on the soul. He had already mentioned, in *Partidas* 2.1.5, that the king is the "heart" and the "soul" of the people, since the "soul lives in the man's heart, and because of it the body can live." Likewise, in the same law, the legislator established that the king is the "head" of the kingdom, insofar as the senses "are born from the head" and they "command all the other limbs of the body."

One can recognize here the presence of Aristotle's (and his commentators') insights into the soul in *De anima*. The references in this first approach to the politics and the legality of the soul (*anima*) are not only clear but also immediate and implicit. In this case, the Aristotelian presence is a resource for, rather than an interpretation of, a philosophical investigation.

The Politics of the Soul

Titles 12 and 13 contain a more in-depth philosophical set of references. They propose a social and political legal reading of the three types of souls: generative or nutritive, sensitive, and rational. It is important to understand that there is no true philosophical investigation in this part of the *Partidas*. The legislator is keen to resolve debates taking place around him and around foundational texts, mostly in the form of glosses and commentaries. He is not interested in contributing to the philosophical debate itself but rather in redirecting it toward the legal statute he wants to institute.

Aristotle's *Περὶ ψυχῆς*, or *De anima* as it was known in scholastic Europe, is one of the foundational texts that philosophers from al-Andalus and all over the Islamic polities were discussing in their debates on incoherence and perplexity: namely, whether the law could be interpreted with the inclusion of pagan philosophy and the exegesis of fictional devices. Philosophers like Averroes, in his commentary to the text, which was promptly translated as part of the *Aristoteles Latinus*, and Bajja Ibn, in his *Kitāb al-nafs* or *Book on the Soul*, contribute psychological and physiological discussions building on the early interests of al-Kindī, al-Rāzī, Avicenna, and al-Fārābī, after the Aristotelian corpus had been translated from Greek and Siriac into Arabic from the ninth century onward. The debates taking place in al-Andalus at the turn of the dynastic successions in the twelfth century cannot be disentangled from the theological-political transformations that these successions entail. Sunni-Sufi philosophers like Ibn Tufayl (c. 1105/504–1185/581), who was also one of the purported teachers of Averroes, wrote the philosophical-theological-political fiction known as *Ḥayy ibn Yaqẓān* —or *Philosophus Autodidactus*, as it was known in Latin—not only as an early Andalusi response to al-Ghazālī's *Tahafut* or *Incoherence* but also as a way to better understand the natural implications of philosophical inquiry and, in particular, the natural and political implications of the location of the soul, as Ḥayy himself, the main character of this narrative, demonstrates by dissecting the doe or gazelle he took to be his mother at the moment of her death.

Many of these commentaries and glosses, often used for pedagogical endeavors—like the various *Commentaries* by Averroes—came to constitute the corpus known as the *Aristoteles Latinus*. The *Aristoteles Latinus* corpus was patiently and laboriously created through translations of Arabic texts, which were very often produced on the Iberian Peninsula, and in the cultural institutions preceding and contemporaneous with Alfonso X. The corpus itself was widely used in Paris, where it had an extraordinary impact on pre-1277 university life among both artists and theologians.[16] The more recent work by Catherine König-Pralong and Ruedi Imbach provides a more complete narrative of the impact of the *Aristoteles Latinus* tradition on the development of intellectual, philosophical, and scholarly life around the key date of 1277.[17]

A similar situation arose with other Aristotelian treatises used and discussed in Alfonso's legislative effort, in particular the nine texts included in the part of the Aristotelian corpus known as *Parva Naturalia*, or "short treatises on nature." Among them are those that fall under the Greek label of αἴσθησις, "aisthesis." Aisthesis is everything related to sensation, perception, and processing such perception at the physiological and psychological levels, giving birth to judgments and decisions. They are treatises that ultimately deal with the affects of the soul, or τὰ πάθε τῆς ψυχῆς.[18] Among those treatises, some are especially important for the legislation in Title 13 in particular, such as *De sensu et sensibile*, *De memoria et reminiscentia*, and *De sopno et vigilia*. These treatises, in their turn, were heavily commented on around the Mediterranean basin, from Baghdadi philosophers and theologians and Andalusi thinkers up to and including Thomas Aquinas, Bartholomew of Glanville, and many others.[19]

The introduction of this aesthetic corpus into the legal and political discourse is yet another way for the legislator to embrace perplexity by engaging emotions. As in the philosophical-legal complex constituted by friendship in the context of the fiction of naturality crowning the *Fourth Partida*, the legislator proceeds to the introduction of affective discourses that serve as counterpoint to the rationality of the law, even the preeminence of dialectics, in order to acquire a legal language that can be more narrative, more affective, more emotional: one of the projects of the theory of power that underpins vernacular jurisdictions. Even in Aristotelian terms, affections and emotions are epistemologically more productive than logical propositions.[20]

Within the legal workshop—the group of individuals who build on the *mens* of the legislator, those who support the *fonction auteur* or even *fonction législateur* that we call Alfonso[21]—there were legal professionals who had taught at the leading universities. We don't know many, and most are *likely* contributors, since none left his name in the *Partidas*. Whereas some of these likely contributors are known for having written other legal corpora, like Fernando Martínez de Zamora, Gonzalo de Toledo, a certain Juan Alfonso, Juan Gil de Zamora, Maestre Roldán, and even Jacobo de Giunta, there is no mention of them in the legislative corpus.[22] At least it is known that Jacobo de Giunta and Juan Gil de Zamora were university people, and it is likely that so were the others. They were conversant and fluent in many of the innovations regarding legal research and commentary, and they were probably not ignorant of the debates and commentaries

concerning Aristotelian philosophy and the dialectic innovations it entailed, even though they decided to remain untouched by dialectics when
composing the *Partidas*.[23] Juan Gil de Zamora, for instance, was a clear
Aristotelian in natural philosophy, to which his comprehensive treatise
Historia Naturalis is a faithful witness.[24]

At any rate, their purpose—the legislator's purpose—was not to *teach*
Aristotelian philosophy about the soul but rather to *think* legally, to *think*
juridically, and to put this thought into legal and political practice. In other
words, the main question was how to articulate, from a legal and political
perspective, concepts that are otherwise essential to the construction of religious anthropologies, and in particular to Christian anthropology in the
Middle Ages (and today): namely, that we humans have a soul, that this
soul is the place of affects and thought from an ethical and political perspective, and that this soul is understood to be immortal and subject to a
different law in the afterlife, a different *persona ficta*, as it were—an *anima
ficta*. In this sense, the politics of the soul is a politics of both the civil and
the metaphysical soul.

This is where Titles 12 and 13 of *Partidas* 2 make a real contribution to
the interaction of philosophy and law from a productive perspective. They
regulate how to use the soul, the political and legal import of the soul, and
to what extent the soul is the location of the legal and political capacities and
responsibilities of the collective subject of the law, of the people.

To deploy this politics of the soul, the legislator presents a legal regulation about the political embodiment of the soul. In the Middle Ages, one
of the debates regarding the soul was linked to hylomorphism, to the metaphysical debate on substance and form and the essence of things. Andalusi
and Parisian thinkers wondered whether or not the soul has substance. The
position that emerged victorious after 1277, and was championed by
Thomas Aquinas, rejects Averroes's theory that the soul shaped the body,
and that therefore the soul was form. The legal response implicitly offered
by Alfonso is that the soul is certainly form, embodied by the body, but
that it is a political-legal body. Souls shape politics and shape the body
politic; that is, they shape the organization and functioning of society. In
Aristotelian terms, they are, like the soul in relation to the person, the
entelechia, the vital principle that animates all. How do they do it? What
are the ways in which this legal thinking can be disseminated throughout
society as if by capillaries?

Three Souls

In *Partidas* 2.12, Alfonso states: "Souls of three kinds—said Aristotle and the
other wise men—exist naturally in all living things" (*Partidas* 2.12, prologue).[25] After this, the lawgiver goes on to explain each of these souls. The
first is the "nutritive," or "generative," soul (*criadera*) common to all living
beings but which Alfonso attributes in particular to plant life. The second is
the sensitive soul (*sentidora*), which is common to all self-moving beings. The
third, specific to humans, is the rational soul (*razonable*).

After he establishes this typology, the legislator mentions "the wise men"
again to assert that "in the same way God gathered all these three souls in
men, men must love three things, from which he expects all the good he may
have in this world as well as in the afterlife. The first is God, the second is
his natural Lord, and the third, his land."[26] Hence, the legislator makes this
the turning point where he can shift from the king to the people, as we stated
before, insisting that "we want to explain, according to what the wise men
said about the three souls, the responsibilities of the people toward God and
toward their king and toward their land." At the same time, however, the
legislator proposes a series of tropological identifications and a change in
order: "The wise men spoke first of the generative soul, which they likened
to the way in which the people must love their land. After that, they spoke
about the sensitive soul, which they likened to the love the people must have
for their king, the people being the king's senses. And finally, they spoke
about the rational soul, which they likened to the love men must have for
God. We, however, understood that we need to mention first the things that
pertain to God, so we will first talk about the rational soul."[27] The legislator
then devotes nine laws to the rational soul and how it can be compared and
used to express the relationship of love from the people to God.

Alfonso carefully avoids identifying the wise men he refers to. When
they are mentioned along with the name of Aristotle, it is possible that he is
simply sweepingly pointing to the host of Aristotelian commentators, including Andalusis and those already included in the growing corpus of *Aristoteles
Latinus*. By not giving any further hints, Alfonso establishes his intellectual
authority without requiring his readers to look for those sources outside the
law itself. In a certain way, this ambiguity has the virtue of keeping the
readers' eyes on the legal text. The law summons external allegations (allegations as defined in Chapter 4) and concordances and establishes a series of
intellectual links with them, an immediate and plausible relationship with

the ideas they present and defend and an invisible narrative that situates the law within a certain genealogy of thought so that from there the law may proceed without giving more details.

The prologue to *Partidas* 2.12 contains a small but important critique of the "wise men" and the order of the discourse on the soul. Alfonso gives priority to the religious interpretation of the rational soul; for him, that should come first, not last, thus contradicting the Aristotelian tradition in *De anima*, including his commentators. This religious priority is all the more important as it is the expression of a civil, not an ecclesiastical, authority.

The religious interpretation of the rational soul is the result of a fictional device, a *semejança*, or comparison (I have translated *semejança* as "likeness"): the rational soul is likened, by legal fiat, to the love people must have toward God. It does not seem that the legal-political tropes—that is, the likenesses (*semejanças*) that stem from the discourse on the soul proposed by the legislator—have any particular source. Early glossators of the *Partidas* such as Alonso Díaz de Montalvo in 1500 and Gregorio López in 1555 were always attentive to concordances and additions that helped consolidate the legal system across the kingdom and the empire over time. They also thought of two different audiences: the courts of justice and the university. They were always eager to pinpoint sources in order to make the legal text more clearly European—a piece that fits neatly within the mythology of the *ius commune*—and therefore more useable not only across the global Iberian Empire but also in Europe. When they got to this point of the *Partidas*, the two early editors and glossators of the *Partidas*, Alonso Díaz de Montalvo and Gregorio López, lacked the resources to identify sources or concordances for this tropological reading of the rational soul and the love of God. This is because the trope of the rational soul and the love of God seems to be an Alfonsine legal creation.[28] The displacement between the rational soul and the love of God—no matter what nature this displacement might have—is not based on dialectical or rhetorical reasoning. The only element of persuasion in this displacement is the regime of sincerity created within the law itself; that is, rather than the configuration of a scientific or rational truth, the law is configured to create its own network of truth, its own space of certainty working within the legal discourse.[29]

The trope establishing the likeness between the rational soul and how the people need to love God is, in fact, an extraordinary step toward an acceptance of the knowledge of God and the experience of faith, hope, and charity, all belonging to the rational side of the crisis between reason and faith studied in depth by Alain de Libera.[30] Alfonso's legislation solves, by fiat, the crisis of reason and faith, since, in fact, there is no gap between the rational soul and the love of God; they are the same thing. There is no need to explore dialectical arguments for the lawgiver's solution to the crisis; the law establishes the direct consequences of its own regulation.

Alfonso asks: How can the soul be the subject of public, civil legislation? What steps should be taken to turn the soul, not the body, into an earthly, temporal interest of the law? How can a law make the connections between the temporal and the eternal, between the political and the theological, and between the earthly and the celestial, with a clear legal interest in the soul? These underlying questions would justify the change in order, and the interest in describing, the rational soul first instead of the others. The projection does not work from earthly to celestial—as a political-theological trope—but rather (and importantly) from celestial to earthly, as a theological-political trope. In this context, the relationship between the rational soul and the people's love for God is, indeed, an important step toward an answer.

The legislator uses this rational soul to introduce the concepts of love, belief, knowledge, and fear in order to make them politically productive, both in and of themselves and as a promise of a tropological understanding. The rational soul, according to the first law of the title, serves two epistemological purposes. The first is the knowledge of God and all things celestial with its concomitant interest in ontology from a theological perspective; everything that exists, exists in God. The second purpose is knowledge of things as they were created and, more important, of their order as it was first established.

Moral-political benefits and social knowledge spring from this order. In particular, men will understand "how to live, and how to order their public affairs [faziendas]" (Partidas 2.12.1).[31] I translate the Spanish noun fazienda as "public affairs" with a purpose, or even as a thesis. Fazienda comes from Latin agenda, "things that need to be done," and it has a political and public meaning in ethical and political texts and fiction from the thirteenth and fourteenth centuries, referring to both material properties (normally in dispute, like lands, buildings, etc.) and political inheritance.[32]

Public life, or fazienda, is precisely what this set of laws is oriented toward. They are not concerned with the private beliefs or individual practices of natural persons but rather with the politics of the soul. The laws are interested in the things that juridical persons, subjects of the law, personae fictae, can do by understanding the public life of the soul, its civil perspective, and how the civil life of the soul can impact the polity itself: the kingdom.

One may interpret this legislation from the point of view of Christian providence and within the discourse of a Christian monarchy that pervades not just the *Partidas* but also other products of his different workshops. Alfonso is, in the end, speaking (legislating) for the advancement of an expansionist monarchy, only one of whose many creative supports is vernacular jurisdiction and its consequences in terms of collaboration from the people. He needed to consolidate such a jurisdiction across the Iberian Peninsula and the growing kingdom he ruled. In the mid-sixteenth century, when Gregorio López, president of the Council of Indies, produced his glossed edition of the *Partidas*, the situation became even clearer: Iberia was not a peninsula anymore, but a global empire. For the ideological construction of this empire, it became necessary to build bridges between the Iberian Visigothic Empire, in a movement known as Gothicism, that could link that Christian past with the Christian present by jumping over the eight centuries of Muslim polities on the peninsula.[33]

From this perspective, those who put their rational soul to work following Alfonso's laws will establish the process of subduing and converting all the other peoples who cannot make use of the politics of the soul. Law and history would share this providential perspective, privileging those "chosen to receive God's inheritance" above those who cannot understand the principles of the rational soul and upon whom "the contrary of all this will come" (*Partidas* 2.12.9).[34]

The title on the rational soul ends with a law about the *timor domini*, or fear of God. The last quotation, from *Partidas* 2.12.9, results precisely from the political and historical-providential reading of the law concerning the fear of God. How does this idea of fear trigger another political reflection on the politics of the soul?

Aesthetics

The next title, *Partidas* 2.13, is specifically dedicated to the sensitive soul of the kingdom. This is the political-aesthetic regime whose responsibility falls on the people's juridical shoulders. There is a figural and tropological relationship between Title 13 and Title 12. Title 13 makes the tropological projection from theology to politics explicit, insofar as it secularizes the legal-theological principles and virtues expressed as part of the people-as-rational-soul trope. Indeed,

Partidas 2.13.15 elaborates on the concept of *timor regis*, or fear of the king. The legislator makes an important distinction here between *temor*, or "fear," and *miedo*, or "fright," inasmuch as the first is both theologically and politically useful for the production of relations of loyalty (*legalitas*) and fidelity (*fides*, faith), whereas the second pertains to a legal tradition in which fright is excluded from legal responsibility, as, for instance, in the laws of the Justinian *Digestum* 4.2.1 that deal with "Quod metus causa gestum erit" (On all those things that are done because of fright). Fear, the law states bluntly, stems from love, while fright comes from horror and implies lack of liberty and an abundance of external pressures.[35]

The legislator explores the legal economy of feelings and affects that constitute the backbone of the fiction of naturality, that is, nature as a legal institution. Love is, in its turn, a political concept, germane but separated from what in theological language is called *charity* (*Partidas* 2.12.6). The theological-political process becomes then consolidated in *Partidas* 2.13.13, where, as the legislator says, the "king . . . was chosen by God and acts on behalf of him on the earth."[36]

The law concerning fear of the king, which allows us to see the theological projection onto the political realm, appears in Title 13 as the political epitome of the eleven laws that establish the aesthetic-legal and aesthetic-political responsibilities of the people. The law also defines the people as the sensitive soul of the kingdom or as the ten senses of the king, while the king is deemed to be the soul and the heart of the kingdom (*Partidas* 2.1.5).

The entire set of laws concerning the sensitive soul of the kingdom and its ten senses is fully legislated again *por semejança* (by means of likeness). This means that it is the result of the articulation of fictional devices that facilitate the interaction between philosophy and law. Without this tropological activity, the connection between these two disciplines would be imperfect.

The fictional device works on two different levels. First, it works at the level of interpretation, in which something is submitted to an allegorical process—turned into something else—and then tropologically interpreted, giving it political and moral significance. Second, it works at the level of the *fictio legis*, insofar as the *semejança* is one of the linguistic procedures of the *as if*, which legally transforms something as if it were then something else. These are two completely different regimes of legal understanding, because the first seems to be central to general, pedagogical communication, while the second has the force of law. The legislation of the *Siete Partidas* is, above all, legislation (a fact I cannot stress enough), although scholars from the nineteenth century onward have had difficulties accepting the code as *only* legislation, so great a challenge does it present to legal positivism and legal scholarship of the twentieth century in particular.

Exploring every tropological and fictional element for each of the ten senses would be a project too great for only one chapter. Besides, this is only a small part of a much larger investigation that would need to be done— perhaps an investigation into the politics of the soul. From this point forward, I will content myself with explaining the ways in which these laws work from the vantage point of tropology and fictional devices.

Each law in *Partidas* 2.13 is structured in three parts. The first part contains a definition of the sense it intends to deal with. There are six laws devoted to the five external senses, because there are two for the sense of taste, and then five more laws regarding the five internal senses. The second part develops the *semejança*, including the tropological reading and the *fictio legis* all at once. In other words, there are no separate linguistic operators to distinguish between these two thinking operations; one turn of phrase performs both operations simultaneously. This second part describes the aesthetic-political responsibilities of the people while, at the same time, it legislates them. The third part of the law expresses the punishment in the case of an infraction of the rule contained and interpreted in the first two parts.

The sense of sight—the legislator explains—is naturally devised to see things from close up and from afar and to distinguish the forms and colors of things. The trope of this sense is that it serves the purpose of seeing the name of the king, who is the projection of God, from different distances. Political and legal sight are fundamental for the protection of the king's name, the king's life, and the king's *fama*, or reputation: the integrity of his dignity. In this sense, the fictional device permits the transformation of physical sight into another kind of surveillance that leads to a legal responsibility with political consequences. The third part of the law addresses the legal responsibilities by identifying the punishment due to those who break the previous two parts of the law. Supporting his argument with the help of the *Fuero antiguo de España*, or "ancient charters of Spain" (that is, the *Liber Iudiciorum*), Alfonso specifies that breaking the legal-perceptive rule contained in the law is punishable by death, or if the life of the convicted person is spared, he must have his eyes removed, thus establishing a final connection between the crime, the tropological reading, and the legal consequences on the organ of the external sense.

By describing each sense, the laws also give a typology of the crimes against the king and the kingdom (*crimen maiestatis* or *lesa maiestatis*). In other words, misperception is what provokes the crime of lèse-majesté. The laws thus regulate how to understand legality. Legality implies learning how to feel politically, how to manage political affects. Feeling politically, or learning how to translate feelings into political thought and political acts, is, in its turn, vital to the role legal concepts play in maintaining the integrity of the kingdom. Conversely, misperception and its political consequences may elicit the inception of a civil inquest. Indeed, notions linked by these laws to the senses, like reputation (*fama*), rumor, public opinion and public knowledge, systems of observation, and perception of the functioning of the kingdom are at the core of a jurisdiction for which civil inquest, as regulated in *Partidas* 3.16, is a method of mutual surveillance of the sensitive souls taking care of the proper perception going on inside other sensitive souls.

Along with political feelings and political aesthetics, these laws also regulate their contrary, thus providing the client of the law with an anti-aesthetics of power. The citizen's virtue is learning how to read natural feelings as political feelings: sensitive stimuli provoke positive political performance. Anti-aesthetic reactions to the same stimuli constitute the frontier of crime against the kingdom itself.

The tension between aesthetics and anti-aesthetics in legal and political terms is the result of the displacement of the concept of pleasure. Indeed, the senses come about by way of perceiving organs, and they are the means of obtaining knowledge. Furthermore, they are also ethically constructed. They are designed to feel pleasure when confronted with appropriate stimuli and displeasure when faced with either inadequate or excessive stimuli. The criminal is the one who confuses these stimuli. In this sense, pleasure and good go hand in hand in the same way that displeasure and evil do. Indeed, the legal subject is not only bound to perceive but also to engage in the production of ethical and political judgments based on his or her perception.

Hearing presents the argument in a poignant way. This sense has been designed to feel good and to feel goodness itself with "pleasant and savory" (*plazenteros e sabrosos*) sounds and must abhor those other sounds that are "heavy and scary" (*fuertes e espantables*). This distinction reinforces the idea that "fright" and "being scared" are feelings that are not linked to love and therefore have no political value. The pleasure of good hearing must be correlated with political feeling regarding what is heard about the king. The trope puts the responsibility of expanding the pleasure of goodness on the people's shoulders, because they must watch out for unpleasant sounds about the king as uttered by other subjects—in order to forbid them from making such utterances. Politically productive hearing will help the subjects be attentive to those who intend to question the king's reputation, so that the culprits can be charged with treason and punished. To feel good about what must be abhorred and to confuse the relationship between pleasure and good is a crime of lèse-majesté (*Partidas* 2.13.3).

Similar readings constitute the legislation pertinent to the olfactory sense, "for those who feel good about the king's being damaged and dishonored, are known traitors, and must suffer the penalty corresponding to those who could have hampered the crime and did not do so" (*Partidas* 2.13.4). Likewise, the other two external senses, taste and touch, build on the central trope of the politics of pleasure, in order to continue with the development of a complete semantic field that permits the people to discuss, and to remember, the relationship between sensing, feeling, good, evil, and their political and criminal counterparts or consequences.

The sense of taste is divided in two parts: taste and tongue, as in speech. Other authors, including Bartholomew of Glanville around 1240 and Juan Gil de Zamora in his *Historia Naturalis* (also a mid-thirteenth-century work) similarly divide this sense. The legislator devotes one law to each of them (*Partidas* 2.13.4–5). The tongue is not only the site for taste but also the organ of speech: "not only to taste, but, furthermore, to speak and to show the man's speech with it." Here, there is a double trope, one of taste in terms of pleasure obtained from healthy tastes, which are immediately related to the health of the king, and one in terms of bad taste as related to bad, unhealthy food, just like the things that can harm the king. The second part of the trope, in Law 5, is directly related to speech, and the bitterness of the lie, in the understanding that the lie is not natural.

This distinction is also important because it introduces the legal concept of *fama* that I am translating as "reputation," as one of the crucial political and legal themes that had helped the growth of "papal government."[37] The introduction of reputation in the systems of social, political, and religious surveillance meant the consolidation of papal jurisdiction, as Julien Théry has demonstrated, in particular from 1215 onward.[38] Alfonso identifies the civil valence of the concept, which is essential in legislation regarding the civil inquisition as presented in the *Third Partida*.

The introduction of the concept of pleasure as a political artifact and as a legal feeling is also present in this second trope of taste. Lying is not natural, it was not created by God, it is man-made, and in this sense, one could say that lying is an institution. Because of that, the mind, the *intellectus*, or even the *anima* (since these concepts can be synonymous in discussions about Aristotelian psychology and aesthetics) feels the greatest and most loyal pleasure in the practice of truth and, consequently, in truth-telling. The people must reject flat out lies (*mentir llanamente*) or, even worse than plain lies, "composite lies told knowingly" (*mentira compuesta a sabiendas*), also called *lisonja*, or flattery, a concept whose semantic genealogy is linked to the political *lauzengier* (flatterer) in Provençal poetry and that seems intertwined with the concept of hypocrisy.

The five internal senses of the sensitive soul are legislated according to the same tripartite structure: description, tropological interpretations, and penal consequences. The horizon of each of these senses is, still, the concept of pleasure, on the one hand, and the complete depiction of the *crimen maiestatis* by means of the tropological relationship between aesthetics and legality in two senses (rhetorical comparison and *fictio legis*), on the other hand.

After legislating the five external senses, *Partidas* 2.13.7 begins with a series of senses "that are within, and are not apparent," beginning with the most important, *common sense*, which, in Aristotelian psychology is theorized after fantasy. Alfonso changes the regular order that puts common sense at the end of the list in order to establish a different hierarchy in the political perception and the critique of political emotions. In this case, the legislator foregrounds the duty of council and the duty of service to the king by the people as a way to establish a tropology of common sense, the infraction of which results in yet another instance of capital crime against the monarch. Fantasy, which appears after common sense, lacks the profound theorization found in Aristotelian philosophy, insofar as the legislator delves into the negativity of unreflective and rash thoughts and actions in order to create, in the following law, a better understanding of imagination. A degree more powerful than fantasy, imagination, the third internal sense, is a psychological counterpart to the ethical virtue of prudence: that is, the legal evaluation of past and present things and their consequences in regard to the observation of monarchical power.

The fourth sense, called *virtud asmadera* in Alfonso's typology, and corresponding to the estimative faculty, has a deeper tropological sense, one that is more crucial to buttressing the construction of the political love that structures the *Partidas*.[39] The *virtud asmadera* is linked to the perception of good feelings, friendship, or goodness in things themselves; the people must be able, with this faculty, to distinguish between friendly and unfriendly, that is, between things that are linked to political love and things that aren't. As the *Siete Partidas* is an integrated system of thought, this *virtud asmadera* links the *Second Partida*, which is essentially political, social, and administrative law, to the *Fourth Partida*, which, as we saw in Chapter 4, is set at the center of the seven insofar as it radially defines the circulation of power through the legislation and theorization of the circulation of love.

The fifth and last internal sense to be regulated, the one at the top of the hierarchy, is memory. It is the most important because it is the repository (*repostura*) and guardian (*guardador*) of the other senses, both internal and external, and it is able to assign a time to each of the things that have been registered and collected; these, in their turn, can be retrieved according to necessity, in due time. The tropological interpretation the legislator implements is, in fact, a powerful *fictio legis* that regulates the two things that need to be remembered.

In the first place, the people must remember power itself, and sovereignty, as the central expression of power, and they must remember that this sovereignty is above the people, as it is practiced by the king. The individual who fails to remember this principle of power will lose all of his property—all of the things that establish his relation to his share of power—as he must be *desapoderado*, or disenfranchised (*Partidas* 2.13.11).

The second thing they must remember is dead voice.[40] In particular, they must remember *mandamientos* and *posturas*. *Mandamientos*, or "commands," are the whole set of rules and laws codified in the *Siete Partidas*. The *posturas*, however, are a larger body of written resolutions, because the word *postura* is widely used in the *Partidas* to designate contracts, documents, and many other legal transactions that can be ascribed to the concept of *dead voice* and that become *new* once they are presented in its written, past form.[41] Remembrance is of the past, but, like dead voice itself, memory makes the past new; retrieving a law by remembrance means to enforce it again by dint of its content in sovereignty and legal power.

In his famous and elegant book, M. T. Clanchy suggested the possibility of writing a history of the production of documents in England between the Norman Conquest and the death of Edward I in 1307.[42] In order to write this history, the history of its materials, systems of communication, languages, and other technologies involved in the phenomenal profusion of documentary and written evidence during this period, Clanchy drew inspiration from H. J. Chaytor's narrative of the history of medieval literature, *From*

Script to Print, when he titled his own book *From Memory to Written Record*.[43] There is no history possible in *from script to print*, because they have coexisted for many centuries (and still do) as different and equally productive creative systems, and for many centuries, some written genres (even literary genres) have preferred script to print.[44] Equally, the relationship between memory and written record has been fraught for centuries, as we know at least from Plato's *Phaedrus* onward. What seems particularly important in the *Partidas* is that the legislator, Alfonso, dissolves this relationship into a different one in which *hypomnemata*, so to speak, is in fact memory, or better yet, memory is equivalent to written record, thus erasing the difference, and even the teleology, of the narrative trope "from memory to written record." This is possible because of the *fictio legis* governing dead voice.

Memory, therefore, is not individual memory. It is the memory of the juridical person like all the other senses that inhere in the sensitive soul—because this soul is the political responsibility of the *persona ficta*. There is a foundational anthropomorphism in the creation of the artificial or juridical person, but this anthropomorphism also becomes the norm, rather than the trope. It is, therefore, counterpointed by another anthropomorphism: the one that gives rise to the soul of the juridical person, a soul defined by the management of legal and political affects, political emotions, and, ultimately, political memory. This is the real consequence of the politics of the soul.

A Royal Inquest

It is very frequently difficult to match the legal construction and codification of the *Partidas* with specific cases from the archives. The amount of documents conveying those judicial cases is scant. It is easier to see allegations to the *Partidas* in early modern, and even modern and contemporary cases, when the *Partidas* had already become a suppletive law in the Alfonsine era. One of the documents that may give us a hint about how an understanding of the *sensitive soul of the kingdom* worked in the later years of the Alfonsine kingdom is a *pesquisa regia*, or royal inquest. The inquest was, at that time, a fairly new judicial system, and Alfonso readapted it as well in the *Partidas*. I suggest reading this readaptation of the inquest and the resulting document as part of the construction of the institutional memory of the sensitive soul of the kingdom.

Inquisitions were enforced by Lateran Council IV in 1215 as a large-scale investigation into things that could not be easily proved but were indeed widely discussed as matters of public opinion. Different kinds of inquisitions could take place, such as those in search of major crimes against papal power (*potestas*), including those falling under the category of *enormitates*, which have been studied by Julien Théry. Crimes of this kind sometimes involved very famous people, but others actually touched only on local matters.

We know some of these inquests, or *inquisitiones*, very well, because some still remain part of popular culture. The inquisition undertaken under the authority of Jacques Fournier, the bishop of Pamiers, part of which took place in Montaillou, was edited by Jean Duvernoy in 1965. Some years later, Emmanuel Le Roy Ladurie wrote the iconic book on the subject, *Montaillou, village occitan de 1294 à 1324* (1972). With the creation of the Pays Cathare by the Conseil Général de Languedoc Roussillon in the Départment d'Aude, who were French authorities under the impetus of the lawyer, historian, and politician Georges Frêche (1938–2010), some of the cities and even hamlets in the Aude and the Languedoc-Roussillon regions took on new names, and Montaillou changed its name to reflect Le Roy Ladurie's book; it is now called Montaillou, Village Occitan. Each year, the village of Fontcalvy celebrates "its legend" with an event called Inquisitor, a "spectacle historique vivant," in which they *play* an inquisition.[45] After Miguel Delibes published his last novel, *El Hereje* (1998), which is about the inquisitions against Protestants burnt at the stake in 1561, the city of Valladolid, Spain, created the Ruta del Hereje (Heretics' Route) for tourists, under the impulse of Alfredo Mateos Paramio, then in the Fundación Municipal de Cultura. The list of other inquisitions that have made their mark on contemporary European geography and culture would be too long to cite here.

If inquisitions have been so well (or at least so intensively) studied it is because scholars like Le Roy Ladurie, Carlo Ginzburg, and Jean-Claude Schmitt and the members of GAHOM (Groupe d'Anthropologie Historique de l'Occident Médiéval) understood the anthropological value of the inquest proceedings and the different kinds of documents created around the inquests, including conversion narratives, preaching treatises, collections of tales to use in sermons, collections of sermons, and theological treatises, among others. With those sources, the members of the GAHOM created the field of *anthropologie historique* (historical anthropology), which has been at the center of medieval historiography in France for over thirty years and has had a clear influence on academic institutions in many nations, including those of Italy, Spain, and the United States. In a certain way, these scholars have gleaned more from the original inquisitorial proceedings than the medieval inquisitors did.

In a lecture at the Banquet du Livre in the Abbey of Lagrasse (Aude), held in 2013, the French scholar Patrick Boucheron wondered why we have such thick manuscripts chronicling inquisitorial procedures and so little documentation of condemnations, or of sentences in general. While the bibliography has underscored the necessity of the research itself, scholars have had difficulty coping with the idea of the importance of research alone.[46] I argue that the proceedings had the purpose of producing, precisely, proceedings. In other words, we have those thick manuscripts from very long inquisitions because there were no precedents, examples, or jurisprudence for a new juridical form and method, and it was necessary to create them. Inquests, just like confession manuals and other texts and cultural artifacts produced during the first hundred years after Lateran Council IV, have the purpose of configuring their own history and knowledge, or, in other words, their own jurisprudence—their own jurisdictional presence across time—which is the only way to consolidate power. That is to say, these proceedings constitute dead voice. In this dead voice, there is at the same time a sort of ethnographic investigation conveying the forms of the subjects' lives, their beliefs and behavior, and the image of authority and sovereign power that underwrites the judicial process itself. These proceedings, therefore, constitute the memory of the juridical subject, the central piece of the constitution of the sensitive soul of the kingdom.

One question that underlies the production of procedures is how the inquisitorial process is to be enforced. In this case, it cannot be enforced without also holding the people, as the sensitive soul of the kingdom, responsible, for which the final document and its presence as dead voice, and as a ghost manuscript, is essential. Dead voice is what makes the proceedings relevant over time. Dead voice is what creates the jurisprudence necessary for the new procedural system and its future usability. In an inquisitorial process, the people need to be the memory of the kingdom by remembering the king, his power, and his sovereignty. They also need to be the legal system described and mandated to perform both the inquest and the final document produced for the involved parties and for the royal archives. In effect, as *Partidas* 3.17.11 states, in some inquests the king or judge must provide the witnesses with a *traslado*, or copy of the proceedings, so that the very legal subjects can be, at least partially, a repository of dead voice—oftentimes, their own voice, now changed from living to written.

The *pesquisa* soon became an important research method. Legal sources from the thirteenth and fourteenth centuries reveal that they were used for diverse ends, for example, to make decisions about many cases, including the regulation of commerce in forbidden exports, such as horses in the Cortes of Valladolid, 1312.[47] Many of those inquests were collected and examined, and then a sentence was issued in accordance with the appropriate legislation; for instance, in 1307, when Louis X Capet was the king of Navarre and France, the civil inquest involving García Sanchiz d'Otiyñano, Iohan Periz d'Areyllano, and Martin Ferrandez was resolved in agreement with both the *Partidas* and the *Fuero de Navarra*.[48] Sentences elicited a negotiation between the king or the Regency Council and city representatives to either remove or carry out a sentence, or even the entire inquest. In 1301, for example, the citizens of Zamora demanded that the king grant them the right to keep the documents of the inquest that he himself had initiated about a debt that was damaging the city's economy, and the king responded that he would reexamine the case and issue a resolution.[49]

The memory of the inquest, and the memory of the other *mandamientos* and *posturas*, is part of the *cortes*, the parliamentary-like meetings across the kingdom in which the king assembled social groups to discuss policy and its enforcement. Indeed, those social groups are the sensitive soul of the kingdom and, as such, express themselves through those meetings.

Legislation also included increasingly more complex regulation of royal inquests. Even local *fueros*, like that of the kingdom of Navarre, the *Fuero de Navarra*, extensively governed civil inquests. So, too, did the *Leyes del Estilo*—which had been promulgated by Sancho IV after the dethronement of Alfonso X in 1282 and intended as a legal explanation for the *Fuero Real*—with broader regulation of royal inquests, in which jurisdictional power was shared by the king and the noblemen who had upheld Sancho in his revolt against his father. The *Ordenamiento de Alcalá*, which was issued by Alfonso XI in 1348 and established a hierarchy of legal sources that includes the *Partidas*, also regulated royal inquests, this time giving more power to the king, according to his clearly monarchical stance.

The document now preserved in the Archivo Histórico Nacional, in Madrid, with the call number Cod. L. 76-B, is a good place to start our analysis because it is such a long and complex judicial piece including, among other things, the interrogation of one hundred witnesses of different social origins, both ecclesiastical and laypeople, and the intervention of notaries (*escribanos, notarios*) and attorneys (*personeros*), all facing the difficult task of deciding the attribution and property of land and places of production. The case has received attention from scholars at the Consejo Superior de Investigaciones Científicas (CSIC), such as Julio Escalona, Cristina Jular, and María Isabel Alonso, primarily with the goal of understanding the case in itself—*Oña v. Frías*—and of undertaking a historical-anthropological investigation into the different actors, with special emphasis on the witnesses. The text was partially edited by Isabel Oceja Gonzalo, along with the other documents from the Monastery of Oña.[50] This edition has the virtue of providing scholars a glimpse of the monastery's archives; however, it does not allow us to see other important issues: namely, the opposing or competing archives performed on the document now preserved in the Archivo Histórico Nacional and, more importantly, the codex as a whole. Reappraising the codex is still essential, because the editor has sequenced and even fragmented it, cutting out parts of the documents she considered superfluous and giving a misleading impression of their role within the original manuscript. However, I will not focus on the whole manuscript; I will simply read one short selection from the text that shows the moments in the process in which the different actors perform a ritual that consists of dusting off their archival items, privileges, and diplomas, a ritual that precedes the long polling of witnesses occupying most of the codex.

Legal proceedings imply the exhibition of documents, because they are essential to proving the case. That the cases included such moments for the presentation of documental proof is not special in and of itself. The *Fuero Real*, the *Espéculo*, and the *Partidas* were very concerned with the regulation and appropriate legislation of documents; these three innovative codes made use of all the recent advances in notarial language and methods for identifying and preventing forgery. Dead voice exists as much in writing as in diplomatic sincerity within legal aesthetics, and in this sense, we could add a second definition of legal aesthetics as the regime of perceptibility of the law as law, and not as legal thinking in general. Dead voice regulates the materiality of the document: the type of paper, seals, colors, script quality, the price of the materials used for writing, even the salaries paid to the scribes according to their expertise in what we can call legal philology. Dead voice is also about the regulation of copies and of the dissemination of documents, about which documents can be considered archival and which ones cannot, about registering the documents, about the graphic elements on the document, and about the whole array of elements that allowed both notaries and laypeople to examine and, if necessary, question the validity of the document. The *pesquisa* conveys how all these procedures take place, how the ritual is presided over by this particular conversation on legal aesthetics, and how legal aesthetics itself is at stake.

Neither the *Fuero Real* nor the *Espéculo* are as systematic as the *Partidas*. The legal workshop also became increasingly acquainted with other European discussions on the notarial arts and with how they engaged with norms of the production and preservation of documents from the Old Testament and from the Qur'an. New technologies were enforced, while other European treatises stayed in the realm of jurisconsultation and as corporate arts within powerful notarial societies. Alfonso created a royal, vernacular legislation that completely reshaped the way in which both professional lawyers and clients of the law faced what we have called legal thinking.

The Archivo Histórico Nacional codex is very careful about what is going on with the proceedings. The archive is fragile, the site of memory in dispute, and parties are ready to defend their archive of dead voices, the ghost manuscripts that come back from death to become alive as if they were new, retrieved from memory to become synchronic facts.

In this codex we see at work the task of the sensitive soul of the kingdom. Memory, indeed, of sovereignty and of dead voice, the sensitive souls of the kingdom need to show, during the *pesquisa*, that they have perceived correctly and that they can reinstate, make new, a chaotic inheritance of the past, ridding it of all those elements that have troubled politics, that have troubled the orderly functioning of the kingdom.

Conclusion

I include this political slippage of the law into aesthetics as a potential way of building legal thinking among people, and in particular among those who are not professional lawyers but cannot escape the pervasiveness of the legal profession and legal languages, those who are inside the lawscape. Law and aesthetics set legal thinking in motion by means of legal operations including tropes, limit cases, allegations, concordances, and *fictiones legum*. In the present case, the "people" as "sensitive soul" is a trope; it is therefore part of a tropological interpretation of natural science with legal consequences.

This trope, even though part of the legislative process and a law in itself, has barely been established. It is, in this sense, an inchoate narrative. It is a way to begin something that has no underlying habitus yet, something that begins to exist only with the production of the law. It appears for the first time, in the *Partidas*, as a poetic artifact, something that can—and ultimately must—modify the perception the *people* have of themselves as juridical and political persons, as *personae fictae*, in legal terminology. In a certain way, vernacular legislations are based on the power of this kind of inchoate narrative. They claim that people play an active role in the formation and transformation of the kingdom according to this new legal code: a public redescription of duties, of the ways in which a person, or *persona*, is fabricated, or *ficta*. Contemporary examples of these inchoate narratives could perhaps further clarify this. Think, for instance, of the motto *Hacienda somos todos* (We all are the IRS) coined in 1978 or even of the Spanish law 52/2007, also known as the Law of Historical Memory (Ley de Memoria Histórica).[51]

The people as the sensitive soul of the kingdom is not a casual trope but rather one that has been well designed and carefully crafted. The title goes, law by law, through the ten senses. The last, in Law 11, is the sense of memory. The legislator briefly discusses cognitive questions related to Aristotelian thinking and debates in *De memoria et reminiscentia* with the purpose of establishing a thesis: the people need to remember the location and identity of central power, the idea of power within the kingdom, and how this power is kept and preserved by means of the *pleitos* and *posturas* produced within the kingdom, that is, by means of the whole body of documentation created as dead voice.

This displacement between the study of the affects and the legal and political must be underlined in the case of the *Partidas*. The *Partidas*, indeed, establish an aesthetic regime—that is, a legal system overtly based on *aisthesis*, which is normally translated as "sense" or "sensibility." This aesthetic regime is in fact crucial for both the codification and the dissemination of the law. The *Partidas* have their own legal science, legal scholarship, and legal propaedeutics inscribed in the law *as* law. They also have their own theories and their own philosophy. This complex was designed for lawyers of very different categories who needed to be able to teach the text, the rationality, and even the very existence of these laws across urban and rural centers that that had been accustomed to regulating themselves with local charters, nobiliary jurisprudence, community usages, or, in many cities of Castile, Leon, New Castile, Aragon, Galicia, and so forth, by nothing other than unwritten customs.[52]

The legislator transformed the people into the sensitive soul of the kingdom. The people were then located at the center of what we could call a constitutional aesthetics: a theory of power in which the affects, the senses, the sensible, τὰ πάθε τῆς ψυχῆς, are legally charged with political and social responsibilities and agencies. The people do not only *perceive* or *sense* but also, by means of this constitutional aesthetics, learn how to perceive and how to separate what is pleasant and therefore politically productive for the kingdom from what is unpleasant to the political senses and can damage the integrity of the kingdom. In this sense, this constitutional aesthetics is a discourse not only on the affects but also on the political responses that the affects must elicit, as regulated by the laws from those who, being legal subjects of the affect, reflect that affect back as political agents.

CONCLUSION

How to write the Law? Many cultures, past and present, would not even consider this a question. There are *unwritten verities*, as Sebastian Sobecki has reminded us with regard to common law.[1] There are also those other laws that were already written before even the clients of the law could realize it. Such clients could become aware of the written law only at the moment they were to be considered subjects of those laws—too late, therefore, to ask the question. There are *acheiropoetic* laws, a Greek word that means that they were not written by physical hands. There are laws predating humankind; laws perhaps written directly in the book of nature in an unknown script. One is free to imagine. So, how the law should be written is a finicky question, and one that could only exist in a distinct, although neither universal nor easily generalizable, set of conditions of possibility.

It is also quite possible that the question may arise not as a question. It may arise as a response. Alfonso X may not have asked the question itself in so many words. He probably didn't nod in front of one of the intellectuals and scholars working for him while asking, "So, Mr. Fulano, how should we write the law?" But he certainly posited it, if not as a question, then as a response.

And it was a multifaceted response at that. Indeed, it was a response to those people in his kingdom who used to scratch the laws, those who treated the law as if the law could be an opportunistic iteration to be appropriated and invented again according to individual interests or to the interests of a group holding consolidated power, a group whose way of lobbying was precisely their ability to erase and rewrite. At least those law-scratchers were conscientious enough, or too complacent, to not simply shred the parchments and papers containing the laws. They used the same ones. They, sophisticated counterfeiters that they were, carefully collected their documents from past eras and refashioned the latter in their image and likeness.

Alfonso's great breakthrough in the history of law and legal thinking was his belief that this was not the right way: laws should not be modified to benefit their subjects, but rather those subjects should modify themselves in front of the mirror of the laws. He knew well, because he had also law scratched and then looked at himself in the mirror of laws.

Far beyond historical and political circumstances, given events, and concrete experiences, Alfonso's was another kind of response. Indeed, this is not the response of Alfonso, a king, a name given to a workshop, a *mens*, an *auctor*, or whatever you want to call it. This response is of a theoretical character, and as such, it is also a time machine that travels to the past and to the future while inhabiting the present, any Alfonsine or post-Alfonsine present. This was the response not of Alfonso, but of the Alfonsine Era, a temporality that opened itself to the time that had just ended and to the time that was to come, theoretically, forevermore. The Spanish adjective *eviterno*, from Latin *aeviternus*, means—unlike the English cognate "eviternal"—something that has had a beginning in time but won't have an end. The Alfonsine Era was sustained by this possibility; it may have had an inception date (June 23, 1252), but it may project itself into eternity.

Opening itself in time, Alfonso's response permeated the debate going on throughout the Mediterranean basin. The primary question of this debate, or rather, crisis, as Alain de Libera has conceptualized it, was whether there could be any reciprocal adequacy between the law on the one hand, and, on the other, philosophical, scientific, poetic, and exegetical bodies of knowledge descended from the pagan past.[2] The history of this debate is discontinuous, fragmentary, multilingual. It has many criss-crossing lines and other lines that fail to intersect with anything. Dialogues inside the debate are sometimes direct and coeval, whereas others are allusive, indirect, oblique, and, oftentimes, across eras.

The debate was already ongoing when Basil of Cesarea (330–379) delivered his homily (the twenty-third) on the education of young boys. His area of influence included Caesarea in Cappadocia (modern Kayseri); Pontus, by the Black Sea; and other places throughout the Anatolian Peninsula and Greece, including Athens. Those boys from the different peninsulas concerned Basil because they seemed to feel some guilt. They seemed to suffer from a sickness in their minds or thought (τὴν τῆς γνώμης νόσον παραπλησίαν) when they realized that their classical baggage interfered with their study of the law and Christian doctrine.[3] This mental sickness, and this was Basil's main cause of distress, may have led them to a certain melancholy, or, in Jean Starobinski's terms, what we would call clinical depression or other indisposition of the soul that seems irremediable (μελανχολίας).[4]

The debate was also flourishing between Milan and the coasts of Northern Africa, and between them and Rome while Augustine (354–430) was writing his work *On Christian Doctrine* (in 397 and in 426), in which he refined the arts of reading, exegesis, and rhetorical commentary for their use in public. Even when he was writing his works on lying and on those who lie (*De mendacio*, ca. 395; *Contra mendacium*, ca. 420), he slipped in ideas on the relationship between biblical parables and falsity in order to disentangle legitimate from illegitimate interventions external to Sacred Scripture and divine law.

Moreover, the debate was also present in Persia and throughout the Islamic world, including the Maghreb, of which al-Andalus was a prominent part. Earlier Persian scholars and intellectuals such as al-Fārābī, Ibn Sīnā, and al-Ghazālī found themselves on the lips and in the codices of Andalusi scholars and intellectuals who either defended or disputed them, including Ibn Tufayl from Guadix, in Granada; Ibn 'Arabī from Murcia; Ibn Bajja from nearby Zaragoza; and Averroes from Cordoba. The debate in al-Andalus viewed the question from the perspective of the possible incoherence and refutation (*tahāfut*) of those philosophers whose theories and research techniques—namely logic—were being increasingly used to interrogate legal sources from the Qu'ran to the latest *fatwa*. Most of their interventions were, indeed, translated on the Iberian Peninsula and included in the corpus we know today as the *Aristoteles Latinus*, which contains not only the texts of the philosopher but also those of the Arabic commentators: Muslim, like those mentioned above, or not, such as the Christian Nestorian Ibn Hunayn, or Ioannitius (808–877), from Bagdad.

The debate/crisis was ongoing among Jewish intellectuals. Maimonides even suggested a concept to characterize the feeling of loss, of disorientation, even sadness—not unlike Basil of Cesarea's words—with which one is overtaken when, confronting the law, one realizes that it is impossible not to philosophize and avoid interpreting the parables, metaphors, and other tropes found in legal texts. This concept was *ḥīrah*, that is, "perplexity." His work was also translated, read, and discussed from the thirteenth century to the early modern period, when his work, now in Latin, was printed under the title *Dux Neutrorum ac Dubitantium, seu Perplexorum*.

In the poem preceding his *Epistle of the Debate*, the Maimonidean philosopher and scholar Shem-Tov Ibn Falaquera (1225–ca. 1290) wrote:

matters of controversy
Between men of intelligence are [matters of] peace.

They are words of delight,
Spoken in the quiet without wrath.

Fools think that between the Law
And Thought there is at all times war.

They think that the hatred of wisdom
Is posited by the Law.

They say that all her foundations
She completely destroys.

They do not understand that wisdom
Is a twin sister of the Law.

He who thinks deeply about these two
Finds that each is a wall for the other.

The man who opens the eye of his mind,
Increases his share in wisdom,

Sees that concerning words of right
And truth, the Law and wisdom agree.

If you want to know this secret,
Arise and hear the Debate.[5]

Ibn Falaquera thought that the best way to hear the debate was to stage it as one of those disputes that Alex J. Novikoff has studied.[6] Pedagogical and institutionalized, the disputation was also used in many different environments to serve political purposes, to perform ideas in front of specific audiences not only to gather support for a certain idea but also to eradicate a particular *idée reçue* from the public sphere. The scholar and the priest's discussion in Ibn Falaquera's *Epistle* ends with the promise of a new book, which might talk about the openness of the debate itself, about the difficulty to end it once and forever.

The Alfonsine Era's response goes in a different way from the other interventions. Alfonso does not foster one position in an explicit way. He does not accumulate arguments in favor or against anything. He moves forward by embracing the challenges of perplexity itself. Instead of suggesting legal exegesis or legal interpretation as the horizon of this controversy or crisis between the Law and the other disciplines, Alfonso legislates with an assumed, intimate correspondence between the law and everything else.

Alfonso's was also a response to the question of whether one could codify an all-encompassing legal system in the vernacular, something none of his contemporaries had ever imagined. Indeed, his response constituted a thesis in vernacular jurisdiction: if one defined power and sovereignty, the results of such definition would necessarily lead toward something visible, understandable, and universal that is perceptible at the level of the senses, external and internal. It had to touch the emotions of all those who were to become subjects before the legal code.

Finally—at least for now—Alfonso's was a response addressing the ways in which the law could make productive use of nature, love, intimacy, friendship, domestic feelings, and emotions as constitutive and constitutional elements. It was a response to the question of how to create a subject that had a soul, that felt passions, and that acted in agreement with them instead of being utterly removed from them. Such a subject could then populate the realm of this vernacular jurisdiction with the king, as a third friend, always in his mind.

It is, if you think of it, a magnificent set of responses. They have an allure, an attraction of their own. They are astonishing. In a certain way, they elicit admiration. And all those feelings are not external to the law but, rather, are central strategies of the Alfonsine Era. These emotional strategies are part of the theory of power devised in Alfonso's political and legal environment. We need to ask—with the past, with the Alfonsine Era in mind, if you wish—to what extent these strategies are still alive, and to what extend these strategies have become normalized in the techniques of law-writing in Spain and elsewhere up through our time.

As a series of techniques for the writing and dissemination of Law, legal science, and legislation, dead voice is a challenge to contemporary politics and to contemporary legal thinking. The techniques encompassed by dead voice, are not there, far away, in history, in some storage room we call the Middle Ages. With their astonishing deployment of sensations, practices of legal love and friendship, everlasting temporalities, and vernacularity, they are, always, as if they were new.

NOTES

1. There are specific difficulties pertaining to quoting the *Partidas* that will be resolved only once we have a definitive edition of this complex text. That day is not yet near. Unless I explicitly state otherwise, I will always quote the Spanish from the 1555 edition of Alfonso X, *Las Siete Partidas,* ed. by Gregorio López Madera. Throughout this book, I use two different but easy ways to refer to Alfonso's text: either *Partidas* part.title.law, all in arabic numerals, never roman (for instance, *Partidas* 2.21.1 refers to the *Second Partida*, title 21, law 1); or, sometimes *Number of Partida* title.law (for instance, *Third Partida* 18.2 is the same as *Partidas* 3.18.2 and *Fourth Partida* 27.7 is the same as *Partidas* 4.27.7). Whenever I am quoting from a manuscript, I give the specific reference to the manuscript and the folio. On many occasions, these references are not equivalent to the Salamanca edition of 1555. When available, the English translations of all citations from the *Partidas* are based on Samuel Parsons Scott's translation (Alphonso X, *Siete Partidas,* 2001). Since Scott's translation is very often problematic, I have silently introduced several changes throughout. Translations from specific manuscripts are mine.

2. I refer to the bibliography mentioned in Chapter 2.

3. See Loveday, "Living Voice." We will have the opportunity for nuanced analysis of some important questions regarding living voice in Chapter 2.

4. The *First Partida* is mainly a collection of legal theory and ecclesiastical, canon law. The *Second Partida* delves into social, political, and administrative questions for both peace and war. The *Third Partida* is fundamentally a procedural legislation. The *Fourth Partida* regulates alliances of both consanguinity and affinity. The *Fifth Partida* devotes its laws to commerce, trade, and all other related issues. The *Sixth Partida* gathers the laws on inheritance in general. The *Seventh Partida* is essentially devoted to criminal law, with some specific titles at the end that regulate legal theory and legal language.

5. Stein, *Roman Law*; Cairns and Plessis, *Creation*; Conte and Miglio, *Il diritto*; Conte, *Tres Libri Codicis*; Hartmann and Pennington, *History*; Hallaq, *Origins*; Hallaq, *History*; Hallaq, *Law and Legal Theory*; Hallaq, *Formation*; Hallaq, *Sharīʿa*; Khadduri and Liebesny, *Origin and Development*; Khan and Ramadan, *Contemporary Ijtihad*; Schacht, *Introduction*; Laldin, *Islamic Law*; Dupret, *La Charia*; Libson, *Jewish and Islamic Law*; Brague, *La Loi de Dieu*; Shemesh, *Halakhah*; Lewittes, *Principles and Development*; Fraade, *Legal Fictions*; Fonrobert and Jaffee, eds., *Cambridge Companion*; Strawn, *Oxford Encyclopedia*; Hezser, *Rabbinic Law*. For the production and negotiation of legal written products (legal opinions, jurisprudence, especially in

the Maliki school of law) in the Islamic context of the Iberian Peninsula, see Safran, *Defining Boundaries in Al-Andalus*.

6. Iglesia Ferreirós, *Una historia del derecho español*; Pérez-Prendes y Muñoz-Arracó, *Historia del derecho español*; Montanos Ferrín and Sánchez-Arcilla Bernal, *Historia del derecho*; Arizaleta, *Les clercs au palais*.

7. Grossi, *History*; Grossi, *L'ordine giuridico*; Bellomo, *L'Europa*. Cf. Emanuele Conte's critique of this perspective on legal history, "Droit médiéval."

8. González Jiménez, *Alfonso X*; Martínez, *Alfonso X*; Kennedy, *Muslim Spain and Portugal*; Linehan, *Spain, 1157–1300*.

9. The *Partidas* have traditionally been an extraordinarily rich source for historical linguists. Hans-Josef Niederehe deemed them to be a long dictionary, among other things. Niederehe, *Alfonso X*, 128. According to Ricardo Escavy Zamora, the number of definitions is more than four hundred. Escavy Zamora, "El contenido lexicográfico"; Sánchez Manzanares, "Razones de nombres"; Rubio Moreno, "Las definiciones léxicas."

10. Even though, as Rubio Moreno has shown (in "Las definiciones léxicas"), there are many glossaries that may be external models for the *Partidas* (and, in any case, there are thousands of lexical glosses in the margins of the *Corpus Iuris Civilis* and the *Corpus Iuris Canonici*), the conceptual map and the lexical contribution of the *Partidas* constitute a radical departure from those models, because the *Partidas* legally constitute a legal language in the vernacular.

11. See Kalmo and Skinner, "Introduction," and Kalmo, "Matter of Fact?"

12. This authorship must be qualified. There is a well-known passage from another work realized in the Alfonsine workshop (in this case, the historiographical workshop) that explains Alfonso's concept of authorship. While commenting on authorship of biblical works, Alfonso writes: "Podemos entender e dezir que compuso Nuestro Señor las razones de los mandados, e que ovo ell autoridad e el nombre dend porque las mando escrivir, mas que las escrivio Moisen, assi como dixiemos nos muchas vezes el rey faze un libro non por quel el escriva con sus manos, mas porque compone las razones del e las emienda e yegua e endereça e muestra la manera de como se deven fazer, e desi escrívelas qui el manda, pero dezimos por esta razon que el rey faze el libro. Otrossi cuando dezimos el rey faze un palacio o alguna obra non es dicho porque lo el fiziesse con sus manos, mas porquel mando fazer e dio las cosas que fueron mester pora ello; e qui esto cumple aquel a nombre que faze la obra, e nos assi veo que usamos de lo dezir." (We can understand and say that it was Our Lord who composed the subjects of the commandments, and that authority and authorial name must befall on Him, because he ordered their writing, but it was Moses who wrote them; in the same guise, we often say that the King makes a book, not because he writes it with his own hands, but because he comes up with the subjects that must be part of it, proposing amendments to them; he also gathers those subjects and outlines them in the way they must be done, and from that moment onward, he decides who must write them. But for all those reasons, we say that the king makes the book. Likewise, when we say that the king makes a palace, or any other thing, we do not intend to say that he does it with his hands, but because he provided both the ideas and the resources to make it. And whoever does that must see his name as the author of the work, and this is how we intend to say it.) *General Estoria*, Part I, MSS/816, Biblioteca Nacional de España, fol. 216r, col. b (the foliation on the manuscript indicates fol. 215). This idea of authorship is in good agreement with some of the debates about the attribution of authorship and ownership regarding the institution of the *tabula picta*, which Alfonso also treats of in the *Third Partida* 28.37.

13. "[Las gentes de nuestro señorío] rayen [las leyes] et escriuien y lo que les semeiaua a pro dellos e a danno de los pueblos, tolliendo a los reyes su poderio e sus derechos e tomandolo

pora ssi lo que non deuie seer fecho en ninguna manera" Alfonso X, *Libro del Fuero*; ms. add. 20787, fol. 1r. The *Libro del Fuero de las Leyes* corresponds to a first redaction of the *First Partida*, that is, the first part of Alfonso X's *Siete Partidas*. The terminology in this part of the code is complicated. *Gentes* seems to refer at the same time those who are used to have a jurisdictional power that competes with the intended central jurisdiction of the king (noblemen, indeed, but also those who hold local powers in the cities), and to the people in a nontechnical way (that is, not considered as legal subjects but rather as natural persons populating a territory under the king's jurisdiction). Then, "people," which he refers to as "los pueblos," consistently implies that the citizens of the kingdom are to be considered as legal subjects (as the law defines "people" in *Partidas* 2.10). Finally, the concept of *señorío* means at the same time "ownership," "jurisdiction," and "domain," among other things.

14. Chapman, *Cancels*; Vismann, *Files*. The English version is an abridgement of the German original, Cornelia Vismann, *Akten: Medientechnik Und Recht*.

15. The notion was common in classical culture and used by the likes of Cicero or Catullus.

16. Teissier-Ensminger, "La loi au figuré." I am enhancing Teissier-Ensminger's concept of *jurisgraphisme*. She coined this term to discuss illustrations *about* legal objects (in her case, the French Penal Code). From this notion—that there is a graphic glossing system that interferes or otherwise establishes a conversation with the law but is not the law—I am building the idea that *jurisgraphisms* have legal value, and this is one of the reasons why legal objects share their legal space (the parchment, the code, the codex) with those nontextual elements.

17. That they are more difficult to interpret in legal terms indicates the enormous difficulties that medieval techniques of legal codification still represent. The materialities of communication of the legal object, including the legal code, are exceedingly challenging and have frequently provoked scholars to separate the text from other material elements, including jurisgraphisms and especially miniatures. Bedos-Rezak changed the paradigm with her work on seals and her conception of the document as a site of mediality. Bedos-Rezak and Hamburger, *Sign and Design*; Bedos-Rezak, *When Ego Was Imago*; L'Engle and Gibbs, *Illuminating the Law*; Casado de Otaola, "Per visibilia ad invisibilia."

18. Foucault developed his ideas on illegalisms in his seminar *La Société punitive*, and then in the resulting book *Surveiller et punir*. Foucault, *La Société punitive*; Foucault, *Surveiller et punir*.

19. Cf. *Partidas* 1.1 and 7, and generally *Partidas* 1.2.

20. *Partidas*, 1555, general prologue, fol. 3v, col. a.

21. Rodríguez-Velasco, "La urgente presencia"; Foronda, "Le Verbe législatif alphonsin."

22. "A privilege means a law given or granted by the king especially to some place or to some man, as a matter of kindness and favor. It should be granted in the following way, according to the custom of Spain; in the first place, it should be begun in the name of God, and afterwards good and proper words should be used, and such as are applicable to the matter with respect to which it is conceded. It should also state that the king, together with his lawful wife and any sons that he may have by her, or by any other wife whom he had married ordered it to be granted, mentioning first the eldest who is to be his heir, and afterwards the other male children, one after another, according to their ages; and if there are no sons the oldest daughter, and after her the other daughters, as we stated in the case of the sons; and if there is neither son nor daughter, naming his brothers, at first the eldest, and then the next, as we specified in the case of sons; and if he has no brother, naming the nearest male relative, as is stated in the Title concerning Lands. The sons, brothers, and other near male relatives are mentioned in

order that, although all of them are bound to observe the privilege, they may do so the better for this reason. After the king has enumerated these, he should state that he grants to the party or parties mentioned in the privilege a certain gift of land or other property, and grants a certain exemption, or a certain fuero, or a certain release, or establishes certain boundaries, or confirms certain acts performed by his predecessors, or which they maintained in their time. When there is a grant of real estate, all its boundaries should be set out as well as the terms of the grant. Where an exemption is granted, it should be stated in what way the party is freed from the performance of what he did, or should do, according to law. Where it concerns a fuero, the reason for making it should be given, as well as the change that is made. Where a release is made, the way in which it is done, as well as the cause should be mentioned, and it should be stated that it is made in order to grant a benefit, or a favor. Where it relates to the establishment of boundaries, the places which are the subject of controversy should be referred to, and the way in which he makes the division from that time forward. Where the privilege is one of confirmation, it should be stated that he had examined the privilege of Such-and-Such king, or of Such-and-Such a man, which he desires to confirm, and everything should be included in the instruments of confirmation." *Partidas* 3.18.2. I always use the word "privilege" to translate the Spanish *privilegio*, according to Scott's translation of the relevant law as transcribed just above.

23. "Recebí dos priuillegios de parte del maestre de Calatraua que ouieron en fieldat por don Henrric, mío ermano, quel auie dado el rey don Ferrando, mío padre. . . . E esto uengo yo conosçudo que reçebí estos dos priuillegios de mano de los freyres de Calatraua e rompílos e so pagado del maestre e de los freyres de Calatraua en razón destos dos priuillegios." (I received two privileges brought to me by the master and the brothers of Calatrava. These documents had been deposited by my brother Henry, and had been given by my father, King Ferdinand. . . . And I want to make known that I received these two privileges from the hands of the brothers of Calatrava, and I tore them up. And I am very grateful to the master and the brothers because they brought these documents to my attention.) González Jiménez, *Diplomatario Andaluz*, doc. 15, March 24, 1253, p. 14. See also González Jiménez and Carmona Ruiz, eds., *Crónica de Alfonso X*, chap. 4, p. 14.

24. Foucault, "Qu'est-ce qu'un auteur?"; Boureau, "Peut-on parler d'auteurs scholastiques?"

25. Menéndez Pidal, "Cómo trabajaron"; Cárdenas, "Alfonso's Scriptorium and Chancery"; Fernández-Ordóñez, "El taller de las 'Estorias'"; Solalinde, "Intervención de Alfonso"; Orazi, "El Rey faze un libro."

26.   *Aservicio de Dios e a pro comunal de las gentes* (*First Partida*: theory of law and canon law);

     La fe católica de nuestro señor Jesucristo habemos mostrado (*Second Partida*: administration, politics, and society);

     Fizo nuestro señor Dios todas las cosas muy complidamente (*Third Partida*: procedural law);

     Onrras señaladas dios nuestro señor Dios al ome (*Fourth Partida*: family law and alliances);

     Nacen entres los omes muchos entecos e grandes contiendas (*Fifth Partida*: commercial law);

     Sesudamente dixeron los sabios antiguos (*Sixth Partida*: last wills);

     Olvidança y atrevimiento son cosas que fazen a los omes errar mucho (*Seventh Partida*: criminal law and rules of law).

27. González Jiménez, *Alfonso X*, 251–52, 261.

28. Alfonso XI, *Ordenamiento de Alcalá*, dated in 1348, MSS Vitrina 15–17, title 18.

29. Craddock, "La cronología." Craddock proposes and thoughtfully demonstrates that the *Espéculo* was presented or promulgated on May 5, 1252. The process of writing the *Partidas* began one year later, on June 23, 1256. For the process of internal creation of the *Partidas*, which was based on a thorough and technical analysis of the textual sources to demonstrate the Alfonsine coherence of the *Partidas*, see Iglesia Ferreirós, "Alfonso el Sabio."

30. González Jiménez, *Alfonso X*, 261.

31. Craddock, "La cronología."

32. Craddock, "La cronología," 53.

33. García Gallo, "Nuevas observaciones." For a thorough critique of the theses of García Gallo, see Craddock, "La cronología"; and Iglesia Ferreirós, "Alfonso el Sabio."

34. Arizaleta, *Les clercs au palais*; Martín Prieto, "Los preámbulos."

35. For a current evaluation of the presence and the translation of the *Liber Iudiciorum*, or *Fuero Juzgo* in Castile see Castillo Lluch, "Las lenguas." Castillo Lluch never published a follow-up on this, part 1 of her research; Maintier-Vermorel, "Étude comparée." On the *Liber Iudiciorum* and the kingdom of Aragon, see Iglesia Ferreirós, *Una historia de la formación*.

36. Iglesia Ferreirós, "La labor legislativa," 296.

37. Szpiech, "From Founding Father." This is, of course, a radically different claim than that made by many historians from the seventeenth to the nineteenth century who did consider that Ferdinand III had actually begun the writing of the *Partidas* and that Alfonso was the one who finished it; see Iglesia Ferreirós, "Alfonso el Sabio, su obra legislativa."

38. Gómez Redondo, *Historia de la prosa*, 304–30; Craddock, "El *Setenario*"; Martin, "Alphonse X"; Martin, "De nuevo"; Alfonso X, *Leyes de Alfonso X*, 123–26.

39. See, for instance, Beit-Arié, "Scribal Re-making."

40. Menéndez Pidal, "Cómo trabajaron."

41. The most updated list of manuscripts of the *Siete Partidas*, with a total of eighty-six items, is on *Biblioteca Española de Textos* Antiguos, or BETA, which is part of *PhiloBiblon*: bancroft.berkeley.edu/philobiblon/index.html; Craddock, *Legislative Works*; Craddock, *Bibliography*. José Manuel Fradejas Rueda is currently building a new digital resource regarding the *Partidas* and unveiling new textual witnesses: https://7partidas.hypotheses.org/testimonios.

42. María e Izquierdo, *Las fuentes*. Montalvo's *compilation* is quite creative, as fewer than half of the laws (of a total of 1,163) are actually medieval regulations. Montalvo's work—and the very concept of *compilation*—acquires a different sense, a process of creative reception in which the lawyer doubles as legislator. Montalvo's text was crucial to future compilations, including the very influential body of the *Leyes de Toro* of 1505 and other compilations of law and jurisprudence that were used across the Iberian Empire during the sixteenth and seventeenth centuries.

43. Alfonso X, *Siete Partidas*, 1501. There are many editions through at least 1550.

44. For a very thorough account of the different editions and versions of the *Siete Partidas*, especially in its printed form, see Berní's letter to Mayans y Ciscar in Berní, *Carta*.

45. Alfonso XI, *Ordenamiento de Alcalá*, fol. 15, col. a. I am quoting from the manuscript Biblioteca Nacional de España MSS Vitrina 15–17, according to my own transcription.

46. Alfonso XI, *Ordenamiento de Alcalá*, fol. 15, col. a.

47. Betancourt-Serna, *La Recepción*; Kabatek, "La lingüística románica histórica"; Ortín García, "Derecho público romano," 626; González Villaescusa, "Renacimiento del vocabulario."

48. See Iglesia Ferreirós, "Una traducción catalana"; and Craddock, *Legislative Works*, with a series of updates on Berkeley eScholarship (http://escholarship.org/uc/item/38r0s439). There are five extant textual witnesses of the Catalan version of the *Partidas*, according to Craddock, Iglesia Ferreirós, and, now, updated, PhiloBiblon/BITECA (bancroft.berkeley.edu/philobiblon/biteca_en.html). In chronological order they are Barcelona, Biblioteca de Catalunya 942; Monastery of El Escorial, M.I.2; Valencia, Biblioteca Histórica Universitaria, 869; Monastery of El Escorial y.III.4; and Barcelona, Biblioteca de Catalunya, 15. The list of Galician and Portuguese translations is longer (a total of forty-three extant copies), so I will simply provide the PhiloBiblon/BITAGAP texid followed by the number of extant manuscripts. Galician: *First Partida*, texid 1214, 2; *Third Partida*, texid 1215, 3; *Fourth Partida*, texid 1211, 2; *Fifth Partida*, texid 1212, 3; *Sixth Partida*, texid 1218, 2; *Seventh Partida*, texid 1217, 1. Portuguese: *First Partida*, texid 1132, 6; *Second Partida*, texid 1133, 7; *Third Partida*, texid 1134, 13; *Fifth Partida*, texid 9709, 1; *Sixth Partida*, texid 9826, 1; *Seventh Partida*, texid 1219, 2. See more recently Gemma Avenoza, "Las *Partidas* en catalán."

49. Real Decreto-ley 1/2015, de 27 de febrero, de mecanismo de segunda oportunidad, reducción de carga financiera y otras medidas de orden social. Jefatura del Estado, Ref: BOE-A-2015–2109, which can be found at *Boletín Oficial del Estado* 51 (February 28, 2015): 19058–19101. (https://www.boe.es/boe/dias/2015/02/28/pdfs/BOE-A-2015-2109.pdf.)

50. See more recently the brilliant doctoral dissertation of Nanu, "La 'Segunda Partida.' "

51. The *tabula differentiarum* appears in the first edition of the Latin version of the *Tablas Alfonsíes*. Alfonso X, *Tabule Astronomice*, fols. 17r-v. See also Craddock, "La nota cronológica."

52. Bravo Lira, "La difusión del código civil." Bravo Lira shows the global importance of Andrés Bellos' code—a code that made an extensive use of the *Partidas*. See also Obregón Tarazona, "Construyendo la Región Americana."

53. Maimonides, *Guide of the Perplexed*, 10.

54. Stern, *Matter and Form*; Stern, "Maimonidean Parable."

55. Dougherty, *Moral Dilemmas*; Wei, "Guy de l'Aumône's *Summa*," 317. Brian Tierney addresses the question of perplexity as part of his inquiry about liberty and law in canon law and theology, in which he focuses on the ideas of Gratian and the canonist Huguccio of Pisa to establish a relationship between *perplexitas* and tolerance. Tierney, *Liberty and Law*, 37–43. Dougherty addresses the question of sin, especially in the first chapter, which is devoted to Gratian, although the scholar is more interested in the logical and intellectual procedures articulated by the theologians to understand the *dilemma* itself, the dialectical quandary. Dougherty quotes a glossary of theological concepts from the thirteenth century, *Declaratio terminorum theologiae*, in which *perplexitas* is defined as "involutio inter opposita ita quod videtur semper vergere in peccatum, quacumque partem eligat," or, as he translates, "an entrapment between opposites to be bound to sin, in whatever side one might choose." Dougherty, *Moral Dilemmas*, 7 and note 9; Bonaventure, *Declaratio terminorum theologiae*, vol. 7: 232–39. The definition of *perplexitas* comes under a larger definition about sins from the heart that have different degrees and involve varied bodily responses; cf. in particular pages 236–37 of Bonaventure's *Declaratio*. There seems to be a difference between how theologians address the question of the perplexity of conscience—by addressing it and suggesting different solutions (like Alexander of Hales, Guy de l'Aumône, or even Thomas Aquinas or Ramon Llull), and the canon lawyers who, reading and commenting on Gratian's ideas on perplexity, deny its existence (cf. Dougherty, *Moral Dilemmas*, 33–37). As for the question of the perplexity *falling onto* an individual, the theologians propose the general question in those terms. The question asked by Guy de l'Aumône (who was, in fact, reading the *Summa Halesiana* and other texts with the intention of

preparing a text for students) is the following: "Item ad pleniorem hius mandate intelligentiam queramus hic de perplexitate conscientie, et primo utrum in homine cadat huius perplexitas," which the manuscript scribe summarizes and refers to as "Utrum in homine cadat perplexitas ad evitandum peccatum." Alexander of Hales addresses the same question with the same verbal choice in *Summa* 3.2.2.q.393. Cf. Wei, "Guy de l'Aumône," 315. The verb *cadere* (to happen, to fall on someone) is the one that addresses the presence of perplexity as a feeling and as an affect. Affect as something that falls in the category of the passion, is part of the research on affect in general but especially in the lineage of thought from Spinoza (*Ethics* 3; and in particular the line of research on definition 3—"Per *affectum* intelligo corporis affectiones, quibus ipsius corporis agendi potentia augetur vel minuitur, iuvatur vel coercetur, et simul harum affectionum ideas") to Nietzsche (see in particular the Heideggerian commentary in Heidegger, *Nietzsche* 1: 44–45). Andreas Philippopoulos-Mihalopoulos (*Spatial Justice*) has studied in particular the affective space of the law within what he calls the lawscape, a concept that defines not only the space where the legal discipline acts but also the legal implications of the spaces where there is no presence of the legal discipline; Spinoza, *Ethica ordine geometrico demonstrata*.

56. Al-Ghazālī, *Incoherence of the Philosophers*. See also the semantic discussion and the translation choices in the introduction of Al-Ghazālī, *Tahafot Al-Falasifat*; Averroes, *Subtilissimus liber Averois*; Geoffroy, "Ibn Rushd (Averroes)"; Hasselhoff, *Dicit Rabbi Moyses*; Hasselhoff, "Maimonides."

57. He advances those elements in the general prologue of the *Partidas* as well as in *Partidas* 1.1 and *Partidas* 1.2.

58. Translating the expression *fictio legis* should not be difficult; however, it now seems to refer to many different legal operations, a problem that somehow blurs the original idea of *fictio legis*. This is why I am not translating it as "legal fiction," because I think the latter refers to an entirely different heuristic realm, which is much more narrative, on the one hand, and less technical, on the other. With *fictio legis* I am instead subscribing to a very precise set of techniques with a distinct set of linguistic operators that imply—formally—a kind of rhetorical comparison ("like," "similar," "as if," etc.) but one that has ontological characteristics; that is, it has the power to change the essence and definition of objects, actions, and persons. As I will discuss later, I am closer to Yan Thomas's works on *fictiones legum* and the definitions and questions he raises, albeit some of his conclusions cannot be easily applied to the legislative and codifying techniques exploited by Alfonso in his *Siete Partidas*. Thomas, "Fictio Legis"; Thomas, "Les artifices de la vérité."

59. Steiner, *Documentary Culture*.

CHAPTER ONE

1. See, for instance, Guyotjeannin, Pycke, and Tock, *Diplomatique médiévale*, 15; Clanchy, *From Memory*.

2. "οὔκουν μνήμης ἀλλ' ὑπομνήσεως φάρμακον ηὗρες." Plato, *Phaedrus* 275b, in Plato, *Euthyphro*, 562.

3. Derrida, *Mal d'archive*; Freshwater, "Allure"; Farge, *Le goût*; in actor-network theory, the archive is one of the so-called *centres de calcul*, a formulation that works very well in the politics of archive and document-exchange and document-negotiation in the period I am analyzing here; Latour, *Inquiry*; Latour, *Reassembling the Social*.

4. Taylor, *Archive*; Stoler, *Along the Archival Grain*. See also Trouillot, *Silencing the Past*.

5. There seems to be an elective affinity between law and an interrelationship of narratology and semiology, maybe because both narratology and semiology present a highly regulated categorization of acting narrative subjects. Cf., for instance, Mikhaïl Xifaras's "Théorie des personnages juridiques" as well as his intervention in *Synesthesia of Law* of 2016 (https://www.youtube.com/channel/UClv7SjwdfQbSQHlOCJL6nUw); and Xifaras, "Figures de la doctrine." Xifaras bases his narratological and semiological approach on the mining of big data—a mining that becomes structurally interpreted to fit the categories of Gérard Genette and, more specifically, Algirdas Julien Greimas. See also Brooks and Gewirtz, *Law Stories*; Binder and Weisberg, *Literary Criticisms*.

6. Clanchy, *From Memory*; Sobecki, *Unwritten Verities*.

7. Alexander, "Living Voice."

8. Piron, "Historien du temps"; Le Goff, "Temps de l'Église"; Le Goff, "L'Occident médiéval"; Schmitt, *Les rythmes*.

9. "(Christus, alfa y omega) In nomine Sancte et indiuidue Trinitatis, Patris et Filii et Spiritus Sancti, amen. Contra multiplices uetustatis insidias cyrographorum munimine nos armamus, obliuionis etenim mater antiquitas lubricitati memoriae nouercatur, et que statuta sunt hodie fortassis crastina euanescent nisi carte beneficio solidentur." González, *El reino de Castilla*, vol. 3, 97. Diego García de Campos, born in the region known as Tierra de Campos, or Campos Góticos (the name used in the Middle Ages), was an extraordinary Latinist who had studied in Paris and was well acquainted with the most important intellectual and theoretical innovations of his time. He entered the Castilian chancery in 1192 and remained there until the end of Alfonso's reign in 1214. See Martínez Gázquez, "Alegorización"; Martínez Gázquez, "El uso simbólico-alegórico"; Martín Prieto, "Los preámbulos."

10. There has been a general tendency to dismiss as unimportant—or useless—some of the formulas contained in documents. Contemporary researchers, however, have successfully reversed that tendency, as we can see in García de Cortázar, "Memoria y cultura"; Agúndez San Miguel, "Memoria y cultura."

11. Martín Prieto, "Los preámbulos"; Martín Prieto, "Invención y tradición."

12. Bedos-Rezak, "Cutting Edge"; Bedos-Rezak, *When Ego Was Imago*.

13. Arizaleta, *Les clercs au palais*; Martín Prieto, "Los preámbulos."

14. "Onde pues que en los titulos antes deste hablamos de los testigos, e de las pesquisas, que es una de las maneras de prueba, que se faze por voz biva, queremos aqui dezir, de todas las escrituras de qual manera quiere que sean, de que pueda nascer prueba o averiguamiento en juyzio, que es otra manera de prueva a que llaman boz muerta." *Partidas* 3.18.pról. For the attribution to Durand, see Orellana Calderón, "La Tercera Partida," 370. My suggestion is that they are following a common model, because Durand's work was compiled in 1271. The concept or idea of *dead voice* may be in relation with the Hellenistic idea that written law is *apsychos*, or lifeless, while the *nómos émpsychos*, or living law, is the human being in charge of holding or upholding the *orthos logos*, or true words of the law. The Hellenistic writers holding such ideas were preserved in Stobaeus's *Anthologia*; Stobaeus gathered those fragments of authors like Pseudo Ecphantus, Pseudo Archytas, Diotogenes, or Sthenides. In English, the treatises were compiled and translated in the work of Thomas Taylor, *Political fragments*. See Squilloni, "Il significato etico-politico"; see also, Velasco, "Lex Animata."

15. "El antigüedad de los tiempos es cosa que faze a los omes olvidar los fechos passados. E porende fue menester que fuesse fallada scritura, porque lo que antes fuera fecho, non se oluidasse, e supiessen los omes por ella las cosas que eran establescidas, bien como si de nuevo fuessen fechas." *Partidas* 3.18.pról.

16. I always use the concept of *fictio legis* as theorized within the medieval glosses and commentaries to the *Corpus Iuris Civilis*. Thomas, "Fictio Legis"; Thomas, "Les artifices de la vérité." I have tried to give an Iberian perspective to the practice of the *fictio legis* in Rodríguez-Velasco, *Plebeyos Márgenes*.

17. It is possible to think about the *fictio legis* from the perspective of Marxist reification. Marx's theory of reification is not applicable in this case, but analogical thinking may be of use in understanding how *fictio* can change the nature of things (by creating facts in specific *fictiones*), in consideration of the fact that things are or can be legal subjects when they become part of a legal process—and that in any case, things are things when they are part of a judicial process. See Thomas, "La valeur des choses"; Thomas, "Les ornements"; Kumler and Lakey, "*Res et significatio.*"

18. Thomas, *Les Opérations du droit*, 40. Thomas understands legal operations as thinking operations, and they include not only fictional devices but also theoretical ones, like casuistry of the relation to nature. The relationship between "legal operation" and "thinking operation" was underscored by Michel Foucault in his *Leçons sur la volonté de savoir*.

19. "E mayormente, porque los pleytos, e las posturas, e las cosas que fazen, e ponen los omes cada dia entresi, los vnos con los otros, non pudiessen venir en dubda, e fuessen guardadas en la manera, que fuessen puestas." *Partidas* 3.18.pról.

20. For the multifaceted legal concept of "exemplum," see Vismann, *Files*.

21. Escalona and Sirantoine, *Chartes et cartulaires*; Azcárate Aguilar-Amat et al., "Volver a nacer"; Escalona Monge, Azcárate Aguilar-Amat, and Larrañaga Zulueta, "De la crítica diplomática"; Peterson, "Reescribiendo el pasado."

22. "E pues que de las scrituras tanto bien viene, que en todos los tiempos tiene pro, que faze membrar lo oluidado, e afirmar lo que es de nueuo fecho, e muestra carreras por do se endereçar, lo que ha de ser: derecho es, que se fagan lealmente, e sin engaño: de manera que se pueda, e entiendan bien, e sean cumplidas, e señaladamente de aquello que podria nascer contienda entre los omes." *Partidas* 3.18.pról.

23. For the criteria of intelligibility of the law, see Rodríguez-Velasco, "Theorizing the Language of Law."

24. "Scriptura de que nace aueriguamento de prueua es toda carta que sea fecha por mano de escriuano publico de concejo, o sellada con sello de Rey, o de otra persona autentica, que sea de creer [e] nace della muy grand pro." The editor and glossator Gregorio López, the president of the Council of the Indies, translates this passage from Spanish into Latin as "Scriptura probatoria" (*Partidas* 3, fol. 87v, gloss a). In this particular case, I have modified Scott's translation in Alfonso X, *Las Siete Partidas*, vol. 3, 692. I may introduce silent emendations to the Spanish text only when necessary and always based on the manuscripts that transmit the *Partidas*.

25. Alfonso X, *Libro del Fuero*, ms. add. 20787, general prologue; Alfonso X, *Espéculo*, Biblioteca Nacional de España, MS 10123, general prologue.

26. To check the proportion of documents confirmed in these circumstances, see Sánchez, *Diccionario*. The examples are quite numerous. On a *privilegio rodado*, Alfonso confirmed fourteen documents dated between 1103 and 1237 to the Council of Burgos. The notary dates this letter of confirmation February 13, in the Spanish era of 1283 (i.e., 1255), after describing and transcribing the documents one by one. González Díez, *Colección*, 89–92. Castilian monasteries preserved confirmations from the king in their archives. Alfonso had either simply confirmed them or their *traslados* or copies, and in some cases the king resealed them. See, for example, the documents preserved at the Augustinian monastery of Santa María de Trianos, a small

monastery that held four such confirmations just for 1255, in Castán Lanaspa, *Documentos*, 117–21.

27. See, for instance, two very different, even opposite perspectives on philology that concur on this matter despite their differences: Blecua, *Manual de crítica textual*; Cerquiglini, *Éloge de la variante*.

28. Alfonso X, *El Fuero Real de España*, 104; Alfonso X, *Fuero Real*, 12.

29. In addition to Bono, *Historia*, see also Brundage, *Medieval Origins*, 371–406, in which he examines the different social extractions and characteristics of the legal profession and the legal professional with specific attention to judges and notaries in chap. 9. The origins of the notarial profession are related to the formation of lobbies and social groups with extraordinary political agency within the cities, as demonstrated in Amelotti and Costamagna, *Alle origini*.

30. Archetype and textual witness are two key notions of textual scholarship (see Blecua, *Manual de crítica textual*).

31. "Dicto de probatione uiuae uocis, quae fit per se testes, dicendum est de probatione mortuae uocis, quae fit per instrumenta." *Speculum*, lib. II, partic. II *De instrumento editione*, pról., 632. The text continues: "dicentes: Quid fit instrumentum, & unde dicatur: Qualiter publicetur, & fiat: Qualiter propria scriptura exemplet publicetur, seu reficiatur: E qualiter aliena, & quid iuris fit de publicatione, seu exemplatione instrumentorum: Quando sint exhibenda instrumenta, & qualiter: Quot sunt eorum species: Quibus instrumentis fides adhibeatur, & quanta: Quibus modus diuersae scripturae in iudicio productae, ualeant impugnari, uel contra eas excipi." Orellana Calderón, "La Tercera Partida," 370.

32. Gloss from the 1555 edition on *Partidas* 3.18.pról.

33. We don't know his exact source for this idea and quotation. Roger Chartier directly quotes Gregorio López's gloss, which he borrowed from the works of Marta Madero (who instead tried to find more about what Innocent really wrote). Chartier, "Jack Cade"; Madero, "Causa, creencia y testimonios"; Madero, "Façons de croire."

34. I am using the 1473 edition of the *Decretals*, a very beautiful printing by Peter Schoeffer. Gregory IX, *Decretales*. See the online reproduction of this edition at the Library of Congress, https://lccn.loc.gov/49040113; Friedberg and Richter, *Corpus Iuris Canonici*. For Innocent, see Innocent IV et al., *Innocentii 4*.

35. "nullus potest facere tabellionem praeter Papam & Imperatorem." Innocent IV, in Gregory IX, *Decretales* 2.22.15.

36. "quia charte animalis mortui non creditur sine adminiculo alio." Innocent IV, in Gregory IX, *Decretales* 2.22.15.

37. See Bono, *Historia* and Amelotti and Costamagna, *Alle origini*. Pilar Ostos Salcedo and María Luisa Pardo have worked on the notaries and notarial offices of Seville and other cities across the Iberian Peninsula and Europe. Ostos Salcedo and Pardo Rodríguez, *Documentos y notarios*; Ostos Salcedo and Pardo Rodríguez, *Estudios*; Ostos Salcedo, Pardo Rodríguez, and Bono y Huerta, *Documentos y notarios*; Pardo Rodríguez, *Señores y escribanos*; Sánchez, *Diccionario*; Murphy, *Rhetoric*, 265; Warhmund, *Rainierius Perusinus*, 75.

38. See Greogrio López's gloss to *Partidas* 3.18.pról.

39. Brundage, *Medieval Origins*, 4.

40. Sinibaldo dei Fieschi, Pope Innocent IV, *Super libros quinque Decretalium*: 22.15, fols. 279v–280r.

41. *Partidas* 3.18.pról., gloss by Gregorio López.

42. Cf. Rutebeuf, *Le Miracle de Théophile*, vv. 245–54. I am also comparing this edition to Rutebeuf, *Œuvres complètes*, 552, and I offer both references: "Et je te refaz un couvant /

Que te ferai si grant seignor / Qu'on ne te vit onques greignor. / Et pui que ainsinques avient, / Saches de voir qu'il te covient / De toi aie lettres pendanz / Bien dites et bien entendanz; / Car maintes genz m'en ont sorpris / Por ce que lor lettres n'en pris. / Por ce les vueil avoir bien dites." The Virgin assures him, "Ta charte te ferai ravoir / Que tu baillas par nonsavoir / Je vois la querre" (The letter I'll bring you back / that you granted as an ignorant / I will go seek it.) (vv. 570–72; Rutebeuf, *Œuvres complètes*, 576–78). The following lines until the end are, in fact, a long discourse on the validity of the letter (vv. 573–663; *Œuvres complètes*, 578–82). Compare the above with the Latin version that might have been the model for Gonzalo de Berceo, *Milagros de Nuestra Señora*, 379, according to the witness preserved at the Biblioteca Nacional, Madrid, ms. 110 (*Miracula Beatae Mariae Virginis et alia*): "Tunc diabolus ad hebreum: 'Abneget–inquit– Filium Marie et ipsam, quia odiosi sunt mihi, firmetque scripto per omnia se eum eamque abnegare, et postea quecumque voluerit a me impetrabit.' Tunc introivit in vicendomnum Sathanas et respondit: 'Abnego Christum et eius Genitricem.' Faciensque cyrographum imposita cera signavit anulo proprio"; Teophilus complains in private of his loss when "feci me servum diaboli per nefande cautionis cirographum" (380). The introspective process, if it can be called that, or rather the rhetorical device whereby Theophilus becomes aware of his loss, his guilt, etc., which is presented as a long series of rhetorical interrogations, is called in the narration an inner "consermocionatio": "Cum diu intra se consermocinaretur cum anima sua hec et multa alia" (381). The letter is always called a *cyrographum scriptum*. In any case, for the Virgin, the words pronounced by Theophilus are more credible than the letter (384); in the end, "Populi autem videntes execrabile cyrographum et abnegatricem cautionem igne combustam ceperunt cum multa profusione lacrimarum diutissime clamare 'Kyrieleison'" (386). "Chirograph" is defined as an informal, scribbled manuscript with no notarial validity and lacking a particular form. In the papal archives it only indicates that the pope has written his name and his ordinal, not necessarily the text. In Latin patrology it refers to a manuscript that is invoked as a witness but that is not identifiable with any of the formal documents—letter, concession, etc.

43. See, below, the section "Voices."

44. Warhmund, *Rainierius Perusinus*; Salatiele, *Ars Notarie, I*; Salatiele, *Ars Notarie, II*; Passaggeri, *Summa totius artis notariae*; Durand, *Speculum iudiciale*.

45. Orellana Calderón, "La Tercera Partida," 269–75, suggests that there is doubt whether the source for this part of the *Third Partida* is Guillaume Durand's *Speculum iudiciale*. In the latter, the transition from oral proof to written proof is presented with the following words: "Dicto de probatione uiuae uocis, quae fit per se testes, dicendum est de probatione mortuae uocis, quae fit per instrumenta." (We have already talked about the proofs by living voice, which are made by witnesses and now we will talk about the proofs by dead voice, which are made with legal instruments.) The expression is, indeed, very close to that used by Alfonso, even though Alfonso's text is much more thorough and explicit, less technical, and includes not only the question of proof but also the principles of research and *inquisitio*. The fact that they are, still, so close does not mean that Durand is Alfonso's source—indeed, there is a problem regarding the dates, because the first edition of the *Speculum* is 1272, a year when Alfonso's *Third Partida* had already been written. It probably means, however, that either Durand used Alfonso's text (a possibility that had never been considered, of course) or that both were using the same set of sources, which already contained those expressions. Both authors would, then, play with them in different terms, because Alfonso and Durand had different views on the proof and the kind of things that can be done in the course of the judicial process. Orellana Calderón has entertained the possibility that both authors were using

similar sources. I am not particularly worried about the textual sources. Even if we accepted that Alfonso's lawyers and law scholars had directly used Durand's text, we already know that the original *Partidas* were fully changed and enhanced many times before 1348, and also afterward, as the manuscripts and editions bear witness to. What interests me is what the Castilian text does from that point forward—in other words, what the vernacular text is able to build with the many different sources with which it is working. For the *Third Partida*, those sources include compilations and scholarly debates on procedural law, as well as notarial arts from the late twelfth century onward and many other technical texts. The *Partidas*, however, are not direct translations of anything, no matter how intensely they exploit their sources. They always use those sources in the middle of their perplexing codification. At the beginning of that prologue is where, in prolepsis, the lawgiver gives an account of the origins of dead voice, or the origins of the written record.

46. Arnulf, the archbishop of Reims, uses the expression to refer to the corroboration of his privilege granted to the abbey of Saint Remigius in 989, modeled according the notarial language of "authentic persons" (*personnarum authenticarum annotatione*), before he attaches his seal (Arnulf of Reims, *Privilegium pro Abbatia S. Remigii*, col. 1547a). Eudes of Sully, in his chapter on the provisions for the organization of a synod, stipulates that only those who have been sent by an "authentic person," like a bishop or an archdeacon, may indeed preach at the synod (Eudes of Sully, *Synodicae Constitutiones*, chap. "Communia Praecepta Synodalia," no. 16, col. 64b–c.) Other authors use the expression for other purposes; in his commentary on the *Book of Revelation*, Richard of Saint Victor comments that John is an authentic person, with clear prestige, and a friend, and therefore he is a guarantor of truth-telling. Richard of Saint Victor, *In Apocalypsim Libri Septem*, chap. 4, "De visione prima," col. 703c. I do not intend to be exhaustive here; suffice it to say that the expression, as well as neighboring expressions, is used until the thirteenth century with a notarial character of transmission of truth.

47. Passeggeri, *De notulis*, in Passeggeri, *Summa totius artis notariae*, 803–4.

48. Passeggeri, "De exemplificatione," in Passeggeri, *Summa totius artis notariae*, 734. The issue of the role of the *persona authentica* is raised because of the necessity of copying and verifying documents that come from a different origin ("quomodo aliena scriptura exemplificatur".)

49. Agamben, *Nudities*; Agamben elaborates a reflection regarding the origin of the mask and its juridical genealogy in order to analyze systems of biometric analysis. As I would argue here, the creation and theorization of the juridical person is the establishment of a set of rules for mutual surveillance based on the identities of the juridical persons and how they can be recognized in public life—including the written world.

50. I borrow the notion of purification from Bruno Latour, *We Have Never Been Modern*. He sets purification in opposition to hybridization, implying that processes of purification, or systematization, are inherent in projects of modernization, especially in the domain of the sciences. The law is a scientific paradigm that requires the formation of an autonomous discipline whose conditions of possibility are based on its ability to purify itself from nonsystematic elements.

51. For instance, how should a "hermafrodite" present him/herself as a public person? "Omnes omines [says Rolandino] aut sunt masculi aut femine aut hermofroditi. Masculi sunt qui agunt et gignunt. Femine qui patiunt et concipunt et pariunt. Hermofroditi qui habent utriusque sexum, masculinum videlicet et femeninum. Sed si magis incale sit et preualet masculinum censet mas. si vero femininum censet femina." *Tractatus de Notulis* from Rolandino's *Summa* chap. 3, "De personis et personarum diuisionibus," fol. 89r (modern foliation, which

is mistaken as starting in fol. 70). This is clearly a topological problem, and one could state that the *census* works when the limits of polarity are in crisis, that is, when there is a particular issue of categorization due to hybridizations—either natural or artificial.

52. Goffmann, *The Presentation of Self.*

53. The fact that the glossator Gregorio López translates "persona authentica alias honrada" is only one more of the instances in which López is either misled or purposefully misleading. He is not interested in simply glossing the *Partidas* text; his work is intended to systematically reconnect Alfonso's text to a more Romanist, imperial kind of law—the only one capable of legitimizing Spanish imperialism in sixteenth-century Europe and the Americas.

54. "En todas las siete Partidas deste nuestro libro fablamos delas personas de los omes, e de los fechos dellos, e de todas las otras cosas que les pertenescen. Mas porque en las palabras e en el declaramiento dellas podrian nascer contiendas entre los omes, sobre las razones que fablamos. Porende queremos en este titulo dezir, en fin de nuestro libro, como se deuen entender, e despaladinar tales dubdas, quando acaescieren. E mostraremos, que quiere dezir significamiento, e declaramiento de palabra. E sobre que razones o cosas puede acaescer. E quien lo puede fazer. E sobre todo diremos delos fechos e de las cosas dubdosas." (In every single one of the seven parts of this book we have talked about the persons of people and their actions, as well as about all the things that belong to this subject. However, and because there may be strife among people regarding the texts we have written, we would like to present this title at the end of our book, which is devoted to the ways in which the laws must be understood and the ways in which doubts may be dispelled. For this reason, we will explain the differences between "meaning" and "interpretation" regarding words. We will also explain what the cases are in which those apply and who can do it. And first and foremost, we will talk about actions and facts that may be doubtful.) *Partidas* 7.33.pról.

55. "Rhythmic-copulative" as in Durand's *Les structures anthropologiques.*

56. The formation of the authentic person implies research in societal foldings and in the ways in which royal jurisdiction can inhabit those foldings by means of archives and the complex bureaucratic system. Bureaucracy itself constitutes, as Max Weber demonstrated, a language and a set of functions that facilitates such research. He thought that bureaucracy was a form of depersonalization and that it was the result of a process whereby societal interactions would be devoid of feelings and passion. Indeed, this is contrary to what the *Partidas* show: the creation of the notarial languages and the expansion of the jurisdiction by such means is a process of personalization, supported by a heavily feeling-bound legislation. Weber, *Protestant Ethic.* See also Rama, *La ciudad letrada*; and Rappaport and Cummins, *Beyond the Lettered City.*

57. For the concept of production of presence I am following Gumbrecht, *Production of Presence.*

58. Ar. *fuhlān* (فلان). Andalusi notarial compilations in Arabic seem to have been *fulan*ized as well; see Ibn al-Áṭṭār, *Formulario notarial hispano-árabe.*

59. In "La Tercera Partida," Raúl Orellana Calderón thinks that a contradiction exists between the general theory of the document and the typology of documents, both in *Partidas* 3.18. By that he means that there are documents in the typology that do not comply exactly with the documental forms established in that title. There is a possible explanation for this in the *Ordenamiento de Alcalá*, 1348, Title 18, where the *Partidas* are promulgated as a suppletive law after the acknowledgment that some textual changes have been made. It could very well be that *Partidas* 3.18 suffered important updates necessary for a growing and more centralized

bureaucracy (256–69); Orellana Calderón's impeccable thesis must be taken into account on this contradiction between theory and practice.

60. Derrida, *Mal d'archive*.

61. Johnson, "Anthropomorphism."

62. Even though Paul de Man considered that anthropomorphism is not a trope. See De Man, "Anthropomorphism."

63. The documents are not Castilian originals but, as Orellana Calderón has demonstrated, adaptations from the models presented by Rolandino de' Passeggeri. The Spanish text changes the name to Urraca, which is a royal name with important notarial presence in Castile (see Monterde Albiac, *Diplomatario de la reina Urraca*). The andromorphism of the archive and the authentic person requires specific research. The foldings and crevices of female agency within the andromorphic archive have been explored in Genoa's case by Jamie Smith in "Women as Legal Agents." For the Castilian case, from the perspective of the legal protection of women, see Arauz Mercado, *La protección jurídica*. Marie Kelleher has dealt with the Aragonese case in relation to female identity as constructed in documents regarding litigation with or by women. Kelleher, *Measure of Woman*.

64. Lucas Álvarez, *Tumbo A*; Fournès, "Iconologie des infantes."

65. All the officers and administrators in the *Partidas* are strictly male: *Partidas* 2.9 and 2.10.

66. Metonymy includes the very theory of the king's body as a "mixed" body: each of the officers is part of the king's body, but this part is and must be taken as the body itself. See, for instance, *Partidas* 2.9.21.

67. Benjamin, "Über den Begriff der Geschichte," thesis no. 6, 692.

68. For a contemporary critical perspective on oaths, see Agamben, *Sacrament of Language*.

69. For instance, Valdés, *Compilación de las instrucciones del Oficio*, articles 10, 11, 58, and 63, among others. Other inquisitors, before and after Valdés, imposed similar limitations to the ability of the prisoners to write about their experiences. Of course, we know about those experiences by other means, including graffiti (like the ones in the inquisitorial prison of Llerena, in Badajoz), poetry composed by memory (as in the cases of Juan de la Cruz or Luis de León), etc.

70. Madero, *Las verdades de los hechos*; Madero, "Causa, creencia y testimonios"; Madero, "Façons de croire."

71. φανερουμενοι οτι εστε επιστολη χριστου διακονηθεισα υφ ημων εγγεγραμμενη ου μελανι αλλα πνευματι θεου ζωντος ουκ εν πλαξιν λιθιναις αλλ εν πλαξιν καρδιας σαρκιναις; cf. Jerome's Latin version: "manifestati quoniam epistula estis Christi ministrata a nobis et scripta non atramento sed Spiritu Dei vivi non in tabulis lapideis sed in tabulis cordis carnalibus." 2 *Corinthians* 3.3.

72. Jerome, *Commentary on Galatians*. I have made some changes to the translation therein. Jerome, *S. Eusebii Hieronymi Stridonensis Presbyteri Commentariorum*, paragraph 2, cols. 386b–c. (Vers. 20.) *Vellem autem esse apud vos modo, et mutare vocem meam, quoniam confundor in vobis.* Scriptura divina aedificat et lecta; sed multo plus prodest, si de litteris vertatur in vocem, ut qui per Epistolam docuerat, praesens instruat audientes. [Col.0386C] Magnam siquidem vim habet vox viva: vox de auctoris sui ore resonans, quae ea pronuntiatione profertur atque distinguitur, qua in hominis sui corde generata est. Sciens itaque Apostolus majorem vim habere sermonem qui ad praesentes fiat, cupit vocem Epistolicam, vocem litteris

comprehensam, in praesentiam commutare: et quia hoc magis expediebat his qui in errore fuerant depravati, vivo eos ad veritatem retrahere sermone."

73. "Si vero aliquid contigeri, quale in Armenia factum est, ut aliud quidem faciat collation litterarum, aliud vero testimonia: tunc nos quidem existimavimus ea, quae viva dicuntur voce, & cum iureiurando: haec digniora fide qum scripturam ipsam secundum se subsistere." Justinian, *Novellae*, 73.3, in *Corpus Iuris Civilis: III*, vol. 3, 365. The Prost & Barlet edition of the *Corpus Iuris* gives a good overview of the marginal commentaries from the *Glossa Ordinaria* to the postglossators: Justinian, *Corpus Iuris Civilis Ivstinianei*, vol. 5, 342–43. The whole *Novella* 73 is essential for the formation of the notarial languages and the discussion regarding documentary forgery. The margins of this *Novella* have two different layers of glosses, but later law scholars, including Bartolus of Sassoferrato and Baldus of Ubaldis, devoted full commentaries to the questions raised in this part of the *Libri Tres*. The gloss "cum iureiurando" discusses the dialectics of voice in more depth: "Item caue tibi, quia tam scriptura que reprobatur quam quae ad reprobandum inducitir, ambo sunt priuatae. Item ota quod ex hoc colligunt quidam ut hodie semper plus credatur voci viuae, quam mortuae. . . . Sed certe hic loquitur quando ex una parte est istrumentum, cui volebat derogari: & testes, qui pro instrument testificabantur: ex alia vero parte sola collationis dissimilitudo: unde non sola vox viua, sed cum instrument iuncta vincit vocem mortuam: & etiam plus est quia scriptura quae vincitur est priuata. Item caue tibi: quia haec instrumenta non contradicunt sibi in sentential: sed diuersa sunt nam primum dicit tea liquid mihi debere: & dico a te scriptum: & tu profer aliud in quo continentur de permutation, vel aliquot alio, quod cum alio fecisti: quod ego Confiteor te fecisse: & si hoc secundum sit dissimile primo in literis, perinde videtur, ac si non sit verum quod contra te induco: sed falsum. Unde melius dicere haec litera, plus voci viuae crei, quam dissimilitudini, quae inducitur per mortuam vocem: id est, per scripturam. Et praedictis patet, quod non plus voci viuae quam mortuae sit credendum: sed aequaliter duobus testibus, et instrumento." Justinian, *Corpus Iuris Civilis Ivstinianei*, vol. 5, 342–43.

74. Lévy, *La hiérarchie des preuves*.

75. Maimonides, *Mishne Torah*, introduction.

76. Wacks, *Double Diaspora*.

77. "& deue entonçe recontar lo que el testigo dixo. E si se acordaren que dixo assi. deue lo luego fazer escriuir el mismo bien & lealmente de guisa que no sea menguada nin cresçida ende ninguna cosa. E despues que fuere todo endereçado. deue lo luego fazer leer antel testigo. E si el testigo entendiere que esta bien deue lo otorgar. E si viere que ay alguna cosa de emendar deue lo luego endereçar. & despues que fuere todo endereçado deuelo fazer leer antel testigo & si el testigo entendiere que esta bien deue lo otorgar E aquel que reçebiere el testigo que dize que sabe el fecho deue le preguntar como lo sabe faziendole dezir por que razon lo sabe. si lo sabe por vista o por oyda o por creençia. E la razon que dixiere deue la fazer escreuir." *Partidas* 3.16.26.

78. See, in addition, Emmanuel Le Roy Ladurie in *Montaillou*, in which he explains the complexity of the process, although he also admits that, in his view, the process can be considered a direct, unmediated one. For an entirely different perspective on the process and the characteristics of its regulated mediations, see Benad, *Domus und Religion in Montaillou*.

79. The Corpus Diacrónico del Español (CORDE) offers several thousand occurrences of the word in this sense for just the time period of 1300–1500 (afterward, the occurrences grow exponentially). Real Academia Española, CORDE, *http://corpus.rae.es/cordenet.html*.

CHAPTER TWO

1. For all details regarding the life and work of Gonzalo de Berceo, see Berceo, *Milagros de Nuestra Señora*, 201–18.

2. Berceo, *Vida de Santo Domingo de Silos*, stanza 2. The translation is from Berceo, *Collected Works*. The translation is perfectly correct, but it does not convey some of the nuances of the original: *prosa* does not mean a poem in general, but a very specific kind of poem with specific rhythmic characteristics, like the *copla cuaderna* in which Berceo writes; moreover, it also indicates the narrative character of the work; I prefer "literate" to "learned," because I believe, as I explain in the text, that he is referring to a very concrete kind of linguistic competence, and not to a general idea of culture or academic training, as "learned" seems to imply. The translation also makes explicit things that are implicit in the Castilian text.

3. Dutton, "Profession"; Dutton, "Gonzalo de Berceo"; Berceo, *Milagros de Nuestra Señora*.

4. For the tradition of the *copla cuaderna* or *cuaderna vía*, see Rico, "La clerecía del Mester."

5. The forty-six first *cuadernas* at the beginning of the *Milagros de Nuestra Señora* constitute a thorough theory and practice of exegesis for the correct understanding of the *Milagros*.

6. "Conplidas deuen ser las leyes & muy cuydadas & muy acatadas: de guisa que sean con razon & sobre cosas que puedan ser fechas segund natura & las palabras dellas que sean buenas & llanas & paladinas: de manera que todo onbre las pueda entender & retener. E otrosi han de ser sin escatima & sin punto & que no sean contrarias las vnas de las otras." *Partidas* 1.1.4.

7. The lexical root *paladin* occurs several dozens of times in the *Partidas* (see the CORDE, http://corpus.rae.es/cordenet.html), always with the meaning of something that is clear, public, and unconcealed; the word occurs sometimes paired with its antonym, like "paladinamente y no en poridad" (openly, and not in secret), *Partidas* 1.5.43. Similarly, the word appears as an adverb opposed to *encubiertamente* (under cover), as in *Partidas* 1.21.pról. For the probable origin and etymology of the word, see Coromines and Pascual, *Diccionario crítico etimológico*, vol. 4, 347–48, s.v. *paladin-*.

8. Martínez, *El humanismo medieval*.

9. Cátedra, "Enrique de Villena"; Lawrance, "Spread of Lay Literacy"; Lawrance, "On Fifteenth-Century"; Miguel-Prendes, *El espejo y el piélago*.

10. Di Camilo, *El humanismo castellano*; Gómez Moreno, *España y la Italia*.

11. It can be debated whether this edition, or Penyafort's work altogether, can be understood as a piece of codification. Certainly, it would be difficult to do so if we read it in accordance with Jeremy Bentham's idea of codification as it has been widely accepted and discussed in common law, even though Bentham's idea, or even claim for codification, could serve greatly to understand Alfonso's work in other ways. Dean Alfange summarized Bentham's process of codification in a classic article on the matter: "(1) Avoid all technical or legal terms wherever possible; (2) if technical terms must be used, define them carefully in the body of the law; (3) define technical terms in "common and known words"; and (4) if the same idea is to be expressed more than once, express it in exactly the same words" (Alfange, "Jeremy Bentham," 72). Alfange then goes on to quote Bentham's *Constitutional Code*, which was, interestingly enough, created at the request of his admirers on the Iberian Peninsula, both in Spain (after the 1812 *Constitución*) and Portugal, and that he extended it not only to those two states but to other nations around the world: "A code formed upon these principles would not require

schools for its explanation, would not require casuists to unravel its subtleties. It would speak a language familiar to everybody: each one might consult it at his need. It would be distinguished from all other books by its greater simplicity and clearness. The father of a family, without assistance, might take it in his hand and teach it to his children, and give to the precepts of private morality the force and dignity of public morals." Alfange, "Jeremy Bentham," 72. I have decided not to use Bentham's understanding of the process of codification. Although it would probably lead to a systematization of Alfonso's process of codification, it would also result in neglecting the other techniques of codification used, with a great deal of experimentation, by the king. Likewise, I am not applying Bentham's idea of codification to any other *code*, and, of course, not to the *Decretals* or the works of Penyafort. And yet, I consider them *codes*, insofar as they are systematized within a codex and are in search of their own invariability as a book of principles to be studied and applied in a universal way as a source of jurisdictional power.

12. The very famous manuscript of the so-called *Smithfield Decretals* (British Library, Royal MS 10 E IV) was produced to be sent to the University of Paris: "Gregorius Episcopus, servus servorum dei dilectis filijs doctoribus et scolaribus uiniuersitatis parisius commorantibus salutem et apostolicam benedictionem" (fol. 4r). Other manuscripts were produced to be sent to other schools and universities from what seems to have been a decentralized network of workshops serving the pope and his envoys and surrogates (including Raymond of Penyafort himself).

13. The particularities of canon Latin and the history of canon law and canon law codifications have been explored in Brundage, *Medieval Canon Law*; and Brundage, *Profession and Practice*.

14. Conte, *Tres Libri Codicis*.

15. See Iglesia Ferreirós, *Una historia de la formación*; Barrero García and Alonso Martín, *Textos de derecho local español*.

16. "Quoniam in plerisque partibus intra eandem ciuitatem atque diocesim permixti sunt populi diuersarum linguarum, habentes sub una fide uarios ritus et mores, districte precipimus ut pontifices huiusmodi ciuitatum siue diocesum prouideant uiros idoneos qui, secundum diuersitates rituum et linguarum, diuina officia illis celebrent et ecclesiastica sacramenta ministrent, instruendo eos uerbo pariter et exemplo." *Constitutiones Concilii quarti Lateranensis, constitutio 9*, 57. The translation is from Schroeder, Disciplinary Decrees, 236–96, as presented in the Fordham University Medieval Sourcebook online: "Since in many places within the same city and diocese there are people of different languages having one faith but various rites and customs, we strictly command that the bishops of these cities and dioceses provide suitable men who will, according to the different rites and languages, celebrate the divine offices for them, administer the sacraments of the Church and instruct them by word and example. But we absolutely forbid that one and the same city or diocese have more than one bishop, one body, as it were, with several heads, which is a monstrosity. But if by reason of the aforesaid conditions an urgent necessity should arise, let the bishop of the locality after due deliberation appoint a prelate acceptable to those races, who shall act as vicar in the aforesaid matters and be subject to him all things. If anyone shall act otherwise, let him consider himself excommunicated; and if even then he will not amend, let him be deposed from every ecclesiastical ministry, and if need be, let the secular arm be employed, that such insolence may be curbed."

17. Naturally, we are still under the colonial spell of two Eurocentric myths: that of the *ius commune* (upheld by the idea of the common legal past of Europe, as in Bellomo, *Common Legal Past*) and that of the Romance-speaking world (the *Romania*) and its fragmentation

(suggested by Wartburg, *La Fragmentation linguistique*). In *L'Aventure des langues*, Henriette Walter developed a better and broader understanding of "Western languages" in the Middle Ages, albeit one still very focused on traditional historical linguistics and philologies. Subsequently, she also grew interested in other non-Romance languages from a moderately (commercially) orientalist perspective: Walter and Baraka, *Arabesques*. A much more interesting look at linguistic, multilingual contact and "translingual writing" in the context of trade, exchange, and commerce, is that of Jonathan Hsy, *Trading Tongues*.

18. Moore, *Formation*; Moore, *War on Heresy*. Moore has, throughout his career, defended a thesis according to which the strategies concerning heresy are similar to those regarding surveillance of other communities like Jews, lepers, or prostitutes and that these strategies can be studied as a superstructure. With this thesis, Moore advocates the formation of what he has called the persecuting society, whose birth he traces. He has tried to combat the common contention that the church persecuted heretics because there were many of them, thus opposing the perspective that heresy is in fact a creation of the very persecuting society that "identified" it. Moore's critics are legion, but his arguments have marked an epoch in the study of heresy. See now the splendid introduction of Barbezat's *Burning Bodies*.

19. "Reduction," here, has a very clear sense of universalization, as studied by Hanks, *Converting Words*.

20. Zink, *La prédication*; Kienzle, *Sermon*; Kienzle, Amos, and Green, *De ore Domini*; Kienzle, *Cistercians, Heresy, and Crusade*; Cátedra, *Los sermones*; Cátedra, *Sermón, sociedad y literatura*; Arizaleta, "La memoria del monarca."; In "*L'exemplum* en pratiques," Nicolas Louis, working with the GAHOM (Group d'Anthropologie Historique de l'Occident Médiéval) at the École des hautes études en sciences sociales, gives an innovative approach to the history of the production and uses of the exemplum as *materia praedicabilis* (themes to preach about) in the context of what the author calls its *âge d'or*, or 1250–1350; his line of questioning goes beyond the consideration common among scholars to regard the books of exempla as mere collections. As Margaret Jennings has emphasized, the proliferation of treatises for sermon composition were also fostered by a specific interest in Ciceronian rhetoric and the development of the *inventio* as the main rhetorical operation. Jennings and Wilson, *Ranulph of Higden*.

21. The southern-France heresies have been considered by European scholars to be heresies par excellence and constituted the center of gravity for the study of the Inquisition—as well as being the very heresies that prompted Gregory IX to deploy apostolic inquisition as a disciplinary device. Even though the concept of heresy is not proper to this particular event, the line between the creation of the *heretica pravitatis* (heretical depravation) and the inquisitorial procedures and devices (including preaching, confession, and many others) was redefined during the fight against the Cathars. The created affinity between heresy and southern France is still in need of deeper investigation, despite the groundbreaking work by scholars like Mark Pegg. See, for example, his *The Corruption of Angels* and *A Most Holy War*. See also Ames, *Righteous Persecution*. Ames examines the concept of heresy on a more global level in *Medieval Heresies*. On the heresies of Southern France and Aragon, see Berlioz, *Le Pays Cathare*.

22. *Lo Codi* is likely an adaptation of the *Summa trecensis*, which condenses *Codex Iustinians*'s books 1–9. Du Plessis, "Creation of Legal Principle."

23. Landau, "Development of Law," especially 124.

24. The vernacular as a concept has gained some importance in the field of postcolonial studies, especially in the social sciences. It has been used to open doors to specific, local forms of citizenship, modernity, etc., as in Will Kymlicka's *Politics in the Vernacular* and in the project led by Brice Knauft from 2000 to 2003 on vernacular modernities, in the middle of a new set

of anthropological, political, and social engagements in the global world (cf. http://www
.anthropology.emory.edu/FACULTY/ANTBK/vernacularModernities/vernacularModernities
.html). Cf. Briguglia and Ricklin, *Thinking Politics in the Vernacular*. Mary Fissel's work, too,
is especially interesting for developing a political conceptualization of the vernacular as she
interconnects the cycle of reproduction with the political metaphors of the body: Fissell, *Vernacular Bodies*.

25. Varro, *De lingua latina*, 5.12.77. Ngũgĩ Wa Thiong'o has proposed a different relationship between theory and poverty in what he calls, based on Grotowski's poor theater, "the
riches of poor theory." Thiong'o, *Globalectics*, 5.

26. At this point, my project also departs radically from the regular conception of the
way in which the Alfonsine workshop functioned. Alfonsine scholars accept the three-tiered
process in the workshop—compilation, the critique of sources, and translation. The order
within this tripartite process may be altered, but it is essentially what constitutes the coherence
of the different workshops—historical, legal, scientific, and even poetic. For this traditional
view of the Alfonsine workshop, see Funes, *El modelo historiográfico alfonsí*; Catalán, *De la silva
textual*; Fernández-Ordóñez, *Las "Estorias" de Alfonso el Sabio*; Gómez Redondo, *Historia de la
prosa*.

27. Noë, *Strange Tools*.

28. Cormack, *Power to Do Justice*. Cormack bases his definition on John Cowell's legal
distinctions of 1607.

29. "Ca *bien asi* como quando la el quiso fazer [la justicia] hobo saber, et querer, et poder
para la fazer, *otrosí* los que la justicia han de fazer por el han menester que hayan en si estas tres
cosas: primeramente voluntad de la querer *et de la amar de coraçon*, parando mientes en los
bienes et en las proes que en ella yacen; la segunda que la sepan fazer como conviene et los
fechos que la demandaren, *los unos con piedad et los otros con recidumbre;* la tercera que hayan
esfuerzo e poder para complirla contra los que la quisieren toller o embargar." *Partidas* 3.pról.
Emphasis in both English and Spanish quotations are mine.

30. I do not conceive of political theologies as an interpretive model according to which
we can look at the processes of secularization of religious concepts in the manner of Carl
Schmitt, *Political Theology*. This interpretive model is, in turn, a political theological strategy
devised to focus on specific forms of power circulation and authoritarianism. I do use the idea
of political theologies as a way to unveil those strategies: as a way to check how modes of
conceptual transaction indicate models of power circulation and versions of authority. See also
Boureau, *Kantorowicz*, 64: "La théologie politique du Moyen Âge se définit comme l'effort
de transposition laïque et juridique des doctrines réligieuses de la communauté des croyants
(l'Église)."

31. "Justitia autem praecipit parcere omnibus, consulere generi hominum, suum cuique
reddere, sacra, publica, aliena non tangere." Cicero, *De re publica*, 3.9.

32. Dodaro, *Christ and the Just Society*. The metaphor of the *fons iustitia* applied to the
king in legal sources (see also Foucault, *Surveiller et punir*), while patristic sources normally
apply the metaphor to God (cf. *Patrologia Latina database*).

33. "La çiençia es como fuente de iustiçia e aprouecha se della el mundo mas que de otra
çiençia." (Science resembles a source of justice, and the world benefits from it more than from
any other science.) *Partidas* 2.31.8. He is talking about legal science.

34. "Asemejaron [la justicia] a la Fuente perenal que ha en si tres cosas: la primera que
asi como el agua que della sale nasce contra oriente, *asi* la justicia cata siempre contra do nasce
el sol verdadero que es dios; et por esto llamaron los santos en las escripturas a nuestro señor

Iesu cristo sol de justicia. La segunda que *asi como* el agua de tal fuente corre siempre, et han los homes mauor sabor de beber della porque sabe mejor et es mas sana que otra, *otrosi* la justicia es en si que nunca se destaja nin mengua, et reciben en ella mayor sabor los que la demandan et la han menester mas que en otra cosa. La tercera que *asi como* el agua desta fuente es caliente en invierno et fria en verano, et la bondad della es contraria a la maldad de los tiempos, *asi* el derecho que sale de la justicia tuelle et contrasta todas las cosas malas et desaguisadas que los hombres fazen." *Partidas* 3.1.1. Emphases are mine.

35. Alfonso X, *Las Siete Partidas*, vol. 3.

36. When I say "Accursian gloss," I do not intend to convey that Accursius was the author but that the gloss was incorporated by Accursius for his *Glossa Ordinaria*.

37. "El que quisiere leer las leyes deste nuestro libro, que pare en ellas bien mientes e que las escodriñe de guisa que las entienda, ca si bien las entendiere . . . uenierle an dos provechos. El uno que sera mas entendido; el otro que se aprovechara mucho dellas. E segun dixeron los sabios, el que lee las escrituras e non las entiende semeja que las desprecia. E otrosi es atal como el que sueña la cosa e cuando despierta non la falla en verdad." *Partidas* 1.1.5.

38. In his political and theological fiction from 1257 to 1263, Thomas of Cantimpré used these words from Psalms 75.6 as a critique of nonattentive scholars, who are too concerned with earthly goods and earthly life: Thomas de Cantimpré, *Bonum universale de apibus*, 180. For the nonattentive versus the engaged reader, see Sweetman, "Beryl Smalley." Corresponds in the Catholic Bible to Psalms 76.6: "All the foolish of heart have been disturbed. They have slept their sleep, and all the men of riches have found nothing in their hands."

39. Cf. *Partidas* 1.1.10, on the benefits derived from the laws.

40. I am here referring to specific Foucauldian ideas developed in the last years of his teaching and research. The technologies of the self include all those procedures of self-examination, of identification of subjecthood. The hermeneutics of the subject implies asking one specific question—namely, what kind of truth can be produced by a subject in the face of a given body of knowledge? For my purposes, the law implies that anybody who wants to be presented as a legal subject must perform those procedures of self-examination and acknowledge the body of knowledge configured in the law itself—according to which, subjecthood is defined. Foucault, *L'herméneutique du sujet*; Foucault, *Technologies of the Self*.

41. For questions on the hermenutics of the subject, self care, and the ultimate goal of giving an account of oneself, I have been inspired by Foucault, *L'herméneutique du sujet*; and Butler, *Giving an Account of Oneself*.

42. "Fezimos señaladamente este libro porque siempre los reyes del nuestro señorio se caten en el ansi como en espejo: e vean las cosas que an en si de enmendar, e las enmienden, e segund aquello que fagan en los suyos."(We wrote this book with the purpose that the kings in our lordship may look at themselves as they would do in a mirror. Like that, they can see all the things they must mend in themselves, and they can then mend them; and afterwards they can also mend their subjects.) *Partidas*, general prologue.

43. Rodríguez-Velasco, *Order and Chivalry*.

44. Foucault, *La Société punitive*, in particular the February 21st session of the seminar; Foucault, *Surveiller et punir*.

45. Costa, *Iurisdictio*.

46. Vallejo, *Ruda equidad, ley consumada*, 42–43.

47. Translating this expression is extremely complex, not because the words themselves have any inherently untranslatable character but because they are surrounded by constant commentaries and specifications regarding their proper meaning and dialectical features in the texts

of the medieval glossators and commentators. It is precisely the translatability—and the constant linguistic, dialectical, and conceptual transactions that take place among law scholars—that makes the expression radically difficult. Rather than adjust my translation according to those circumstances and debates, I, like medieval legal scholars, underscore the expressions in order to suggest a set of new meanings: in this case, *potestas iuris dicendi* as "the power to claim rights."

48. In her translation of Marsilius of Padua's *Defensor Pacis*, Annabel Brett translates *merum imperium* as "unmixed command," which is an extraordinarily literal way of translating the notion. However, the footnote is very clarifying: "The translation offered in the text does not remotely capture the full sense of this term. Essentially, *merum imperium* is what we might call absolute sovereignty, including (crucially) the power of the sword, i.e. over life and death (capital jurisdiction)," and she partially translates the definition in *Digest* 2.1.3, which glossators commented on and discussed for a number of centuries, although they were much more interested in other parts of the definition.

49. Vallejo, *Ruda equidad, ley consumada*, 59–60.

50. Cf. Vallejo, *Ruda equidad, ley consumada*, 132–33; Mochi Onory, *Fonti canonistiche*; Calasso, *I glossatori*. The territorialization of jurisdictional power is an important index entry that occupies several lines in Esteban Daoiz's index to the *Corpus Iuris Civilis*, which we use throughout this book; not all indexes are equal, though; the *Gema Legalis*, a Venetian index to the works of Bartolus of Sassoferrato, does not devote as much space to this question of territorialization, but it is particularly concise and precise in addressing it in the following way: "Iurisdictio cohaeret territorio" (Jurisdiction makes the territory cohere.) Bassani, *Gemma legalis seu Compendium*, vol. II, s.v. "iurisdictio."

51. The question of language and the obtention of a discourse in plebeian experience is one of the pillars of Breaugh, *L'expérience plébeienne*.

52. A crucial study of this indirect ethnographic and cultural enterprise is Schmitt, *Le saint Lévrier*. Jamie Taylor has studied, from a different perspective, the value of interrogation and witnessing after 1215, arguing that they "were designed to produce a unified devotional or political community." Taylor, *Fictions of Evidence*, 7. From a different perspective, but in my opinion an extremely important perspective for understanding the investigative power of jurisdictional methods of interrogation, cf. Kumler, *Translating Truth*.

53. Carré, *Le baiser sur la bouche*.

54. Referring the *Bible with Ordinary Gloss* is almost a metaphysical impossibility, because of the amount of manuscripts and their internal differences. I am using printed editions, and in particular the considered *edition princeps* of 1480–1481.

55. Heidegger, *Nietzsche*, 1: *The Will to Power as Art*, 48.

CHAPTER THREE

1. Trithemius, *Beati Rabani Mauri Vita*, col. 92c.

2. Schmitt, *Les revenants*, 229. For Gui of Corvo, see Gobi, *Dialogue avec un fantôme*, 59 and 156.

3. Kagan, *Lucrecia's Dreams*; Ginzburg, *Il formaggio e i vermi*; Davis, *Return of Martin Guerre*.

4. Siger de Brabant disputed six *impossibilia* between 1270 and 1273. Siger de Brabant, *Siger de Brabant: Écrits*. Norman Kretzmann studied the genre of the *impossibilium* by stating

that the importance of these logical utterances, essentially *sophismata*, constituted ways to call attention to specific issues of a larger relevance. Kretzmann considers that those issues are of an abstract nature, but in my opinion they are also of a political character, especially if one considers those that belong in the realm of the historiographical (Siger's war on Troy, for instance) or those that deal with existence and metaphysics, like some of the *sophismata* Jean Buridan included in his *Summula de Dialectica*. Cf. Kretzmann, "Socrates Is Whiter"; Buridan and Dorp, *Summula de dialectica*.

5. *Cortes* constitute the center of gravity for those exchanges of documents, exhibitions of privileges, and other written instruments. Castilian and Leonese *Cortes* are available in thick manuscripts that were copied and disseminated among local powers, city archives, and so on. The Real Academia de la Historia undertook the publication of those *Cortes* from 1883 onward: *Cortes de los Antiguos Reinos de León y de Castilla*. For Aragón, Catalonia, and Valencia, see *Cortes de los Antiguos Reinos de Aragón y de Valencia y Principado de Cataluña*. Collections of documents from monasteries and other institutions and local archives, which were mainly published during the second half of the twentieth century in the wake of the interest on economic and social history, show the precise way in which they kept records of their different documents successively exhibited to new kings, with the confirmation and sometimes accompanied by dorsal notes that explain the circumstances of the confirmation, the copy, etc. There are dozens of those collections, which are unnecessary to list here (I give some examples within this chapter), but perhaps one of the most important is *Diplomatario Andaluz de Alfonso X*. González Jiménez, *Diplomatario Andaluz*.

6. Lowenthal, *Past Is a Foreign Country*; Fabian, *Time and the Other*; Hartley, *Go-Between*; Brown, "In the Middle."

7. Aristotle, *Poetics*, 1451b, where the philosopher claims that poetry is more philosophical than history (see the Introduction).

8. Rodríguez-Velasco, "Diabólicos quirógrafos." Shakespeare's *King Lear* is a good example of the spectral life of the document that changes the life of the characters. At the beginning of *King Lear*, Edmund shows the audience a sealed letter:

> Well, then,
> Legitimate Edgar, I must have your land:
> Our father's love is to the bastard Edmund
> As to the legitimate: fine word,—legitimate!
> Well, my legitimate, if this letter speed,
> And my invention thrive, Edmund the base
> Shall top the legitimate. I grow; I prosper:
> Now, gods, stand up for bastards!

The letter in his hand—a false letter, a false ghost indeed—forces Gloucester to read it, transforming the legitimate Edgar into a person without identity, a "philosopher," a nameless poor man, who will come back from among the dead at the end of the play to destroy the letter and, with it, falsehood itself. The revenant letter can only contain something urgent and definitive. It is more than a literary resource: procedures and procedural documents are never entirely dead, even though they are dead voice. Looking at these documents from afar, from the historical perspective, gives the sensation that these documents are the real agents of history, not the people behind them—in a sort of spectrality and fetishization similar to what Marx said in discussing the commodity. Marx, *Capital*; Derrida, "Apparition de l'inapparent."

9. The different processes of *iussio* and *redactio* in the notarial world of the thirteenth century in Castille have been described and studied by Marina Kleine, who has also been able to document the roles of over 150 actors in the notarial offices of the king. Kleine, *La cancillería real de Alfonso X*.

10. This is in no way a criticism of those disciplines that have been and are fundamental to the different processes of historical knowledge. I am just highlighting that these disciplines are not neutral and that they have also played an important role in the development of political discourse and judicial procedure. However, handbooks and compilations regarding the technologies that form the discipline rarely, if ever, raise this question. See Ruiz, *Introducción a la codicología*; Guyotjeannin, "Le vocabulaire de la diplomatique"; Guyotjeannin, Pycke, and Tock, *Diplomatique médiévale*.

11. Justinian, *Novellae* 73, in *Corpus Iuris Civilis: III, Novellae*. There is an English translation of the *Novellae* at http://www.uwyo.edu/lawlib/blume-justinian/ajc-edition-2/novels/61 –80/novel%2073_repacement.pdf.

12. Justinian, *Novellae* 73, in *Corpus Iuris Civilis: III, Novellae*.

13. Iglesia Ferreirós, *Una historia de la formación*, vol. 2, 3n13. It is interesting to note that while the process whereby the substitution of an *aequitas constituta* for the *aequitas ruda* in Castile and León gave birth to the introduction of the *Liber Iudiciorum*, and afterward the different Romanistic projects led by Alfonso X—as a way to fight against the *fueros de albedrío* that claimed competing jurisdictional power against the king—in Aragon the movement was the opposite when Jaume I removed the *Liber Iudiciorum* from the legal landscape, promoting local charters like the *Usatges* of Barcelona.

14. *Fuero Juzgo en latín y castellano* 2.4, 33. All references to the *Liber Iudiciorum* and the *Fuero Juzgo* come from *Fuero Juzgo en latín y castellano*. Translations of the *Liber Iudiciorum* / *Fuero Juzgo* are mine.

15. *Liber Iudiciorum*, 2.4, 23.

16. *Liber Iudiciorum* / *Fuero Juzgo* 2.5, 27–32 in Latin; in Spanish: "De los escriptos que deven valer e non, et de las mandas de los muertos," 2.5, 38–45.

17. "Cada un omne debe escrevir su manda con su mano, e diga special mientre que manda fazer de sus cosas, o a quien las manda, e notar y el dia y el anno en que faze la manda, e depues que tod esto oviere escripto, escriva en fondon de la carta que lo confirma con su mano. E depues que los herederos e sus fijos ovieren esta manda, fasta XXX annos muestrenla al obispo de la tierra o al iuez fasta VI. meses, y el obispo o el iuez tomen otros tales tres escriptos, que fuesen fechos por su mano daquel que fizo la manda: e por aquellos escriptos, si semeiare la letra de la manda, sea confirmada la manda." *Fuero Juzgo*, 2.5.15, 42.

18. Gayoso Carreira, *Historia del papel en España*; Burón Castro, "Papel hispano-árabe"; Mármol Bernal, "El papel a través"; Mármol Bernal, "Papel en Córdoba"; Barletta, *Covert Gestures*.

19. A pioneer study of medieval French documents as sites of mediality was undertaken in Bedos-Rezak, "Cutting Edge"; and Bedos-Rezak, *When Ego Was Imago*. See also Bedos-Rezak, *Form and Order*.

20. Vismann, *Files*, 25–29; Chapman, *Cancels*. When I call them legal philologists, I am also putting forth the following thesis: that the discipline of philology is a legal operation that has worked as a central support of religious and even civil law. This is, I believe, what underpins Giabattista Vico's idea of a philology as a "coscienza del certo" (consciousness of certainty) that is essential to both the history of the church and the history of the state and that buttresses his

project for a *scienza nuova* (new science). Although philology became an academic discipline in the nineteenth century, I don't think it ever lost this juridical and political character.

21. "Don Alfonso, por la gracia de Dios rey de Castiella, de Toledo, de Leon, de Gallizia, de Seuilla, de Cordoua, de Murzia e de Iahen, a todos los ommes de mio regnio que esta mi carta vieren, salut e gracia. Sepades que los ommes de Villaluiella uinieron a mi a Toledo e mostraronme su priuilegio que tienen del Emperador, e pidieronme merced que ge lo conformasse. E yo, por otras priessas que auia, non ge lo pud confirmar. Ond uos mando que ge lo tengades e que ge lo guardedes asi como les fue tenido e guardado en tienpo del rey don Alfonso, mio visauuelo, e del rey don Ferrando, fata su muerte. E esto sea fasta que yo salga alla a la tierra; et entonce ueerlo he e sabre como les fue tenido e dare lo que touiere por bien." Archivo de la Catedral de Burgos, V-37, Catalog of the Archivo Histórico de la Catedral de Burgos, vol. 37, doc. 4. https://www.fundacioncajacirculo.es/AHCB_D.php?cod = 21624V& nombre = Villalbilla%20de%20Burgos).

22. González Díez, *Colección*, 89–92.

23. Archivo de la Catedral de Burgos V-37, fol. 7, p. 8, doc. 5. There are later copies of this document with the confirmations by Sancho IV, 1286; Alfonso XI, 1332; and Peter I, 1353. Alfonso X's confirmation, on January 6, 1255, explains how the king "has seen" a letter "lacking the Emperor's seal . . . that they say they were always kept" (vi . . . sin sello del emperador don Alfonso . . . que dicen que les valio siempre). However, Alfonso refused to add his seal.

24. The king sanctioned Alvaro Martín, García Martín de Zumel, and Juan de Piliella's sales of the possessions that had belonged to Don Alvaro Fernández. "I saw a leaded letter from King Ferdinand, my father . . . and so it stands firmer, I commanded my lead seal be added" (vi carta plomada del rey don Ferrando, mío padre . . . porque sea mas firme mande poner en ella mi sello de plomo). Archivo de la Catedral de Burgos, vol. 32, fol. 51, p. 9, doc. 6.

25. Manuscripts of the *Espéculo* containing this prologal piece are Real Biblioteca MS II/ 101 (manid 3182), Biblioteca National de España, MS 10123 (manid 1158), Real Academia de la Historia, MS 9–30–3/6112 (manid 3750). The most impressive manuscript containing the first edition of the *Partidas*, and presenting the same narrative, is British Library Add. MS 20787 (manid 1112); also Hispanic Society of America MS HC 397/573 (manid 115).

26. Thomas, "El sujeto de derecho."

27. Rama, *La ciudad letrada*. See the critique of vernacular literacy and the lettered city trope and paradigm in Rappaport and Cummins, *Beyond the Lettered City*. A fascinating critique of literacy as an apparatus of power, as discussed in Chapter 2, may be read in Clanchy, *From Memory*, 11–20; Vismann, *Files*.

28. "Un privilejo escripto en pergamino de cuero e seellado con seello de plomo pendiente en filos de seda vermejos e amariellos, que es del papa Bonifacio, segund que por él parescía." Vaca Lorenzo, *Documentación medieval*, docs. 20–21, p. 43–45.

29. Guyotjeannin, Pycke, and Tock, *Diplomatique médiévale*.

30. "Martes, dos días de mayo, era de mille e trezientos e quarenta e çinco annos. [1307] Este día, Corroçano de Berviesca veno ante don Pero Bonifaz, alcallde del rey en Burgos, et mostró una carta escripta en pergamino de cuero signada con signo de Johan Peres, notario que se dizie de la villa de Carrión, et seellada con seello pendiente de çera en cuerda de seda prieta, el seello en sennal de escudo et en él sennales de lobos e quarterones en quadra e en las letras de enderredor dizie 'S. de Gonzalo Gómez,' la qual carta era sana, non rayda nin rota nin corrupta nin dubdosa en ninguna parte." Echániz Sans, *El monasterio femenino*, doc. 31, pp. 59–60.

31. Aristotelian fantasy was also redefined as one of the aesthetic responsibilities of the people in *Partidas* 2.13.

32. The discussion regarding the adequacy of the idea of literature for the Middle Ages is as long as the resistance to the discussion, precisely because of all the national and identitary implications of the literary institution. Paul Zumthor gave a very technical explanation of the inadequacy by focusing on the oral components of medieval poetry, music, epic, etc. Zumthor, "Y a-t-il une 'littérature' médiévale?" See also Marino, *Biography*. I am not particularly interested in addressing this question. There is a modern process of institutionalization of literature that is proper to the bourgeois cultural system. See also Casanova, *La République mondiale*. This institution is not independent from the pre-Enlightenment idea and practices of the Republic of Letters. Medieval literature had its own processes of institutionalization, which, in their turn, are closely related to legal spaces and the production of those legal spaces (the court, the church, the market, the commons, etc.).

33. Dahan, *Notes et textes sur la poétique*. In his commentaries on Aristotle's *Poetics*, Averroes always connects it with syllogisms and logic. For the question of the exemplum: "Exemplar dicitur originalis scriptura, genus videlicet ex quo generatur uel sumitur exemplum; quod quidem exemplar apellatur etiam originale et autencticum . . . unde uersus: Exemplar pater est, exemplum quod generatur." Passeggeri, *Summa totius artis notariae*, book III, chap. 10. For exemplum as a precedent, see Vismann, *Files*, 48.

34. Crampon, "Un sermon prêché." Cf. Also Zink, *La prédication*, 568.

35. Boureau, *Satan Hérétique*; see also Pasciuta, *Il diavolo in Paradiso*.

36. ¹³ et vos cum mortui essetis in delictis et praeputio carnis vestrae convivificavit cum illo donans vobis omnia delicta ¹⁴ delens quod aduersum nos erat *chirografum decretis* quod erat contrarium nobis et ipsum tulit de medio adfigens illud cruci 15 expolians principatus et potestates traduxit palam triumphans illos in semet ipso. (¹³ και υμας νεκρους οντας εν τοις παραπτωμασιν και τη ακροβυστια της σαρκος υμων συνεζωποιησεν συν αυτω χαρισαμενος ημιν παντα τα παραπτωματα ¹⁴ εξαλειψας το καθ ημων χειρογραφον τος δογμασιν ο ην υπεναντιον ημιν και αυτο ηρκεν εκ του μεσου προσηλωσας αυτο τω σταυρω.) Emphases are mine.

37. Cf. Horozco, *Emblemas morales*, 3.34, 168.

38. Gautier de Coincy, *Le Miracle de Théophile*, vv. 1316–18.

39. Berceo, *Milagros de Nuestra Señora*, vv. 820a–b.

40. Ibn Aḥmad Ibn al-'Aṭṭār, *Kitab al-watha'iq wa-l-sijillat*. This is a tenth-century Andalusi notarial compilation in which names have been all replaced by *fulān* in the Arabic original by a Cordovan judge and expert in jurisprudence. For Galicia, Gutiérrez Aller, *Formulario notarial*. For Aragón, Blasco and San Vicente, *Formulario notarial de Gil de Borau*. Apart from the *Notas del Relator*, there are other Castilian compilations of notarial models, such as the notes edited by Luisa Cuesta Gutiérrez, *Formulario notarial castellano del siglo XV*. Notarial treatises became increasingly important and increasingly present during the sixteenth and seventeenth centuries, in part because of the expansion of the *lettered city*.

41. Díaz de Toledo, *Notas del relator*; for other printings, see PhiloBiblon, http://bancroft .berkeley.edu/philobiblon/index.html.

42. "Sepan quantos esta carta vieren como yo fulano & yo fulano fijos que somos de fulano vezino de tal lugar nosotros & cada uno de nos no costreñidos ni apremiados ni enduzidos por persona alguna que sea ni ser pueda mas de nuestras propias & libres voluntades otorgamos & conoscemos por esta carta que por quanto dezimos que vos fulano fijo de fulano vezino que soys de tal lugar fuestes o ovistes seydo acusado sobre razon de la muerte que fulano

nuestro hermano hovo en un ruydo & pelea en que se acaecio & por quanto nos todos los sobredichos & cada uno de nos avemos seyedo ciertos & certificados por omes buenos dignos de fe & de creer en que vos el dicho fulano & nuestro hermano fuera & fue causa de la dicha su muerte & que vos que erades & soys sin culpa y el dicho fulano fuera reboluidor de la dicha pelea." Díaz de Toledo, *Notas del relator*.

43. Ong, *Orality and Literacy*, 79.

44. Escalona and Sirantoine, *Chartes et cartulaires*, 9.

45. Marx, "Die Tradition aller toten Geschlechter lastet wie ein Alp auf dem Gehirne der Lebenden," in *Der achtzehnte Brumaire des Louis Bonaparte*, chap. 1, www.marxists.org. Only after that, does he discuss the "ghost [*Gespenst*] of the old revolution." Obviously, *ghost* is a crucial concept in Marxist economy and in Marxist politics.

CHAPTER FOUR

Note to epigraph: "To the government of nations [Here Scott translates *gentes* as "nations," very technically, but Alfonso means the people in general] appertain the laws which unite the hearts of men through love, and this is right and reason [another possibility is, as I believe, that Alfonso is giving a definition: love is *derecho* and it is rationality itself]; for, from these two things [*derecho y razón*, as definitions of "love"] proceed perfect justice, which causes men to live properly one with another. Those who live in this manner have no reason to hate [Alfonso says "unlove," which is to break the love relations that gathered them before; it is not hate] each other but to like ["love" is a better translation for *querer*] each other well. Wherefore laws which are just cause the good will of one man to be united to that of another by means of friendship." For the specific problems surrounding the translation of *gentes*, see Brett, *Changes of State*, chaps. 3 and 4.

1. "Haec igitur lex in amicitia sanciatur, ut neque rogemus res turpis nec faciamus rogati." Cicero, *Laelius de amicitia*, 12.40, 150–51.

2. Aristotle, *Nicomachean Ethics*, 1155a.

3. Averroes, "Aristotelis Stagiritae Moralivm Nichomachiorvm," fol. 54v.

4. Harcourt, *Exposed*.

5. Lear, *Treason*. It is the question of treason that leads Lear to talk about friendship not as a legal category or as legislation but as the horizon of social peace abbreviated as friendship. During the Roman Republic, long before the development of Germanic law, the idea of *lex amicitiae* constituted a general expression, not a regulation at all; friendship received, however, a political and ethical interpretation that turned it into a powerful concept for international relations and the development of diplomatic rapprochements between the republic and other polities in the Mediterranean and Europe. Cf. Burton, *Friendship and Empire*.

6. Foucault, *Le Pouvoir psychiatrique*, 59.

7. Masciandaro, *Stranger as Friend*.

8. Chauí, "Amizade."

9. Hägglund, *This Life*, 10–11.

10. Foucault, *La Société punitive*.

11. Foucault's project, as expressed in his *Leçons sur la volonté de savoir*, studied French penality and the complex processes whereby penal law became interested in the use of other sciences in inquests and legal examinations and how this use ultimately also fostered the development of some of those sciences. Here, we see how the legal discipline comes to require a

series of external disciplines and theoretically promotes a different interpretation of those external disciplines themselves.

12. "El saber de las leyes non es tan solamente en aprender e decorar las letras dellas, mas el verdadero entendimiento dellas" (the knowledge of the laws is not only learning and knowing them by heart, but the true understanding of them) *Partidas* 1.1.13.

13. Villadiego Vascuñana y Montoya, *Forus antiqus gothorum Regum Hispaniae*, lib. 3 ("De las nacencias de los casamientos"), tit. 1 ("De las bodas"), rub. 68, fol. 174r. The rubrics were created by Villadiego himself and refer to his own commentaries on the *Liber*. Villadiego made an interesting point in his disentanglement of the concepts of *sotius*, a kind of friendship (attested in Latin as one of the nouns for "friend," as in "partner" or "ally"—s.v. Lewis and Short, *A New Latin Dictionary*) reserved for married partners, from the idea of a friend as one's best ally in hard times, who is worth more than gold, and an alter ego. Villadiego's rubric depends on Aristotle, *Ethics*, 9, 1166a. But as I have said, none of this actually appears in the legal text on which he is commenting.

14. For instance, and only as an example, cf. *Liber Iudiciorum*, lib. 2, tit. 4, "Titulus de testibus et testimoniis." *Fuero Juzgo en latín y castellano*, 23–27.

15. Daoiz's index to Iustinian *Corpus Iuris Civilis*, s.v. "amicvs," d. gl. Fi.

16. Daoiz, s.v. "Amicitia," gl. fi. in l. latae culpae.

17. Cf. Durand, *Speculum iudiciale*, 1.4, rubrica "De teste," where he excludes both enemies and friends from testifying. The edition I am using also includes the discussions of glossators and commentators up to the so-called *mos italicus*, that is, the school led by Bartolus of Sassoferrato during the fourteenth century. The *additiones* give a very complete map of the consensus about this and about how friends should be excluded from testifying: Durand, *Speculum Iuris*, 127v–28r. *Partidas* 3.16.8 gathers a long and explicit typology of those who cannot be witnesses in the process, and although this list includes very extreme cases, it does not include friendship as a case for exclusion.

18. Literature on friendship and true friendship, however, is an extremely important tradition not only in treatises on predication and collections of exempla but also in historiography and other narratives, including knightly romances. Epic poetry, including the *Cantar de Mio Cid*, is specifically interested in the meaning of friendship; similarly, Arabic sources translated at the behest of both Alfonso X and his brother Fadrique, such as *Sendebar* or *Calila e Dimna*, include various tales on the nature of friendship. Models for many tales interested in the question of friendship are, in particular, the tales that serve as the opening of Petrus Alfonsi, *Disciplina Clericalis*, namely the "Exemplum de dimidio amico," and the "Exemplum de integro amico." Victor Chauvin provided a complete map of the medieval European texts that adopted, translated, or adapted these two exempla: Chauvin, *Bibliographie des ouvrages arabes*, vol. 9.

19. "Onde porque esta orden del matrimonio establescio dios mismo por si, por esso es uno de los mas nobles e mas honrrados de los siete sacramentos. E por ende deve ser honrrado e guardado como aquel que es el primero que fue fecho e ordenado por dios mismo en el parayso, que es como su casa señalada. E otro si como aquel que es mantenimiento del mundo, e que faze alos omes bevir vida ordenada naturalmente e sin pecado, e sin el qual los otros seys sacramentos non podrían ser mantenidos nin guardados." *Partidas* 4, pról.

20. "E por esso lo pusimos en medio delas siete partidas deste libro, assi como el coraçon es puesto en medio del cuerpo, do es el spiritu del ome, onde va la vida a todos los miembros. Et otrosi como el sol que alumbra todas las cosas, e es puesto en medio de los siete cielos, do son las siete estrellas que son llamadas planetas. . . . E por esso lo pusimos en la quarta partida

deste libro, que es en medio de las siete, assi como puso nuestro señor el sol en el quarto cielo, que alunbra todas las estrellas, segun cuenta la su ley." *Partidas* 4, pról.

21. Ibn Tufayl, *Ḥayy Ibn Yaqẓān*, 111–15.

22. Vismann, *Files*, 21–25.

23. Vismann, *Files*, 22; Derrida, "Before the Law."

24. Vismann, *Files*, 22. The quote continues: "which is why it makes sense to leave their composition to authors like Christa Wolf, who in 1990 wrote the preamble for the draft of the constitution of the 'Round Table' involving civil rights groups and the tottering bureaucracy of the old East German regime."

25. I emphasize that I refer to the institution of literature that helps consolidate the public sphere in modern societies, in particular from the eighteenth century onward; see Casanova, *La République mondiale des lettres*.

26. Here, I am referring to the question of possible and logical worlds as expressed in Chapter 3.

27. Rico, *El pequeño mundo del hombre*.

28. Auerbach, *Time, History, and Literature*, 65–112.

29. Anidjar, *Blood*.

30. The distinction between the two kinds of power (authority and *potestas*), as well as the metaphor of the production and reflection of light, were published by Pope Gelasius I in his letter to the Emperor Atanasius, usually known as *Dua sunt. Epistula VIII: Ad Atanasium Imperatorem*, cols. 41b–47a.

31. Jager, *Book of the Heart*; Carruthers, *Book of Memory*; "Aristotle didn't enter into the narrow straits of mechanisms. Thus, 'man thinks with his soul' means that man thinks with Aristotle's thought. In that sense, thought is on the winning side." Lacan, *On Feminine Sexuality*, 111 (section "On the Baroque").

32. Cicero also establishes central connections between friendship and the law in his dialogue, *De legibus*.

33. *Partidas* 4.27.6.

34. Freud, *Mass Psychology*, 57–63.

35. Manuel González Jiménez partially describes the different distributions of land in *Alfonso X el Sabio*, 60–67, 195–204. In order to understand the horizontal and political strategies of Alfonso's idea and legislation of chivalry, see Rodríguez-Velasco, "Invención y consecuencias."

36. See Conte, "*Ordo iudicii* et *regula iuris*."

37. The reference for this law is Gratian's *Decretum*, part 3 ("De consecratione"), distinction 1, canon 39 ("Vestimenta"). Gratian does not cite Daniel's passage, but it is in the *Glossa ordinaria*. A frequent course of action for Alfonso is to include glosses as part of his legislation, dissolving the difference between *scholarship and gloss* on the one hand and *legislation* on the other.

38. Such a digital catalog does not yet exist, but I have spearheaded a project to create it, along with other digital resources for the study of medieval law (TheLegalWorkshop).

39. Thomas, *Les Opérations du droit*, 21–40. See also Conte, *La fuerza del texto*

40. Thomas, *Les Opérations du droit*, 208.

41. Thomas, *Les Opérations du droit*, 236.

42. Thomas, *Les Opérations du droit*, 215.

43. I have translated "men" as "humans" on account of Alfonso's clarification that when he says "men" he means "both men and women" (*Partidas* 7.33.6), rather than using Scott's translation.

44. See also Madero, *La loi de la chair.*

45. "Padre, assai ci fia men doglia / se tu mangi di noi: tu ne vestisti / queste misere carni, e tu le spoglia." Dante, *Inferno*, 516, canto 33, vv. 55–63.

46. Alfonso X, *Las Siete Partidas*, 1491 ed..

47. Sherman, *Used Books.*

48. Dagenais, *Ethics of Reading.*

49. Augustine of Hippo, *La ciudad de Dios*, 16–17, 19.2, 549–59.

50. Alfonso X, *Las Siete Partidas*, Biblioteca Nacional, Madrid, MSS Vitr. 4–6; Biblioteca Nacional, Madrid, MS 12793; and Monasterio de San Lorenzo de El Escorial, Z.I.15.

51. Alfonso X, *Las Siete Partidas*, Monasterio de San Lorenzo de El Escorial Y.II.5 (copied before 1389); and Biblioteca Capitular, Toledo, 43–13.

52. Alfonso X, *Las Siete Partidas,* Monasterio de San Lorenzo de El Escorial, Y.II.5, fol. 89va. The same reader left other marks, as on fol. 90vb, in which the reader leaves another *manicula* where the legislator indicates how friends need to know each other very well in order to keep the integrity of friendship and avoid its coming to an end, and on fol. 91vb, in which the legislator states the ways in which friends need to share their belongings with their friends.

53. Alfonso X, *Las Siete Partidas* Monasterio de San Lorenzo de El Escorial. Y.II.5, fol. 92va.

54. Thomas, *Les Opérations du droit*, 137–186, 183.

55. Thomas, *Les Opérations du droit*, 134–35.

56. Thomas, *Les Opérations du droit*, 137.

57. Cf. Ost, *Raconter la loi*, 19–20.

58. "Naturaleza tanto quiere dezir como debdo que han los onbres vnos con otros por alguna derecha razon en se amar & en se querer bien & del departimiento que ha entre natura & naturaleza es este. Ca natura es vna virtud que haze ser todas las cosas en aquel estado que dios las ordeno. Naturaleza es cosa que semeja a la natura & que ayuda a ser & mantener todo lo que desçende della." *Partidas* 4.24.1.

59. Paul was the one who established the difference between literal and spiritual interpretation, concluding that "the letter killeth, but the spirit giveth life," or, if you prefer the Greek, which is the language he wrote in, "το γαρ γραμμα αποκτεινει το δε πνευμα ζωοποιει" (2 Corinthians 3.6).

60. Scalia and Garner, *Reading the Law*; Garner, *A Dictionary of Modern* American; David Foster Wallace, *Consider the Lobster*, loc. 907. Cf. Korb, "Words Mean Things." Garner also wrote a legal dictionary, *A Dictionary of Modern Legal*. Posner, the author of the polemic *Law and Literature* (for the 1998 edition he dropped the "misunderstood relation" subtitle from the original edition), then produced a harsh critique of Scalia and Garner, in Posner "The Incoherence of Antonin Scalia."

CHAPTER FIVE

1. Dolezalek, "Lexiques de droit et autres outils."

2. Philippopoulos-Mihalopoulos, *Spatial Justice.*

3. The Arabic genealogy of the denomination "internal senses" was first established by Harry Austryn Wolfson, "Internal Senses." See also Harvey, *Inner Wits.*

4. Vallejo, *Ruda equidad, ley consumada*, 79–80.

5. Orellana Calderón, " 'Contra los de dentro tortizeros e sobervios.' "

6. Vallejo, *Ruda equidad, ley consumada*, 75.

7. González Jiménez, *Alfonso X el Sabio*, 120–23, 273–93; Martínez, *Alfonso X, the Learned*, 148–211. See Simon R. Doubleday's 2015 biography *The Wise King*.

8. "Cuydan algunos quel pueblo es llamado la gente menuda assi como menestrales e labradores e esto no es ansi ca antiguamente en babilonia e en troya. e en roma. que fueron lugares muy señalados ordenaron todas estas cosas con razon e pusieron nonbre acada vna segund que conuiene pueblo llaman el ayuntamiento de todos los onbres comunalmente delos mayores e delos medianos e delos menores ca todos son menester: e no se pueden escusar porque, se han de ayudar vnos a otros porque pueden bien beuir e ser guardados e mantenidos." *Partidas* 2.10.1. It is important to note here that the *Partidas* always reads "hombres," or "men." Sometimes I translate this as "men," literally following the text and following Scott, and other times I translate this as "humans," following the specification made by Alfonso in *Partidas* 7.33.6, in which he explains that "man" means both "man and woman." *Partidas* 1.2.5 also defines the concept of *pueblo*: "Pueblo tanto quiere dezir como ayuntamiento de gentes de todas maneras de aquella tierra do se allegan. E desto no sale ome ni muger, ni clerigo ni lego." (Pueblo is the gathering of all the people from all categories in the land on which they converge. And there is no exception as to whether it is man or woman, cleric or secular.)

9. Senellart, *Les arts de gouverner*, part 3. See also Santamaria, *Le secret du prince*.

10. See Auerbach, *Time, History, and Literature*, 65–113.

11. "Los officiales del rey (que han de juzgar, e an de ser ayudadores a complir la justicia) son como labradores, los ricos omnes e los cavalleros son como a soldadados, para guardar la, e las leyes e los fueros, e los derechos, son como valladar, que la cerca. E los juezes, e justicias, como paredes e setos porque se amparen que non entre ninguno a fazer daño." *Partidas* 2.10.3.

12. Philippopoulos-Mihalopoulos, *Spatial Justice*.

13. In fact, Alfonso, like many other political theorists in the Middle Ages, does not limit himself to the same metaphors to organize society. He experiments with different tropes. He prefers a trifunctional one, for instance, at the beginning of *Partidas* 2.21, when he legislates chivalry, although he had used other tropes elsewhere, such as the theory of *estamentos*, or estates, rather than of the three orders, before *Partidas* 2.21.

14. The literature about the knightly code is extensive. Historians of chivalry have frequently created some sort of codification of chivalry in the Middle Ages, as common denominator of the discourses they could find in literary texts or in political treatises to control the activities of chivalry. The common denominator that leads, in different ways, to the knightly code only hides the enormous productivity of the internal debates and reinventions of the *ordo militum* throughout the Middle Ages and beyond. Rodríguez-Velasco, "Invención y consecuencias de la caballería."

15. See Baschet, *Corps et âmes*.

16. Libera, *La Double révolution*.

17. König-Pralong, *Le bon usage*; Imbach and König-Pralong, *Le défi laic*.

18. Aristotle, *On the Soul*, 403b.

19. For a general outline of the question of the senses, with special interest in England (many of the philosophers of the senses traveled between the latter and the Continent quite often, beginning with Richard Rufus, who, in the early thirteenth century taught both at Oxford and in Paris); see Woolgar, *Senses in Late Medieval England*; Palazzo, *L'invention chrétienne des cinq sens*; Jørgensen, Laugerud, and Skinnebach, *Saturated Sensorium*.

20. According to Aristotle, people in general learn more quickly and more easily by means of paradigms than by means of enthymemes, because the latter are mere demonstrations.

Stories (μῦθοι, λόγοι) and paradigms, however, "are more like witnesses [μαρτύρων] and the proofs that come from witnesses are easy [ῥᾴδιοι]." This is because, according to Aristotle, people find pleasure in analogies or similarities, and "paradigms and tales [μῦθοι] display similarities [τὸ ὅμοιον δεικνύουσιν]." Aristotle, *Problems, Books 1–19*, 18.7.

21. I am obviously getting inspiration for the idea of the *fonction législateur* from Foucault, "Qu'est-ce qu'un auteur?"; Foucault, *Dits et Écrits*, 817–48; and Boureau, "Peut-on parler d'auteurs scholastiques?"

22. The best known are Juan Gil de Zamora, whose intellectual work includes political theory, historiography, and natural history, and, of course, Jacobo de Giunta, better known as Jacobo of the Laws (el de las Leyes), who received various benefits from King Alfonso, including lands and properties during the division of Murcia after its conquest. See González Jiménez, *Alfonso X el Sabio*, 123.

23. In this sense, they remain in the intellectual idiom that Gilles of Rome considered "political idiocy," because it is not founded on logic but on narrativity. See Rodríguez-Velasco, "Political Idiots and Ignorant Clients."

24. Heusch, "Index des commentateurs." The Fundación Larramendi, through the microsite "Comentaristas de Aristóteles" of its *Biblioteca Virtual de Polígrafos* (http://www.larra mendi.es) also constitutes a major resource for understanding the intensive processes of Aristotelian commentary during the Middle Ages and beyond. Among the commentators who were part of the Iberian Alfonsine era we find Domingo Gundisalvo, translator and author of three treatises on *De anima*; Toledan translators working under Cerebruno; the School of Toledo; Gerardo de Cremona; and Alvarus Toletanus, who translated Averroes' *De intellectu humano*. This is only a short list.

25. "Almas de tres maneras, dixo Aristoteles e los otros sabios, que son naturalmente en las cosas que biuen."

26. "Onde dixeron los sabios que assi como ayunto dios en el ome estas tres maneras de almas, que segund aquesto deue el amar tres cosas, de que le deue venir todo bien que espera auer en este mundo e en el otro. La primera cosa es a dios. La segunda a su señor natural. La tercera a su tierra." *Partidas* 2.12. pról.

27. "Queremos aqui dezir, segund lo ellos [los sabios antiguos] departieron, qual deue el pueblo ser a dios, e a su rey, e a su tierra. E como quier que los sabios fablaron primeramente del alma criadera, de que fizieron semejança de como el pueblo deue amar a su tierra, e de si fablaron de la sentidora de que fizieron semejança al amor que el pueblo deue auer al rey que es como sentido del. E apostre mas fablaron de la razonable a que fizieron semejança del amor quel pueblo deue auer a dios. E nos, catando que las cosas que fablan en el [dios] deuen ser ementadas primero: porende touimos por bien e por guisado de fablar primeramente del alma razonable." *Partidas* 2.12.pról.

28. It is hard to say whether there are other possible sources for Alfonso, but in this case, one likely source—the only one I can think of—would be Shem-Tov ibn Falaquera's treatise *Re'shit Ḥokhmah* (*The Beginning of Knowledge*) on Psalm III.10 (*Initium sapientiae est timor domini*), which is devoted to the rational soul. Ibn Falaquera announces this treatise in his *Epistle of the Debate*, on the controversy between philosophy and law, a treatise that was translated into Latin (Bibliothèque nationale de France, manuscrit fonds Latin. 6691A), although, of course, some of the scholars working in the Alfonsine workshop were conversant and fluent in both Hebrew (the language of ibn Falaquera) and Arabic (most of the works regarding the controversy in question). At any rate, the correspondence that *timor domini* and rational soul are in a relation of affinity is both in ibn Falaquera and Alfonso.

29. Rodríguez-Velasco, "Theorizing the Language of Law."

30. Libera has studied the philosophical and theological consequences of this crisis in depth, exploring the arguments between Albert the Great and Pope John-Paul II. Libera, *Raison et foi.*

31. "E conosciendolo assi conoscera como el mismo deue biuir e ordenar su fazienda."

32. This meaning and its semantic field is attested to in many different kinds of text, including those of historiography, fiction, and law. See, for instance, the statistics presented by the CORDE (corpus.rae.es).

33. The Iberian Gothicist idea implies that al-Andalus is only a fault within a continuous history of Roman and Christian Spain. One of the first theorizations of Gothicism is Saavedra Fajardo, *Corona Gothica, Castellana y Austriaca*; Álvarez Alonso, "Un rey, una ley, una religión"; Teillet, *Des goths à la nation gothique*; Fontaine and Pellistrandi, *L'Europe héritière de l'Espagne wisigothique.*

34. "Bien auenturada es la gente de quies es dios su señor: ca este es pueblo que escogio por su heredad. E los que lo non fizieren venir les ha el contrario de todo esto."

35. Compare the laws on fear of God and fear of the king in *Partidas* 2.12.6–7 and *Partidas* 2.13.14.

36. "El rey . . . escogido de dios e en su nome tiene lugar en tierra." This law, and this particular conclusion of the law, has been considered to be the foundation for the construction of a sacred monarchy, a theocracy, similar to the French one. There is an open debate regarding the sacred monarchy in medieval Spain, and while Teófilo F. Ruiz considers the Spanish monarchy to be *unsacred*, there are elements of sacredness that have been raised by José Manuel Nieto Soria and Peter Linehan. My position is that the ritual of sacredness is part of a legal strategy in which the *Partidas* occupies a central place; in other words, the question is less to know whether the Spanish monarchy considered itself a sacred institution than what the circumstances were in which the sacredness of the monarchy was invoked. Ruiz, "Unsacred Monarchy"; Ruiz, "Une royauté sans sacré"; Ruiz, *City and the Realm*, preface; see also Rodríguez-Velasco, *Order and Chivalry*, chap. 1; Foronda, *El espanto y el miedo.*

37. In addition to the classic book by Walter Ullman, *Growth of Papal Government in the Middle Ages*, see Sisson and Larson, *Companion to the Medieval Papacy*; Théry, "Le triomphe de la théocratie pontificale." Whalen's book on *The Two Powers* is a crucial new contribution to the question from the perspective of the opposition between the popes and Frederick II.

38. Théry, "'Fama'"; Théry, "*Atrocitas/enormitas.*"

39. Because the different commentators on Aristotle's aesthetics analyze the internal senses differently, it is crucial to understand that, from a philosophical point of view, they are dealing with the autonomy of the soul in relation to theological debates. Alfonso's take is entirely different, because every single political goal is already inscribed in the legislation; therefore, he does not need to engage in any philosophical debate, but, rather, in the normativity of his own design as expressed in the legal code. See Black, "Estimation in Avicenna"; Black, "Mental Existence"; Black, "Estimation and Imagination."

40. The necessity of keeping a memory of the penal and the criminal is legislated in *Partidas* 7, prologue.

41. A quick way to review this is via the linguistic corpus of the Real Academia Española: "Banco de datos (CORDE). Corpus diacrónico del español," Real Academia Española, http://www.rae.es. There are over 220 occurrences of the words *postura* and *posturas*, which always refer to agreements, contracts, local customs, documents, litigations, and procedures. Similarly, the noun *mandamiento*, which appears over 200 times in the *Partidas*, refers to different bodies

of legislation, or to regulations that must be enforced in particular spaces and territories (including the home).

42. Clanchy, *From Memory to Written Record*.

43. Chaytor, *From Script to Print*.

44. See Bouza, *Corre manuscrito*; Chartier, *Inscrire et effacer*. Interestingly, there are some very crucial genres that seem to have preferred manuscript transmission even after the invention of the printing press, including of historiography, *ejecutorias de nobleza de sangre* (documents that certify nobility of blood), other nobiliary treatises, genealogies, etc.

45. http://lhistoireenspectacles.fr/fontcalvy.html.

46. Weis, *Yellow Cross*; Benad, *Domus und Religion in Montaillou*; Pegg, *Most Holy War*; Pegg, *Corruption of Angels*; Moore, *War on Heresy*; Ames, *Righteous Persecution*; Laurendeau, "'Le village et l'inquisiteur.'"

47. Cortes de Valladolid, 1312, art. 74, in *Cortes de los antiguos reinos de León y de Castilla*, vol. 1, 215.

48. *Sentencia dictada por Guillem de Chaudenay*.

49. Cortes de Zamora, 1301, art. 128, in *Cortes de los Antiguos Reinos de León y de Castilla*, vol. 1, 158.

50. Oceja Gonzalo, *Documentación*.

51. *Boletín Oficial del Estado* 310 (December 27, 2007): 53410–16. https://www.boe.es/boe/dias/2007/12/27/pdfs/A53410-53416.pdf.

52. Guilarte, *Castilla país sin leyes*; González Jiménez, *Alfonso X el Sabio*, 90–96.

CONCLUSION

1. Sobecki, *Unwritten Verities*.

2. Libera, *Raison et foi*.

3. Basil, *Letters*, 4, 432, l. 5.

4. Basil, *Letters*, 4, 434, l. 4; Starobinski, *L'encre de la mélancolie*; Klibansky, Panofsky, and Saxl, *Saturn and Melancholy*.

5. Quoting (with a small change in translation) from Harvey, *Falaquera's Epistle of the Debate*, 13–14.

6. Novikoff, *Medieval Culture of Disputation*.

BIBLIOGRAPHY

PRIMARY SOURCES

Alexander of Hales [attributed]. *Summa universis theologiae (Summa fratris Alexandri)*, ed. Bernardini Klumper and the Quarracchi Fathers. Rome: Collegii S. Bonaventurae, 1924–1948, 4 vols.

Alfonso X. *Espéculo*. Biblioteca Nacional de España, Madrid, MSS 10123 (manid 1158).

Alfonso X. *Espéculo*. Real Biblioteca, Madrid, MS II/101 (manid 3182).

Alfonso X. *Espéculo*. Real Academia de la Historia, Madrid, MS 9–30–3/6112 (manid 3750).

Alfonso X. *Fuero Real*, ed. Azucena Palacios Alcaine. Madrid: Promociones y Publicaciones Universitarias, 1991.

Alfonso X. *El Fuero Real de España: Diligentemente hecho por le noble Rey Don Alfonso IX*, ed. Alonso Díaz de Montalvo. Madrid: En la oficina de P. Aznar, 1781.

Alfonso X. "General Estoria I," ed. Francisco Gago Jover. In *Prose Works of Alfonso X el Sabio. Digital Library of Old Spanish Texts*. Hispanic Seminary of Medieval Studies, 2011. http://www.hispanicseminary.org/t&c/ac/index-en.htm.

Alfonso X. *General Estoria*, First Part. Biblioteca Nacional de España, Madrid, MSS 816.

Alfonso X. *Leyes de Alfonso X. I, Espéculo*, ed. Gonzalo Martínez Díez. Ávila: Fundación Sánchez Albornoz, 1985.

Alfonso X. *Libro del Fuero de las Leyes*. British Library, London, Add MS 20787 (manid 1112).

Alfonso X. *Las Siete Partidas*. British Library, London, Add MS 20787 (manid 1112).

Alfonso X. *Las Siete Partidas*. Hispanic Society of America, New York, MS HC 397/573 (manid 115).

Alfonso X. *Las Siete Partidas*. Biblioteca Nacional de España, Madrid. MSS Vitrina 4–6.

Alfonso X. *Las Siete Partidas*. Biblioteca Nacional de España, Madrid, MSS 12793.

Alfonso X. *Las Siete Partidas*. Real Biblioteca del Monasterio de San Lorenzo de El Escorial, Z.I.15.

Alfonso X. *Las Siete Partidas*. Real Biblioteca del Monasterio de San Lorenzo de El Escorial, Y.II.5.

Alfonso X. *Las Siete Partidas*. Biblioteca Capitular, Toledo, 43–13.

Alfonso X. *Las Siete Partidas*. Sevilla: Meinardo Ungut and Stanislao Polono, 1491.

Alfonso X. *Las Siete Partidas*, ed. Alonso Díaz de Montalvo. Venice: Lucantonio Giunta, 1501.

Alfonso X. *Las Siete Partidas*, ed. Gregorio López [Madera], President of the Council of Indies. Salamanca: Andrea de Portonariis, 1555.

Alfonso X. *Las Siete Partidas*, ed. Robert I. Burns, trans. Samuel Parsons Scott. Philadelphia: University of Pennsylvania Press, 2001, 5 vols.

Alfonso X. *Tabule Astronomice*. Venice: Erhard Ratdolt, 1483.

Alfonso XI. *Ordenamiento de Alcalá*. Biblioteca Nacional de España, Madrid, MSS Vitrina 15–17.

Apuleius. *Apologia; Florida; De deo Socratis*, ed. and trans. Christopher P. Jones. Loeb Classical Library 534. Cambridge, MA: Harvard University Press, 2017.

Aristotle. *Nicomachean Ethics*, trans. H. Rackham, rev. ed. Loeb Classical Library 73. Cambridge, MA: Harvard University Press, 2003.

Aristotle. *The Poetics. "Longinus": On the Sublime. Demetrius: On Style*, ed. and trans. Stephen Halliwell. Loeb Classical Library 199. Cambridge, MA: Harvard University Press, 1995.

Aristotle. *Problems, Books 1–19*, ed. and trans. Robert Mayhew. Loeb Classical Library 316. Cambridge, MA: Harvard University Press, 2011.

Arnulf of Reims. *Privilegium pro Abbatia S. Remigii*. In *Patrologia Latina Database*, ed. Jacques-Paul Migne, vol. 139. Ann Arbor, MI: ProQuest Information and Learning Company, 1996 [1844–55], 221 vols.

Augustine of Hippo. *La ciudad de Dios*. In *Obras completas de san Agustín*, ed. J. Morán. Madrid: BAC, 1988.

Averroes. "Aristotelis Stagiritae Moralivm Nichomachiorvm cvm Averrois Cordvbensis Expositione." In *Aristotelis Stagiritae Omnia Qvae Extant Opera: Nunc primum selectis translationibus, collatisque cum graecis emendatissimis exemplaribus, Margineis scholijs illustrate, & in nouum ordinem digesta, Additis etiam nonnullis libris nunquam antea latinitate donates*, vol. 3, *Libri Moralem Totam Philosophiam Complectentes*. Venice: Iuntas, 1550.

Averroes. *Subtilissimus liber Averois qui dictur Destructio Destructionum philosophiae Algazelis*, trans. Calo Calonymus. Venice: Iuntas, 1527.

Azo. *Summa Azonis, locvples ivris civilis thesavrvs*, ed. Henricus Dresij. Venice: Gaspare Bindonum, 1584.

Basil. *The Letters, Letters 249–368, On Greek Literature*, ed. Roy Deferrari. Loeb Classical Library 270. Cambridge, MA: Harvard University Press, 1934.

Bassani, Luciano. *Gemma legalis seu Compendium aureum propositionum, sententiarum, regularumque omnium memorabilium, quas tum Bartolus a Saxoferrato, . . . in suis commentarijs, consilijs, quaestionibus, tractatibus, atque etiam alijs omnibus / nunc recens emissis, scriptas reliquit tum Alexander, Barbatia, Parisius, Pomates, Claudius, Seysellius, Io. Franciscus Ruuerensis, Menochius, atque prater eos veteres, etiam recentiores, ij que celeberrimi, videlicet Iacobus Anellus de Bottis, . . . [et] Petrus Mangrella . . . ad ipsum conscripsere . . . ; opus . . . excultum a Luciano Bassano*. Venice: Iuntas, 1590.

Berceo, Gonzalo de. *The Collected Works of Gonzalo de Berceo in English Translation*, trans. Jeannie K. Bartha, Annette G. Cash, and Richard T. Mount. Tempe: Arizona Center for Medieval and Renaissance Studies, 2008.

Berceo, Gonzalo de. *Milagros de Nuestra Señora*, ed. Fernando Baños Vallejo. Madrid/Barcelona: RAE/Galaxia Gutenberg, 2011.

Berceo, Gonzalo de. *Vida de Santo Domingo de Silos*, ed. Teresa Labarta de Chaves. Madrid: Castalia, 1972.

Biblia Latina cum Glossa Ordinaria: Facsimile Reprint of the Edition Princeps Adolph Rusch of Strassburg, 1480/81. Turnhout: Brepols, 1992.

Bonaventure. *Declaratio terminorum theologiae*, ed. Adolphe Charles Peltier, *S. R. E. cardinalis S. Bonaventuræ . . . Doctor Seraphici Ecclesiae . . . Opera omnia Sixti V . . . jussu diligentissime emendata; accedit sancti doctoris vita, una cum diatriba historico-chronologico-critica*, vol. 7. Paris: Louis Vivès, 1866.

Catálogo del Archivo Histórico de la Catedral de Burgos, Sección Actas Capitulares, Burgos: Cajacírculo, 2007–2015, 41 vols.

Cicero. *De re publica. De legibus*, trans. Clinton Walker Keyes. Loeb Classical Library 213. Cambridge, MA: Harvard University Press, 1928.

Cicero. *De senectute. Laelius de amicitia. De divinatione*, trans. W. A. Falconer. Loeb Classical Library 154. Cambridge, MA: Harvard University Press, 1923.

Constitutiones Concilii quarti Lateranensis una cum Commentariis glossatorum, ed. Antonio García y García. Vatican City: Biblioteca Apostolica Vaticana, 1988.

Cortes de los Antiguos Reinos de Aragón y de Valencia y Principado de Cataluña. Madrid: Real Academia de la Historia, 1896, 2 vols.

Cortes de los Antiguos Reinos de León y de Castilla. Madrid: Ribadeneyra, 1883–1884, 5 vols.

Dante. *Inferno*, ed. Robert M. Durling. Oxford: Oxford University Press, 1996.

Daoiz, Esteban. *Index Iuris Civilis Copiosus*. Lyon: Prost & Barlet, 1627.

Díaz de Montalvo, Alonso. *Copilación de las Leyes del Reyno*. Huete: Álvaro de Castro, 1484.

Díaz de Toledo, Fernando. *Notas del relator*. Valladolid: Jean de Francour, 1493.

Durand, Guillaume. *Speculum iudiciale illustratum et repurgatum a Giovanni Andrea et Baldo degli Ubaldi [1574]*. Aalen: Scientia, 1975.

Durand, Guillaume. *Speculum Iuris*. Lyon: Filippo Tinghi, 1577.

Eudes of Sully, Bishop of Paris. *Synodicae Constitutiones*. In *Patrologia Latina Database*, ed. Jacques-Paul Migne, vol. 212. Ann Arbor, MI: ProQuest Information and Learning Company, 1996 [1844–55], 221 vols.

Fuero Juzgo en latín y castellano, cotejado con los mas antiguos y preciosos códices por la Real Academia Española. Glossarium vocum barbararum et exoticarum quæ in Libro Judicum continentur. Glosario de voces antiqüadas y raras que se hallan en el texto castellano. Madrid: Joaquín Ibarra, Impresor de Cámara del Rey, 1815.

Gautier de Coincy. *Le Miracle de Théophile, ou comment Théophile vint à la pénitence*, ed. Annette Garnier. Paris: Honoré Champion, 1998.

Gelasius I. *Dua sunt. Epistula VIII: Ad Anastasium Imperatorem*. In *Patrologia Latina Database*, ed. Jacques-Paul Migne, vol. 59. Ann Arbor, MI: ProQuest Information and Learning Company, 1996 [1844–55], 221 vols.

Al-Ghazālī, Abu Hamid Muhammad. *The Incoherence of the Philosophers: Tahāfut Al-Falāsifah; A Parallel English-Arabic Text*, trans. Michael E. Marmura. Provo, UT: Brigham Young University Press, 1997.

Al-Ghazālī, Abu Hamid Muhammad. *Tahafot Al-Falasifat*, trans. Maurice Bouyges. Beirut: Imprimérie catholique, 1927.

Gratian. *Decretum*. In *Patrologia Latina Database*, ed. Jacques-Paul Migne, vol. 187. Ann Arbor, MI: ProQuest Information and Learning Company, 1996 [1844–55], 221 vols.

Gregory IX. *Decretales*. Mainz: Peter Schoeffer, 1473.

Gregory IX. *Smithfield Decretals*, with gloss of Bernard of Parma. British Library, London, Royal MS 10 E IV.

Horozco, Juan de. *Emblemas morales*. Madrid: Juan de la Cuesta, 1589.

Ibn al-'Aṭṭār, Muḥammad ibn Aḥmad. *Kitāb al-Wathā'iq wa'l-sijillāt: Formulario notarial hispano-árabe*, ed. Pedro Chalmeta Gendrón and Federico Corriente. Madrid: Academia Matritense del Notariado, Instituto Hispano-Árabe de Cultura, 1983.

Ibn Tufayl. *Ḥayy ibn Yaqẓān: A Philosophical Tale*, trans. Lenn Evan Goodman. Chicago: University of Chicago Press, 2009.

Innocent IV. *Super libros quinque Decretalium*. Frankfurt am Main: Sigismundus Feiereabend, 1570.

Innocent IV, Lucio P. Rosello, Baldo de Ubaldi, and Tommaso Diplovatazio. *Innocentii 4. Pont. Max. in Quinque Libros Decretalium, Necnon in Decretales Per Eundem Innocentium Editas, Quae Modo in Sexto Earundem Volumine Sunt Insertae, & in Huius Operis Elencho, . . . Adnotatae, Commentaria Doctissima. Cum Pauli Roselli, Adnotationibus, Et Loco Indicis, Baldi Margarita. Nunc Verò Diligentiori Quàm Antea Studio Recognita, . . . Integritati Suae Restituta. Summas Etiam Rerum Notabilium Quàm Plurimis in Locis Vbi Deerant Adijci Curauimus. Additis Insuper Vita Eiusdem Auctoris, Ac Nouo Indice Ita Locupleti.* Venice: Iuntas, 1578.

Jerome. *Commentary on Galatians*, trans. Andrew Cain. Washington, DC: Catholic University of America Press, 2014.

Jerome. *S. Eusebii Hieronymi Stridonensis Presbyteri Commentariorum In Epistolam Ad Galatas Libri Tres.* In *Patrologia Latina Database*, ed. Jacques-Paul Migne, vol. 26. Ann Arbor, MI: ProQuest Information and Learning Company, 1996 [1844–55], 221 vols.

Justinian. *Corpus Iuris Civilis: III, Novellae*, ed. Rudolph Schoell. Zurich: Weidmann, 1972.

Justinian. *Corpus Iuris Civilis Ivstinianei, cvm commentariis Accvrsii, scholiis Contii, et D. Gothofredi lvcvblationibus ad Accvrsium, in quibus Glossae obscuuriores explicantur, similes & contrariae afferuntur, vitiosa notantur.* Lyon: Prost & Barlet, 1627, 6 vols.

Maimonides, Moses. *The Guide of the Perplexed*, trans. Shelomoh Pines. Chicago: University of Chicago Press, 2010.

Maimonides, Moses. *Mishne Torah*. A new translation with commentaries, notes, tables, charts, and index by Eliyahu Touger. New York: Moznaim, 1986. http://www.chabad.org/library/article_cdo/aid/901656/jewish/Introduction-to-Mishneh-Torah.htm.

Marsilius of Padua. *The Defender of the Peace*, ed. Annabel Brett. Cambridge: Cambridge University Press, 2005.

Miracula Beatae Mariae Virginis et alia. Biblioteca Nacional de España, Madrid, MS 110.

Passeggeri, Rolandino de'. *Summa totius artis notariae Rolandini Rodulphini Bononiensis [1546].* Bolonia: Consiglio Nazionale del Notariato, 1977.

PhiloBiblon. Bancroft Library. University of California, Berkeley, 1997–. http://vm136.lib.berkeley.edu/BANC/philobiblon/index.html.

Plato. *Euthyphro. Apology. Crito. Phaedo. Phaedrus*, ed. H. N. Fowler. Loeb Classical Library 36. Cambridge, MA: Harvard University Press, 1990.

Raymond of Penyafort. *Summa de casibus pœnitentiae. Summa de matrimonio.* n.d., ca. 1230.

Richard of Saint Victor. *In Apocalypsim Libri Septem.* In *Patrologia Latina Database*, ed. Jacques-Paul Migne, vol. 196. Ann Arbor, MI: ProQuest Information and Learning Company, 1996 [1844–55], 221 vols.

Rutebeuf. *Le Miracle de Théophile.* In *Œuvres complètes de Rutebeuf*, ed. Edmond Faral and Julia Bastin. Paris: A. et J. Picard, 1959–1960.

Rutebeuf. *Œuvres complètes*, ed. Michel Zink. Paris: Lettres Gothiques, 1990.

Saavedra Fajardo, Diego de. *Corona Gothica, Castellana y Austriaca*. Antwerp: Juan Bautista Verdussen, 1681.

Salatiele. *Ars Notarie, I, I frammenti della prima stesura dal codice bolognese dell'Archiginnasio B 1484*, ed. Gianfranco Orlandelli. Milano: Giuffrè, 1961.

Salatiele. *Ars Notarie, II, La seconda stesura dai codici della Biblioteca Nazionale di Parigi lat. 4593 e lat. 14622*, ed. Gianfranco Orlandelli. Milano: Giuffrè, 1961.

Sánchez de Valladolid, Fernán. *Crónica de Alfonso X*, ed. Manuel González Jiménez and María Antonia Carmona Ruiz. Murcia: Real Academia Alfonso X el Sabio, 1998.

Sinibaldo dei Fieschi, Pope Innocent IV. *Super libros quinque Decretalium.* Frankfurt: Sigismundus Feiereabend, 1570.

Schroeder, H. J., trans. *Disciplinary Decrees of the General Councils: Text, Translation and Commentary.* St. Louis: B. Herder, 1937.

Sentencia dictada por Guillem de Chaudenay, ed. José María Lacarra and Ángel J. Martín Duque. Pamplona: Gobierno de Navarra (Documentos de la Colección Diplomática de Irache, II), 1986.

Siger de Brabant. *Siger de Brabant: Écrits de logique, de morale, et de physique; édition critique*, ed. Bernardo Carlos Bazán. Louvain: Publications Universitaires, 1974.

Spinoza, Baruch. *Éthique*. Ed. and trans. Bernard Pautrat. Paris: Seuil (L'Ordre Philosophique), 1988.

Taylor, Thomas. *Political fragments of Archytas, Charondas, Zaleucus, and other ancient Pythagoreans, preserved by Stobaeus, and also, Ethical fragments of Hierocles, the celebrated commentator on the golden Pythagoric verses, preserved by the same author, translated from the Greek.* Chiswick: Taylor, 1882.

Thomas de Cantimpré. *Bonum universale de apibus*, ed. George Colveneere. Douai: Balthazar Beller, 1627.

Trithemius, Johannes. *Beati Rabani Mauri Vita*. In *Patrologia Latina Database*, ed. Jacques-Paul Migne, vol. 197. Ann Arbor, MI: ProQuest Information and Learning Company, 1996 [1844–55], 221 vols.

Valdés, Fernando de. *Compilación de las instrucciones del Oficio de la santa Inquisición, hecha en Toledo año de mil quinientos sesenta.* [Madrid?], [1561?].

Varro, Marcus Terentius. *De lingua latina*, ed. M. Nisard. Paris: Firmin Didot, 1875.

Villadiego Vascuñana y Montoya, Alonso de. *Forus antiqus gothorum Regum Hispaniae, olim liber iudicum, hodie Fuero Juzgo nuncupatus XII libros continens.* Madrid: Ex Officina Petri Madrigal, 1600.

SECONDARY LITERATURE

Agamben, Giorgio. *Homo Sacer: Sovereign Power and Bare Life.* Stanford, CA: Stanford University Press, 1998.

Agamben, Giorgio. *Nudities.* Palo Alto, CA: Stanford University Press, 2011.

Agamben, Giorgio. *The Sacrament of Language: An Archeology of the Oath.* Vol. 2, part 3 of *Homo Sacer.* Palo Alto, CA: Stanford University Press, 2012.

Agúndez San Miguel, Leticia. "Memoria y cultura en la documentación del monasterio de Sahagún: La respuesta de las fórmulas 'inútiles' (904–1230)." *Anuario de estudios medievales* 40, no. 2 (2010): 847–88.

Alexander, Loveday. "The Living Voice: Skepticism Towards the Written Word in Early Christian and in Greco-Roman Texts." In *The Bible in Three Dimensions*, ed. D. J. A. Clines, S. E. Fowl, and S. E. Porter, 221–47. Sheffield: Sheffield Academic Press, 1990.

Alfange, Dean, Jr. "Jeremy Bentham and the Codification of Law." *Cornell Law Review* 55, no. 1 (1969): 58–77.

Álvarez Alonso, Clara. "Un rey, una ley, una religión: Goticismo y constitución histórica en el debate constitucional." *Historia Constitucional* 1 (2000). http://www.historiaconstitu cional.com/index.php/historiaconstitucional/article/view/106/90.

Amelotti, Mario, and Giorgio Costamagna. *Alle origini del notariato italiano*. Milan: Giuffrè, 1975.

Ames, Christine Caldwell. *Medieval Heresies: Christianity, Judaism, and Islam*. New York: Cambridge University Press, 2015.

Ames, Christine Caldwell. *Righteous Persecution: Inquisition, Dominicans, and Christianity in the Middle Ages*. Philadelphia: University of Pennsylvania Press, 2009.

Anidjar, Gil. *Blood*. New York: Columbia University Press, 2015.

Arauz Mercado, Diana. *La protección jurídica de la mujer en Castilla y León*. Valladolid: Junta de Castilla y León, 2007.

Arizaleta, Amaia. *Les clercs au palais: Chancellerie et écriture du pouvoir royal (Castille, 1157–1230)*. Paris: SEMH, 2010. https://journals.openedition.org/e-spanialivres/154.

Arizaleta, Amaia. "La memoria del monarca: Alfonso X testigo de Pedro Marín." *Cahiers d'Études Hispaniques Médiévales* 32 (2009): 267–300.

Auerbach, Eric. *Time, History, and Literature: Selected Essays of Erich Auerbach*, ed. and intr. by James I. Porter, and Jane O. Newman. Princeton, NJ: Princeton University Press, 2014.

Avenoza, Gemma. "Las *Partidas* en catalán." In *7 Partidas Digital. Edición crítica digital de las "Siete Partidas."* https://7partidas.hypotheses.org/1015 [2017.12.21].

Azcárate Aguilar-Amat, Pilar, Julio Escalona, Cristina Jular Pérez-Alfaro, and Miguel Larrañaga. "Volver a nacer: Historia e identidad en los monasterios de Arlanza, San Millán y Silos (siglos XII–XIII)." *Cahiers d'Études Hispaniques Médiévales* 29 (2006): 359–94.

Barbezat, Michael D. *Burning Bodies. Communities, Eschatology, and the Punishment of Heresy in the Middle Ages*. Ithaca, NY: Cornell University Press, 2018.

Barletta, Vincent. *Covert Gestures: Crypto-Islamic Literature as Cultural Practice in Early Modern Spain*. Minneapolis: University of Minnesota Press, 2005.

Barrero García, Ana María, and María Luz Alonso Martín. *Textos de Derecho local español en la Edad Media. Catálogo de Fueros y Costums municipales*. Madrid: Consejo Superior de Investigaciones Científicas and Instituto de Ciencias Jurídicas, 1989.

Baschet, Jérôme. *Corps et âmes: Une histoire de la personne au Moyen Âge*. Paris: Flammarion, 2016.

Bedos-Rezak, Brigitte-Miriam. "Cutting Edge. The Economy of Mediality in Twelfth-Century Chirographic Writing." *Das Mittelalter* 15, no. 2 (2010): 134–61.

Bedos-Rezak, Brigitte-Miriam. *Form and Order in Medieval France*. Aldershot: Variorum/ Ashgate, 1993.

Bedos-Rezak, Brigitte-Miriam. *When Ego Was Imago*. Leiden: Brill, 2010.

Bedos-Rezak, Brigitte-Miriam, and Jeffrey F. Hamburger. *Sign and Design. Script as Image in Cross-Cultural Perspective (300–1600 CE)*. Baltimore: Dumbarton Oaks, 2016.

Beit-Arié, Malachi. "Scribal Re-making: Transmitting and Shaping Texts." In *Hebrew Manuscripts of East and West: Towards a Comparative Codicology*, 79–103. The Panizzi Lectures. London: British Library, 1993.

Bellomo, Manlio. *The Common Legal Past of Europe, 1000–1800*, trans. Lydia G. Cochrane. Washington, DC: Catholic University of America Press, 1995.

Bellomo, Manlio. *L'Europa del diritto comune*. Roma: Il cigno Galileo Galilei, 1989.

Benad, Mathias. *Domus und Religion in Montaillou: Katholische Kirche und Katharismus im Uberlebenskampf der Familie des Pfarrers Petrus Clerici am Anfang des 14. Jahrhunderts*. Tübingen: Mohr, 1990.

Benjamin, Walter. "Über den Begriff der Geschichte." In *Gesammelte Werke*, ed. Hermann Schweppenhäuser and Rolf Tiedemann, 690–708. Frankfurt: Suhrkamp, 1991.

Bentham, Jeremy. *The Works of Jeremy Bentham*, ed. J. Bowring. Edinburgh: William Tait, 1838–1843, 11 vols.

Berlioz, Jacques. *Le Pays Cathare: Les religions médiévales et leurs expressions méridionales*. Paris: Éditions du Seuil, 2000.

Berní, Josep. *Carta, que escrive Joseph Berni y Catalá al señor Gregorio Mayans, y Siscar, sobre que las leyes de partida fueron hechas en Sevilla por el mismo Alonso el Sabio, y doce juezes españoles*. Valencia: Francisco Burguete, 1773.

Betancourt-Serna, Fernando. *La Recepción del Derecho Romano en Colombia (saec. XVIII): Fuentes Codicológicas Jurídicas I; Ms. Nº 274 BnC*. Sevilla: Universidad de Sevilla, Secretariado de Publicaciones, 2007.

Binder, Guyor, and Robert Weisberg. *Literary Criticisms of Law*. Princeton, NJ: Princeton University Press, 2000.

Black, Deborah. "Estimation and Imagination: Western Divergences from an Arabic Paradigm." *Topoi* 19 (2000): 59–75.

Black, Deborah. "Estimation in Avicenna: The Logical and Psychological Dimension." *Dialogue* 32 (1993): 219–58.

Black, Deborah. "Mental Existence in Thomas Aquinas and Avicenna." *Mediaeval Studies* 61 (1999): 45–79.

Blasco, Asunción, and Ángel San Vicente. *Formulario notarial de Gil de Borau, Zaragoza, siglo XIV*. Zaragoza: Justicia de Aragón, 2001.

Blecua, Alberto. *Manual de crítica textual*. Madrid: Castalia, 1983.

Bono, José. *Historia del Derecho Notarial español: La Edad Media. 2: Literatura e Instituciones*. Madrid: Junta de Decanos de los Colegios Notariales de España, 1982.

Boureau. Alain. *Kantorowicz. Histoires d'un historien*. Paris: Les Belles Lettres, 2018.

Boureau, Alain. "Peut-on parler d'auteurs scholastiques?" In *Auctor et Auctoritas: Invention et conformisme dans l'écriture médiévale; Actes du colloque tenu à l'Université de Versailles-Saint-Quentin-en-Yvelines, 14–16 juin 1999*, ed. Michel Zimmermann, 267–79. Paris: École des Chartes, 2001.

Boureau, Alain. *Satan Hérétique: Naissance de la démonologie dans l'Occident Médiéval*. Paris: Odile Jacob, 2004.

Bouza, Fernando. *Corre manuscrito: Una historia cultural del Siglo de Oro*. Madrid: Marcial Pons, 2002.

Brague, Rémi. *La Loi de Dieu. Histoire philosophique d'une alliance*. Paris: Gallimard, 2005.

Bravo Lira, Bernardino. "La difusión del Código Civil de Bello en los países de derecho castellano y portugués." *Revista de Estudios Histórico-Jurídicos* 7 (1982): 71–106.

Breaugh, Martin. *L'expérience plébeienne: Une histoire discontinue dela liberté politique*. Paris: Rivages/Payot, 2007.

Brett, Annabel. *Changes of State: Nature and the Limits of the City in Early Modern Natural Law*. Princeton, NJ: Princeton University Press, 2011.

Briguglia, Gianluca, and Thomas Ricklin. *Thinking Politics in the Vernacular: From the Middle Ages to the Renaissance*. Fribourg: Academic Press, 2011.

Brooks, Peter, and Paul Gewirtz, eds. *Law Stories. Narrative and Rhetoric in the Law*. New Haven, CT: Yale University Press, 1998.

Brown, Catherine. "In the Middle." *Journal of Medieval and Early Modern Studies* 30, no. 3 (2000): 547–74.

Brundage, James. *Medieval Canon Law*. London: Longman, 1995.

Brundage, James. *The Medieval Origins of the Legal Professions: Canonist, Civilians, and Courts.* Chicago: University of Chicago Press, 2008.

Brundage, James. *The Profession and Practice of Medieval Canon Law.* Aldershot: Ashgate/ Variorum, 2004.

Buridan, Jean, and Johannes Dorp. *Summula de dialectica.* Venice: Petrus de Quarengiis, Burgomensis, 1499.

Burón Castro, Taurino. "Papel hispano-árabe en el Archivo de la Catedral de León." In *Actas del V Congreso Nacional de Historia del Papel en España,* 93–103. Girona: Ajuntament de Sarrià de Ter, 2003.

Burton, Paul J. *Friendship and Empire: Roman Diplomacy and Imperialism in the Middle Republic (353–146 BC).* Cambridge: Cambridge University Press, 2011.

Butler, Judith. *Giving an Account of Oneself.* New York: Fordham University Press, 2008.

Cairns, John W., and Paul J. Plessis. *The Creation of the Ius Commune: From Casus to Regula.* Edinburgh: Edinburgh University Press, 2010.

Calasso, Francesco. *I glossatori e la teoria della sovranità: Studio di diritto comune pubblico.* Milano: Giuffrè, 1957.

Cárdenas, Anthony J. "Alfonso's Scriptorium and Chancery: Role of the Prologue in Bonding the *Translatio Studii* to the *Translatio Potestatis.*" In *Emperor of Culture: Alfonso X the Learned of Castile and His Thirteenth-Century Renaissance,* ed. R. I. Burns, 90–108. Philadelphia: University of Pennsylvania Press, 1990.

Carré, Yannick. *Le baiser sur la bouche au Moyen Âge: Rites, symboles, mentalités (XIᵉ–XVᵉ siècles).* Paris: Le Léopard d'Or, 1992.

Carruthers, Mary. *The Book of Memory.* Cambridge: Cambridge University Press, 2008.

Casado de Otaola, Luis. "Per visibilia ad invisibilia: Representaciones figurativas en documentos altomedievales como símbolos de validación y autoría." *Signo* 4 (1997): 39–56.

Casanova, Pascale. *La République mondiale des lettres.* Paris: Editions du Seuil, 1999.

Castán Lanaspa, Guillermo. *Documentos medievales del Monasterio de Santa María de Trianos.* Salamanca: Universidad de Salamanca, 1992.

Castillo Lluch, Mónica. "Las lenguas del *Fuero juzgo*: Avatares históricos e historiográficos de las versiones romances de la Ley visigótica (I)." *e-Spania* 13 (June 2012). doi: 10.4000/ e-spania.20994.

Catalán, Diego. *De la silva textual al taller historiográfico alfonsí: Códices, crónicas, versiones y cuadernos de trabajo.* Madrid: Fundación Ramón Menéndez Pidal, 1997.

Cátedra, Pedro M. "Enrique de Villena y algunos humanistas." *Academia Literaria Renacentista* 3 (1981): 187–203.

Cátedra, Pedro M., ed. *Los sermones atribuidos a Pedro Marín. Van añadidas algunas noticias sobre la predicación castellana de san Vicente Ferrer.* Salamanca: Universidad de Salamanca, 1990.

Cátedra, Pedro M. *Sermón, sociedad y literatura en la Edad Media: San Vicente Ferrer en Castilla (1411–1412); Estudio bibliográfico, literario y edición de los textos inéditos.* Valladolid: Junta de Castilla y León, 1994.

Cerquiglini, Bernard. *Éloge de la variante: Histoire critique de la philologie.* Paris: Éditions du Seuil, 1989.

Chapman, Robert William. *Cancels.* London: Constable, 1930.

Chartier, Roger. *Inscrire et effacer.* Paris: Seuil/Gallimard, 2005.

Chartier, Roger. "Jack Cade, the Skin of a Dead Lamb, and Hatred of the Written Word." *Shakespeare Studies* 34 (2006): 77–89.

Chauí, Marilena. "Amizade. Recusa do servir." *Contra a servidão voluntária.* Belo Horizonte, MG: Autêntica; São Paulo, SP: Editora Fundação Perseu Abramo, 2013

Chauvin, Victor. *Bibliographie des ouvrages arabes ou relatifs aux arabes publiés dans l'Europe chrétienne de 1810 à 1885.* Liège: Vaillant-Carmanne, 1905, 12 vols.

Chaytor, H. J. *From Script to Print: An Introduction to Medieval Literature.* Cambridge: Cambridge University Press, 1945.

Clanchy, Michael T. *From Memory to Written Record: England 1066–1307.* Malden, MA: Wiley-Blackwell, 2012.

Conte, Emanuele. "Droit médiéval: Un débat historiographique italien." *Annales HSS* 57, no. 6 (2002): 1593–1613.

Conte, Emanuele. *La fuerza del texto: Casuística y categorías del derecho medieval.* Madrid: Universidad Carlos III, 2016.

Conte, Emanuele. "*Ordo iudicii* et *regula iuris*: Bulgarus et les origines de la culture juridique (XIIᵉ siècle)." In *Frontières des savoirs en Italie à l'époque des premières universités (XIIᵉ–XVᵉ s.),* ed. Joël Chandelier and Aurélien Robert, 157–79. Rome: École Française de Rome, 2015.

Conte, Emanuele. *Tres Libri Codicis: La ricomparsa del testo e l'esegesi scolastica prima di Accursio.* Frankfurt am Main: V. Klostermann, 1990.

Conte, Emanuele, and Massimo Miglio. *Il diritto per la storia: Gli studi storico giuridici nella ricerca medievistica.* Roma: Istituto storico italiano per il Medio Evo, 2010.

Cormack, Bradin. *A Power to Do Justice: Jurisdiction, English Literature, and the Rise of Common Law, 1509–1625.* Chicago: University of Chicago Press, 2007.

Coromines, Joan, and José Antonio Pascual, *Diccionario crítico etimológico castellano e hispánico.* Madrid: Gredos, 1980–1991, 6 vols.

Costa, Pietro. *Iurisdictio: Semantica del potere politico nella pubblicistica medievale (1100–1433).* Milano: A. Giuffrè, 1969.

Craddock, Jerry R. *A Bibliography of the Legislative Works of Alfonso X el Sabio (1986) with update (1981–1990).* Berkeley: Department of Spanish and Portuguese, University of California Berkeley, 2011. https://escholarship.org/uc/item/38r0s439.

Craddock, Jerry R. "La cronología de las obras legislativas de Alfonso X el Sabio." In Jerry R. Craddock, *Palabra de rey: Selección de estudios sobre legislación alfonsina,* ed. Heather Bamford and Israel Sanz Sánchez, 43–101. Salamanca: Semyr, 2008. Originally published in *Anuario de Historia del Derecho Español* 51 (1981): 365–418.

Craddock, Jerry R. *The Legislative Works of Alfonso X, el Sabio: A Critical Bibliography.* London: Grant & Cutler, 1986.

Craddock, Jerry R. "La nota cronológica del prólogo de las *Siete Partidas.*" In Jerry R. Craddock, *Palabra de rey: Selección de estudios sobre legislación alfonsina,* ed. Heather Bamford and Israel Sanz Sánchez, 103–43. Salamanca: SEMYR, 2008.

Craddock, Jerry R. "El *Setenario*: Última e inconclusa refundición alfonsina de la primera *Partida.*" *Anuario de Historia del Derecho Español* 56 (1986): 441–66.

Crampon, A. "Un sermon prêché à Amiens vers l'an 1260." *Mémoires de la Société des Antiquaires de Picardie* 5, no. 3 (1876): 551–601.

Cuesta Gutiérrez, Luisa. *Formulario notarial castellano del siglo XV.* Madrid: Instituto Nacional de Estudios Jurídicos, 1947.

Dagenais, John. *The Ethics of Reading in Manuscript Culture: Glossing the "Libro de buen amor."* Princeton, NJ: Princeton University Press, 1994.

Dahan, Gilbert. *Notes et textes sur la poétique au Moyen Âge*. Paris: Librairie philosophique J. Vrin, 1981.

Davis, Natalie Z. *The Return of Martin Guerre*. Cambridge, MA: Harvard University Press, 1983.

De Man, Paul. "Anthropomorphism and Trope in the Lyric." In Paul de Man, *The Rhetoric of Romanticism*, 239–62. New York: Columbia University Press, 1984.

Derrida, Jacques. "Apparition de l'inapparent. L'escamotage phénoménologique." In Jacques Derrida, *Spectres de Marx: L'état de la dette, le travail du deuil et la nouvelle Internationale*, 201–79. Paris: Galilée, 1993.

Derrida, Jacques. "Before the Law." In *Acts of Literature*, ed. Derek Attridge, 181–220. New York: Routledge, 1992.

Derrida, Jacques. *Mal d'archive: Une impression freudienne*. Paris: Galilée, 1995.

Di Camilo, Ottavio. *El humanismo castellano del siglo XV*. Valencia: Fernando Torres, 1976.

Dodaro, Robert. *Christ and the Just Society in the Thought of Augustine*. Cambridge: Cambridge University Press, 2004.

Dolezalek, Gero R. "Lexiques de droit et autres outils pour le *ius commune* (XIIe–XIXe siècle)." In *Les manuscrits des lexiques et glossaires de l'antiquité tardive à la fin du Moyen Âge*, ed. Jacqueline Hamesse, 353–76. Louvain: Université de Louvain-la-Neuve, 1996.

Doubleday, Simon R. *The Wise King: A Christian Prince, Muslim Spain, and the Birth of the Renaissance*. London: Basic Books, 2015.

Dougherty, M. V. *Moral Dilemmas in Medieval Thought: From Gratian to Aquinas*. Cambridge: Cambridge University Press, 2011.

Du Plessis, J. P. "The Creation of Legal Principle." *Roman Legal Tradition* 4 (2008): 46–69.

Dupret, Baudouin. *La Charia: Des Sources à la pratique, un concept pluriel*. Paris: La Découverte, 2014.

Durand, Gilbert. *Les structures anthropologiques de l'imaginaire: Introduction à l'archetypologie générale*. Paris: Bordas, 1969.

Dutton, Brian. "Gonzalo de Berceo: unos datos biográficos." In *Actas del I Congreso de la Asociación Internacional de Hispanistas (Oxford, 6–11 septiembre 1962)*, ed. Frank Pierce and Cyril Jones, 249–54. Oxford: Dolphin Book, 1964.

Dutton, Brian. "The Profession of Gonzalo de Berceo and the Paris Manuscript of the *Libro de Alexandre*." *Bulletin of Hispanic Studies* 37 (1960): 137–45.

Echániz Sans, María. *El monasterio femenino de Sancti Spíritus de Salamanca. Colección diplomática (1268–1400)*. Salamanca: Universidad de Salamanca, 1993.

Escalona, Julio, Pilar Azcárate Aguilar-Amat, and Miguel Larrañaga Zulueta. "De la crítica diplomática a la ideología política: Los diplomas fundacionales de san Pedro de Arlanza y la construcción de una identidad para la Castilla medieval." In *Actas del VI Congreso Internacional de Historia de la Cultura Escrita*, coord. Carlos Sáez Sánchez, vol. 1, 159–206. Alcalá de Henares: Universidad de Alcalá de Henares, 2002.

Escalona, Julio, and Hélène Sirantoine. *Chartes et cartulaires comme instruments de pouvoir (Espagne et Occident Chrétien, VIIIe–XIIe siècles)*. Toulouse: CNRS/Université de Toulouse le Mirail, 2013.

Escavy Zamora, Ricardo. "El contenido lexicográfico de las *Partidas*." In *La lengua y la literatura en tiempos de Alfonso X. Actas del Congreso Internacional. Murcia, 5–10 marzo 1984*, ed. Fernando Carmona Fernández and Francisco Flórez Arroyelo, 195–210. Murcia: Universidad de Murcia, 1985.

Fabian, Johannes. *Time and the Other: How Anthropology Makes Its Object*. New York: Columbia University Press, 1983.

Farge, Arlette. *Le goût de l'archive*. Paris: Seuil, 1998.

Fernández-Ordóñez, Inés. *Las "Estorias" de Alfonso el Sabio*. Madrid: Istmo, 1992.

Fernández-Ordóñez, Inés. "El taller de las 'Estorias.'" In *Alfonso X el Sabio y las Crónicas de España*, ed. Inés Fernández-Ordóñez, 61–82. Valladolid: Fundación Central-Hispano y Centro para la Edición de los Clásicos Españoles, 2000.

Fissell, Mary E. *Vernacular Bodies: The Politics of Reproduction in Early Modern England*. Oxford/New York: Oxford University Press, 2006.

Fonrobert, Charlotte E., and Martin S. Jaffee, eds. *Cambridge Companion to the Talmud and Rabbinic Literature*. Cambridge: Cambridge University Press, 2007.

Fontaine, Jacques, and Christine Pellistrandi, eds. *L'Europe héritière de l'Espagne wisigothique: Colloque international du C.N.R.S. tenu à la Fondation Singer-Polignac, Paris, 14–16 mai 1990*. Madrid: Casa de Velázquez, 1992.

Foronda, François. *El espanto y el miedo: Golpismo, emociones políticas y constitucionalismo en la Edad Media*. Madrid: Dykinson, 2013.

Foronda, François. "Le Verbe législatif alphonsin: Hypothèses de lecture de quelques miniatures du manuscrit Add. 20787 de la British Library." In *La parole des rois. Couronne d'Aragon, royaume de Castille, XIIIᵉ–XVᵉ siècle*, ed. Stéphane Péquignot, Sophie Hirel, and François Foronda. *e-Spania* 4, 2007. http://e-spania.revues.org/document17o3.html.

Foster Wallace, David. *Consider the Lobster*. New York: Little Brown and Company, 2005 (kindle edition).

Foucault, Michel. *Dits et Écrits*, I, 1954–1988, ed. Daniel Defert and François Ewald. Paris: Gallimard, 2001.

Foucault, Michel. *L'herméneutique du sujet: cours au Collège de France 1981–1982*, ed. Frédéric Gros, François Ewald, and Alessandro Fontana. Paris: Gallimard/Seuil, 2001.

Foucault, Michel. *Leçons sur la volonté de savoir: Cours au Collège de France (1970–1971); Suivi de Le savoir d'Œdipe*, ed. François Ewald, Alessandro Fontana, and Daniel Defert. Paris: Gallimard/Seuil, 2011.

Foucault, Michel. *Le Pouvoir psychiatrique: Cours au Collège de France, 1973–1974*, ed. François Ewald, Alessandro Fontana, and Jacques Lagrange. Paris: Gallimard/Seuil, 2003.

Foucault, Michel. "Qu'est-ce qu'un auteur?" *Bulletin de la Société Française de Philosophie* 63, no. 3 (1969): 73–104.

Foucault, Michel. *La Société punitive: Cours au Collège de France*, ed. Bernard Harcourt. Paris: Seuil, 2013.

Foucault, Michel. *Surveiller et punir: Naissance de la prison*. Paris: Gallimard, 1975.

Foucault, Michel. *Technologies of the Self: A Seminar with Michel Foucault*, ed. Luther H. Martin, Huck Gutman, and Patrick H. Hutton. London: Tavistock, 1988.

Fournès, Ghislaine. "Iconologie des infantes (*Tumbo* A et *Tumbo* B de la cathédrale de Saint-Jacques de Compostelle et *Tumbo* de Touxos Outos)." *e-Spania* 5 (juin 2008). https://journals.openedition.org/e-spania/12033.

Fraade, Steven D. *Legal Fictions: Studies of Law and Narrative in the Discursive Worlds of Ancient Jewish Sectarians and Sages*. Leiden: Brill, 2011.

Fradejas Rueda, José Manuel. "Testimonios." In *7 Partidas Digital. Edición crítica digital de las "Siete Partidas."* https://7partidas.hypotheses.org/testimonios.

Freshwater, Helen. "The Allure of the Archive." *Poetics Today* 24, no. 4 (2003): 729–58.

Freud, Sigmund. *Mass Psychology and Other Writings*, trans. J. A. Underwood, with an introduction by Jacqueline Rose. London: Penguin Books, 2004.

Friedberg, Emil, and Aemilius L. Richter, eds. *Corpus Iuris Canonici*. Lipsiae: Ex officina Bernhardi Tauchnitz, 1879.

Funes, Leonardo. *El modelo historiográfico alfonsí: Una caracterización*. Papers of the Medieval Hispanic Research Seminar, 6. London: Department of Hispanic Studies, Queen Mary and Westfield College, 1997.

García de Cortázar, José Ángel. "Memoria y cultura en la documentación del monasterio de Arlanza: La respuesta de las fórmulas 'inútiles' (años 912–1233)." In *La Península en la Edad Media: Treinta años después; Estudios dedicados a José Luis Martín*, ed. José María Mínguez Fernández and Gregorio del Ser Quijano, 143–58. Salamanca: Universidad de Salamanca, 2006.

García Gallo, Alfonso. "Nuevas observaciones sobre la obra legislativa de Alfonso X." *Anuario de Historia del Derecho Español* 46 (1976): 609–70.

Garner, Bryan. *A Dictionary of Modern Legal Usage*. New York: Oxford University Press, 1995.

Garner, Bryan. *A Dictionary of Modern American Usage*. New York: Oxford University Press, 1998.

Gayoso Carreira, Gonzalo. *Historia del papel en España*. Lugo: Diputación de Lugo, 2006.

Geoffroy, Marc. "Ibn Rushd (Averroes), Latin Translations of." In *Encyclopedia of Medieval Philosophy*, ed. Henrik Lagerlund, 501–7. Springer: Dordrecht, 2011.

Ginzburg, Carlo. *Il formaggio e i vermi: Il cosmo di un mugnaio del '500*. Torino: G. Einaudi, 1976.

Gobi, Jean. *Dialogue avec un fantôme*, ed. Marie-Anne Polo de Beaulieu. Paris: Les Belles Lettres, 1994.

Goffman, Erwin. *The Presentation of Self in Everyday Life*. New York: Anchor Books, 1959.

Gómez Moreno, Ángel. *España y la Italia de los Humanistas: Primeros ecos*. Madrid: Gredos, 1994.

Gómez Redondo, Fernando. *Historia de la prosa medieval castellana. I. La creación del discurso prosístico: el entramado cortesano*. Madrid: Cátedra, 1998.

González, Julio. *El reino de Castilla en la época de Alfonso VIII*. Madrid: CSIC, 1960, 3 vols.

González Díez, Emiliano. *Colección diplomática del Concejo de Burgos*. Burgos: Ayuntamiento de Burgos, 1984.

González Jiménez, Manuel. *Alfonso X el Sabio*. Barcelona: Ariel, 2004.

González Jiménez, Manuel. *Diplomatario Andaluz de Alfonso X*. Sevilla: El Monte, Caja de Huelva y Sevilla, 1991.

González Jiménez, Manuel, and María Antonia Carmona Ruiz, eds. *Crónica de Alfonso X: Según el Ms. II/2777 de la Biblioteca del Palacio Real (Madrid)*. Murcia: Real Academia Alfonso X el Sabio, 1999.

González Villaescusa, Ricardo. "Renacimiento del vocabulario técnico agrimensor de la antigüedad y recepción del derecho romano en el siglo XIII." *Agri centuriati* 5 (2008): 21–31.

Grossi, Paolo. *A History of European Law*, trans. Laurence Hooper. Chichester, UK: Wiley-Blackwell, 2010.

Grossi, Paolo. *L'ordine giuridico medievale*. Roma: Laterza, 1995.

Guilarte, Alfonso María. *Castilla país sin leyes*. Valladolid: Ámbito, 1989.

Gumbrecht, Hans Ulrich. *Production of Presence: What Meaning Cannot Convey*. Palo Alto, CA: Stanford University Press, 2007.

Gutiérrez Aller, Victorino. *Formulario notarial*. Galicia: Xunta de Galicia, Dirección Xeral de Política Lingüística, 1998.

Guyotjeannin, Olivier. "Le vocabulaire de la diplomatique en latin medieval." In *Vocabulaire du livre et de l'écriture au moyen âge: Actes de la table ronde, Paris 24–26 septembre 1987*, ed. Olga Weijers, 120–34. Turnhout: Brepols, 1989.

Guyotjeannin, Oliver, Jacques Pycke, and Benoît-Michel Tock. *Diplomatique médiévale*. Turnhout: Brepols, 2006.

Hägglund, Martin. *This Life: Secular Life and Spiritual Freedom*. New York: Pantheon Books, 2019.

Hallaq, Wael B. *The Formation of Islamic Law*. Aldershot: Ashgate/Variorum, 2004.

Hallaq, Wael B. *A History of Islamic Legal Theories: An Introduction to Sunnī Uṣūl Al-Fiqh*. Cambridge: Cambridge University Press, 1997.

Hallaq, Wael B. *Law and Legal Theory in Classical and Medieval Islam*. Aldershot: Ashgate/Variorum, 1994.

Hallaq, Wael B. *The Origins and Evolution of Islamic Law*. Cambridge: Cambridge University Press, 2005.

Hallaq, Wael B. *Sharī'a: Theory, Practice, Transformations*. Cambridge: Cambridge University Press, 2009.

Hanks, William F. *Converting Words: Maya in the Age of the Cross*. Berkeley: University of California Press, 2010.

Harcourt, Bernard E. *Exposed: Desire and Disobedience in the Digital Age*. Cambridge, MA: Harvard University Press, 2015.

Hartley, L. P. *The Go-Between*. London: H. Hamilton, 1953.

Hartmann, Wilfried, and Kenneth Pennington. *The History of Medieval Canon Law in the Classical Period, 1140–1234: From Gratian to the Decretals of Pope Gregory IX*. Washington, DC: Catholic University of America Press, 2008.

Harvey, E. Ruth. *The Inward Wits: Psychological Theory in the Middle Ages and the Renaissance*. London: Warburg Institute, 1975.

Harvey, Steven. *Falaquera's Epistle of the Debate: An Introduction to Jewish Philosophy*. Cambridge, MA: Harvard University Press, 1987.

Hasselhoff, Görge K. *Dicit Rabbi Moyses: Studien zum Bild von Moses Maimonides im lateinischen Westen vom 13. bis 15. Jahrhundert*. Würzburg: Königshausen & Neumann, 2004.

Hasselhoff, Görge K. "Maimonides in the Latin Middle Ages: An Introductory Survey." *Jewish Studies Quarterly* 9 (2002): 1–20.

Heidegger, Martin. *Nietzsche*. London: Routledge and Kegan Paul, 1981, 2 vols.

Heusch, Carlos. "Index des commentateurs espagnols médiévaux d'Aristote (XIIᵉ–XVᵉ siècles)." *Atalaya* 2 (1992): 157–75.

Hezser, Catherine. *Rabbinic Law in Its Roman and Near Eastern Context*. Tübingen: Mohr Siebeck, 2003.

Holsinger, Bruce. "Of Pigs and Parchment: Medieval Studies and the Coming of the Animal." *PMLA* 124, no. 2 (2009): 616–23.

Holsinger, Bruce. "Written on Beasts." *New York Review of Books*, November 25, 2015. http://www.nybooks.com/daily/2015/11/25/parchment-beasts/.

Howe, C. J., et al. "Manuscript Evolution." *Trends in Genetics* 17, no. 3 (2001): 147–52.

Hsy, Jonathan. *Trading Tongues: Merchants, Multilingualism, and Medieval Literature*. Columbus: Ohio State University Press, 2013.

Iglesia Ferreirós, Aquilino. "Alfonso el Sabio, su obra legislativa y los historiadores." *Historia, Instituciones, Documentos* 9 (1982): 9–112.

Iglesia Ferreirós, Aquilino. "Alfonso el Sabio y su obra legislativa." *Anuario de Historia del Derecho Español* 50 (1980): 531–62.

Iglesia Ferreirós, Aquilino. *La creación del derecho: Una historia de la formación de un derecho estatal español.* Madrid: Marcial Pons, 1996, 2 vols.

Iglesia Ferreirós, Aquilino. *La creación del derecho: Una historia del derecho español; Lecciones.* Barcelona: Gráficas Signo, 1989, 2 vols.

Iglesia Ferreirós, Aquilino. "La labor legislativa de Alfonso X el Sabio." In *España y Europa, un pasado jurídico común: Actas del I simposio internacional del instituto de derecho común, Murcia, 26–28 de marzo de 1985,* ed. A. Pérez Martín, 275–599. Murcia: Instituto de Derecho Común, 1986.

Iglesia Ferreirós, Aquilino. "Una traducción catalana de la *Segunda Partida.*" *Anuario de Historia del Derecho Español* 17 (1987): 265–78.

Jager, Eric. *The Book of the Heart.* Chicago: University of Chicago Press, 2000.

Jennings, Margaret, and Sally A. Wilson, eds. *Ranulph of Higden. Ars Componendi Sermones.* Paris: Peeters, 2003.

Johnson, Barbara. "Anthropomorphism in Lyric and Law." *Yale Journal of Law and the Humanities* 10, no. 2 (1998): 549–74.

Jørgensen, Hans Henrik Lohfert, Henning Laugerud, and Laura Katrine Skinnebach, eds. *The Saturated Sensorium: Principles of Perception and Mediation in the Middle Ages.* Aarhus: Aarhus University Press, 2015.

Kabatek, Johannes. "La lingüística románica histórica: Tradición e innovación en una disiciplina viva." *La corónica* 31, no. 2 (2003): 35–40.

Kagan, Richard L. *Lucrecia's Dreams: Politics and Prophecy in Sixteenth-Century Spain.* Berkeley: University of California Press, 1990.

Kalmo, Hent. "A Matter of Fact? The Many Faces of Sovereignty." In *Sovereignty in Fragments: The Past, Present and Future of a Contested Concept,* ed. Hent Kalmo and Quentin Skinner, 114–31. Cambridge: Cambridge University Press, 2010.

Kalmo, Hent, and Quentin Skinner. "Introduction: A Concept in Fragments." In *Sovereignty in Fragments: The Past, Present and Future of a Contested Concept,* ed. Hent Kalmo and Quentin Skinner, 1–25. Cambridge: Cambridge University Press, 2010.

Kay, Sarah. "Legible Skins: Animals and the Ethics of Medieval Reading." *Postmedieval: A Journal of Medieval Cultural Studies* 2, no. 1 (2011): 13–32.

Kelleher, Marie A. *The Measure of Woman: Law and Female Identity in the Crown of Aragon.* Philadelphia: University of Pennsylvania Press, 2011.

Kennedy, Hugh. *Muslim Spain and Portugal: A Political History of Al-Andalus.* London: Longman, 1996.

Khadduri, Majid, and Herbert J. Liebesny. *Origin and Development of Islamic Law.* New York: AMS Press, 1984.

Khan, L. Ali, and Hisham M. Ramadan. *Contemporary Ijtihad: Limits and Controversies.* Edinburgh: Edinburgh University Press, 2011.

Kienzle, Beverly Mayne. *Cistercians, Heresy, and Crusade in Occitania, 1145–1229: Preaching in the Lord's Vineyard.* Woodbridge: York Medieval Press, 2007.

Kienzle, Beverly Mayne. *The Sermon.* Turnhout: Brepols, 2000.

Kienzle, Beverly Mayne, Thomas L. Amos, and Eugene A. Green. *De ore Domini: Preacher and Word in the Middle Ages.* Kalamazoo, MI: Medieval Institute, 1989.

Kleine, Marina. *La cancillería real de Alfonso X: Actores y prácticas en la producción documental.* Sevilla: Universidad de Sevilla, 2015.

Klibansky, Raymond, Erwin Panofsky, and Fritz Saxl. *Saturn and Melancholy: Studies in the History of Natural Philosophy, Religion and Art*. London: Nelson, 1964.

Korb, Scott. "Words Mean Things." *Slate*, August 3, 2012.

König-Pralong, Catherine. *Le bon usage des savoirs: scolastique, philosophie et politique culturelle*. Paris: Vrin, 2011.

Kretzmann, Norman. "Socrates Is Whiter Than Plato Begins to Be White." *Noûs* 11 (1977): 3–15.

Kumler, Aden. *Translating Truth: Ambitious Images and Religious Knowledge in Late Medieval France and England*. New Haven, CT: Yale University Press, 2011.

Kumler, Aden, and Christopher R. Lakey. "*Res et significatio*: The Material Sense of Things in the Middle Ages." *Gesta* 51, no. 1 (2012): 1–17.

Kymlicka, Will. *Politics in the Vernacular: Nationalism, Multiculturalism, and Citizenship*. Oxford: Oxford University Press, 2001.

Lacan, Jacques. *On Feminine Sexuality: The Limits of Love and Knowledge: Encore 1972–1973*, trans. Bruce Fink. New York: Norton, 1999.

Laldin, Mohamad Akram. *Islamic Law: An Introduction*. Kuala Lumpur: International Islamic University Malaysia, 2006.

Landau, Peter. "The Development of Law." In *The New Cambridge Medieval History*, ed. David Luscombe and Jonathan Riley-Smith, vol. 4, 113–47. Cambridge: Cambridge University Press, 2004, 7 vols.

Latour, Bruno. *An Inquiry into Modes of Existence*. Cambridge, MA: Harvard University Press, 2013.

Latour, Bruno. *Reassembling the Social: An Introduction to Actor-Network-Theory*. Oxford: Oxford University Press, 2007.

Latour, Bruno. *We Have Never Been Modern*. Cambridge, MA: Harvard University Press, 1989.

Laurendeau, Danielle. "'Le village et l'inquisiteur': Faire parler et savoir taire au tribunal d'Inquisition de Pamiers (1320–1325)." *Histoire & Sociétés Rurales* 34 (2010–12): 13–52.

Lawrance, Jeremy. "On Fifteenth-Century Spanish Vernacular Humanism." In *Medieval and Renaissance Studies in Honour of Robert Brian Tate*, ed. Ian Michael and Richard A. Cardwell, 63–79. Oxford: Dolphin Book, 1986.

Lawrance, Jeremy. "The Spread of Lay Literacy in Late Medieval Castile." *Bulletin of Hispanic Studies* 62, no. 1 (1985): 79–94.

Lear, Floyd S. *Treason in Roman and Germanic Law: Collected Papers*. Houston: University of Texas Press, 1965.

Le Goff, Jacques. "L'Occident médiéval et le temps." In Jacques Le Goff, *Un autre Moyen Âge*, 597–613. Paris: Gallimard, 1999.

Le Goff, Jacques. "Temps de l'Église, temps du marchand." *Annales ESC* 15, no. 3 (1960): 417–33.

L'Engle, Susan, and Robert Gibbs. *Illuminating the Law: Legal Manuscripts in Cambridge Collections*. London: H. Miller, 2001.

Le Roy Ladurie, Emmanuel. *Montaillou, village occitan de 1294 à 1324*. Rev. ed. Paris: Gallimard, 1982.

Lévy, Jean-Philippe. *La hiérarchie des preuves dans le droit savant du Moyen-Âge depuis la Renaissance du Droit Romain jusqu'à la fin du XIVe siècle*. Paris: Librairie du Recueil Sirey, 1939.

Lewis, Charlton T., and Charles Short. *A New Latin Dictionary*. New York: Harper and Brothers, 1891. Accessible through perseus.tufts.edu.

Lewittes, Mendell. *Principles and Development of Jewish Law: The Concepts and History of Rabbinic Jurisprudence from Its Inception to Modern Times.* New York: Bloch, 1987.

Libera, Alain de. *La Double révolution.* Book 1 of *L'Acte de penser,* vol. 3 of *Archéologie du sujet.* Paris: Vrin, 2014.

Libera, Alain de. *Raison et foi: Archéologie d'une crise d'Albert le Grand à Jean-Paul II.* Paris: Seuil, 2003.

Libson, Gideon. *Jewish and Islamic Law: A Comparative Study of Custom During the Geonic Period.* Cambridge, MA: Harvard University Press, 2003.

Linehan, Peter. *Spain, 1157–1300: A Partible Inheritance.* Malden, MA: Blackwell, 2008.

Louis, Nicolas. "L'*exemplum* en pratiques: Production, diffusion et usages des recueils d'*exempla* latins aux XIIIᵉ–XVᵉ siècles." *L'Atelier du Centre de recherches historiques* (2013). https://journals.openedition.org/acrh/5600.

Lowenthal, David. *The Past Is a Foreign Country.* Cambridge: Cambridge University Press, 1985.

Lucas Álvarez, Manuel, ed. *Tumbo A de la Catedral de Santiago.* Santiago de Compostela: Seminario de Estudios Gallegos and Cabildo de la S.A.M.I. Catedral, 1998.

Madero, Marta. "Causa, creencia y testimonios. La prueba judicial en Castilla durante el siglo XIII." *Bulletin du Centre d'études médiévales d'Auxerre,* special ser. no. 2 (2008). https://journals.openedition.org/cem/9672.

Madero, Marta. "Façons de croire: Les témoins et le juge dans l'œuvre juridique d'Alphonse X le sage, Roi de Castille." *Annales: Histoire, Sciences Sociales* 54, no. 1 (1999): 197–218.

Madero, Marta. *La loi de la chair: Le droit au corps du conjoint dans l'œuvre des canonistes.* Paris: Sorbonne, 2015.

Madero, Marta. *Las verdades de los hechos.* Salamanca: Universidad de Salamanca, 2004.

Maintier-Vermorel, Estelle. "Etude comparée du *Liber Judiciorum* et du *Fuero Juzgo.*" *e-Spania* 6 (December 2008). https://journals.openedition.org/e-spania/16833.

María e Izquierdo, María José. *Las fuentes del ordenamiento de Montalvo.* Madrid: Dykinson, 2004.

Marino, Adrian. *The Biography of "the Idea of Literature" from Antiquity to the Baroque.* Albany: State University of New York Press, 1995.

Mármol Bernal, Eduardo. "El papel a través de la ruta de la seda." *Actas del XI Congreso Nacional de Historia del Papel,* 153–63. Sevilla: Ayuntamiento de Sevilla, 2015.

Mármol Bernal, Eduardo. "Papel en Córdoba." *Actas del II Congreso Nacional de Historia del Papel en España,* 65–69. Cuenca: Diputación de Cuenca, 1997.

Martin, Georges. "Alphonse X ou la science politique (*Septénaire,* 1–11)." *Cahiers de linguistique hispanique médiévale* 18–19 (1993–1994): 79–100, and 20 (1995): 7–33.

Martin, Georges. "De nuevo sobre la fecha del *Setenario.*" *e-Spania* 2 (2006). doi: 10.4000/e-spania.381.

Martínez, H. Salvador. *Alfonso X, el Sabio: una biografía.* Madrid: Ediciones Polifemo, 2003.

Martínez, H. Salvador. *Alfonso X, the Learned: A Biography.* Leiden: Brill, 2010.

Martínez, H. Salvador. *El humanismo medieval y Alfonso X el Sabio: ensayo sobre los orígenes del humanismo vernáculo.* Madrid: Ediciones Polifemo, 2016.

Martínez Gázquez, José. "Alegorización de la declinación latina en el *Planeta* de Diego García de Campos (1218)." *Revista de Estudios Latinos* 2 (2002): 137–47.

Martínez Gázquez, José. "El uso simbólico-alegórico de los números en el Planeta (1218) de Diego García de Campos." *Butlletí de la Reial Acadèmia de Bones Lletres* 50 (2005–2006): 365–77.

Martín Prieto, Pablo. "Invención y tradición en la cancillería real de Alfonso VIII de Castilla (1158–1214)." *Espacio, Tiempo y Forma. Serie III. Historia Medieval* 26 (2013): 209–44.

Martín Prieto, Pablo. "Los preámbulos de los documentos reales bajo Alfonso VIII de Castilla (1158–1214): Relaciones entre el formulario y el personal de la cancillería." *Cahiers d'Études Hispaniques Médiévales* 35, no. 1 (2012): 27–43.

Marx, Karl. *Capital: A Critique of Political Economy*, vol. 1. New York: Penguin, 1976.

Marx, Karl. *Der achtzehnte Brumaire des Louis Bonaparte*. Hambrug: Meissner, 1869.

Masciandaro, Franco. *The Stranger as Friend: The Poetics of Friendship in Homer, Dante, and Boccaccio*. Firenze: Firenze University Press, 2013.

Menéndez Pidal, Gonzalo. "Cómo trabajaron las escuelas alfonsíes." *Nueva Revista de Filología Hispánica* 5, no. 4 (1951): 363–80.

Miguel-Prendes, Sol. *El espejo y el piélago: La "Eneida" castellana de Enrique de Villena*. Kassel: Reichenberger, 1998.

Mochi Onory, Sergio. *Fonti canonistiche dell'idea moderna dello stato: Imperium spirituale, iurisdictio divisa, sovranità*. Milano: Vita e pensiero, 1951.

Montanos Ferrín, Emma, and José Sánchez-Arcilla Bernal. *Historia del derecho y de las instituciones*. Madrid: Dykinson, 1991.

Monterde Albiac, Cristina, ed. *Diplomatario de la reina Urraca de Castilla y León (1109–1126)*. Zaragoza: Anubar, 1996.

Moore, Robert I. *The War on Heresy*. Cambridge, MA: Belknap Press of Harvard University Press, 2012.

Moore, Robert I. *The Formation of a Persecuting Society: Power and Deviance in Western Europe, 950–1250*. Oxford: B. Blackwell, 1987.

Murphy, James Jerome. *Rhetoric in the Middle Ages: A History of Rhetorical Theory from Saint Augustine to the Renaissance*. Berkeley: University of California Press, 1981.

Nanu, Irina. "La 'Segunda Partida' de Alfonso X el Sabio y la tradición occidental de los 'specula principum.'" Ph.D. diss., Universidad de Valencia, 2013.

Niederehe, Hans-Josef. *Alfonso X el Sabio y la lingüística de su tiempo*. Madrid: SGEL, 1987.

Nirenberg, David. *Neighboring Faiths: Christianity, Islam, and Judaism in the Middle Ages and Today*. Chicago: University of Chicago Press, 2014.

Noë, Alva. *Strange Tools: Art and Human Nature*. New York: Hill and Wang, 2016.

Novikoff, Alex J. *The Medieval Culture of Disputation: Pedagogy, Practice, and Performance*. Philadelphia: University of Pennsylvania Press, 2014.

Obregón Tarazona, Liliana. "Construyendo la Región Americana: Andrés Bello y el Derecho Internacional." *Revista de Derecho Público* 24 (2010): 2–22.

Oceja Gonzalo, Isabel. *Documentación del monasterio de San Salvador de Oña*. Burgos: J. M. Garrido Garrido, 1983.

Ong, Walter J. *Orality and Literacy: The Technologizing of the Word*. London: Methuen, 1982.

Orazi, Veronica. "'El Rey faze un libro, non porquel escriva con sus manos' (*General Estoria*, I, 216r). Alfonso X e le *escuelas alfonsíes*: Paradigma di autorialità multipla." In *L'autorialità plurima: Scritture collettive, testi a più mani, opere a firma multipla*, ed. Alvaro Barbieri and Elisa Gregori, 431–41. Padova: Essedra, 2015.

Orellana Calderón, Raúl. "'Contra los de dentro tortizeros e sobervios': Los otros 'defensores,' jurisdicción y poder en el proyecto político alfonsí." *e-Spania* 1 (2006). https://journals.openedition.org/e-spania/331.

Orellana Calderón, Raúl. "La Tercera Partida de Alfonso X el Sabio: Estudio y edición crítica de los títulos XVIII al XX." Ph.D. diss., Universidad Complutense de Madrid, 2006.

Ortín García, Carmen. "Derecho público romano y recepción del derecho romano en España, Europa e Iberoamérica." *Revista de Estudios Histórico-Jurídicos* 26 (2004): 626–33.

Ost, François. *Raconter la loi: Aux sources de l'imaginaire juridique.* Paris: Odile Jacob, 2004.

Ostos Salcedo, Pilar, and María Luisa Pardo Rodríguez. *Documentos y notarios de Sevilla en el siglo XIV (1301–1350).* Sevilla: Universidad de Sevilla, 2003.

Ostos Salcedo, Pilar, and María Luisa Pardo Rodríguez. *Estudios sobre el notariado europeo (siglos XIV–XV).* Sevilla: Universidad de Sevilla, 1997.

Ostos Salcedo, Pilar, María Luisa Pardo Rodríguez, and José Bono y Huerta. *Documentos y notarios de Sevilla en el siglo XIII.* Sevilla: Universidad de Sevilla, 1989.

Palazzo, Éric. *L'invention chrétienne des cinq sens dans la liturgie et l'art au Moyen Âge.* Paris: Éditions du Cerf, 2014.

Pardo Rodríguez, María Luisa. *Señores y escribanos: El notariado andaluz entre los siglos XIV y XVI.* Sevilla: Universidad de Sevilla, 2002.

Pasciuta, Beatrice. *Il diavolo in Paradiso.* Roma: Viella, 2015.

Pegg, Mark. *The Corruption of Angels: The Great Inquisition of 1245–1246.* Princeton, NJ: Princeton University Press, 2001.

Pegg, Mark. *A Most Holy War: The Albigensian Crusade and the Battle for Christendom.* Oxford: Oxford University Press, 2008.

Pérez-Prendes y Muñoz-Arracó, José Manuel. *Historia del derecho español.* Madrid: Servicio de Publicaciones, Facultad de Derecho, Universidad Complutense, 1999, 2 vols.

Peterson, David. "Reescribiendo el pasado: El Becerro Galicano como reconstrucción de la historia institucional de San Millán de la Cogolla." *Hispania* 69, no. 233 (2009): 653–82.

Philippopoulos-Mihalopoulos, Andreas. *Spatial Justice: Body, Lawscape, Atmosphere.* London: Routledge, 2015.

Piron, Sylvain. "Historien du temps." In *Une autre histoire: Jacques Le Goff (1924–2014),* ed. Jacques Revel and Jean-Claude Schmitt, 71–78. Paris: EHESS, 2015.

Posner, Richard A. *Law and Literature: A Misunderstood Relation.* Cambridge, MA: Harvard University Press, 1988.

Posner, Richard A. "The Incoherence of Antonin Scalia." *The New Republic,* August 24, 2012.

Rama, Ángel. *La ciudad letrada.* Hanover: Ediciones del Norte, 1984.

Rappaport, Joanne, and Tom Cummins. *Beyond the Lettered City: Indigenous Literacies in the Andes.* Durham, NC: Duke University Press, 2012.

Real Academia Española. "CREA (Corpus de referencia del español actual)." http://www.rae.es.

Rico, Francisco. "La clerecía del Mester." *Hispanic Review* 53 (1985): 1–23 and 127–50.

Rico, Francisco. *El pequeño mundo del hombre: Varia fortuna de una idea en la cultura española.* Madrid: Alianza Editorial, 1986.

Rodríguez-Velasco, Jesús. "Diabólicos quirógrafos: O cómo creer la piel de un animal muerto." *El Cronista del Estado Social y de Derecho* 40 (2014): 38–47.

Rodríguez-Velasco, Jesús. "Invención y consecuencias de la caballería." In *La caballería y el mundo caballeresco,* ed. Josef I. Fleckenstein, J. Rodríguez-Velasco, and Thomas Zotz, xi–lxiv. Madrid: Siglo XXI, 2006.

Rodríguez-Velasco, Jesús. *Order and Chivalry: Knighthood and Citizenship in Late Medieval Castile.* Philadelphia: University of Pennsylvania Press, 2010.

Rodríguez-Velasco, Jesús. *Plebeyos Márgenes: Ficción, Industria del Derecho y Ciencia Literaria (siglos XIII–XIV).* Salamanca: SEMYR, 2011.

Rodríguez-Velasco, Jesús. "Political Idiots and Ignorant Clients: Vernacular Legal Language in Thirteenth-Century Iberian Culture." *Digital Philology: A Journal of Medieval Cultures* 2, no. 1 (2013): 86–112.

Rodríguez-Velasco, Jesús. "Theorizing the Language of Law." *Diacritics* 36, no. 3–4 (2006): 64–86.

Rodríguez-Velasco, Jesús. "La urgente presencia de las *Siete Partidas*." *La Corónica* 38, no. 2 (2010): 97–134.

Rubio Moreno, Laura María. "Las definiciones léxicas de *Las Partidas* y de los actuales *Código Civil y Penal*." *Revista de Lexicografía* 12 (2005–2006): 223–38.

Ruiz, Elisa. *Introducción a la codicología*. Madrid: Fundación Germán Sánchez Ruipérez, 2002.

Ruiz, Teófilo F. *The City and the Realm: Burgos and Castile, 1080–1492*. London: Variorum, 1992.

Ruiz, Teófilo F. "Une royauté sans sacré: La monarchie castillane au bas Moyen Âge." *Annales ESC* 3 (1984): 429–53.

Ruiz, Teófilo F. "Unsacred Monarchy: The Kings of Castile in the Late Middle Ages." In *Symbolism, Ritual, and Politics Since the Middle Ages*, ed. Sean Wilentz, 108–44. Philadelphia: University of Pennsylvania Press, 1985.

Safran, Janina M. *Defining Boundaries in Al-Andalus: Muslims, Christians, and Jews in Islamic Iberia*. Ithaca, NY: Cornell University Press, 2013.

Sánchez, María Nieves, dir. *Diccionario español de documentos alfonsíes*. Madrid: Arco/Libros, 2000.

Sánchez Manzanares, María del Carmen. "Razones de nombres en *Las partidas* de Alfonso X." In *Caminos actuales de la historiografía lingüística*, ed. Antonio Roldán Pérez, 1421–34. Murcia: Universidad de Murcia, Sociedad Española de historiografía lingüística, 2006.

Santamaria, Jean-Baptiste. *Le secret du prince: Gouverner par le secret; France, Bourgogne, XIIIᵉ– XVᵉ siècle*. Ceyzériey: Champ Vallon, 2018.

Scalia, Antonin, and Bryan Garner. *Reading the Law: The Interpretation of Legal Texts*. New York: Thomson/West, 2012.

Schacht, Joseph. *An Introduction to Islamic Law*. Oxford: Clarendon Press, 1964.

Schmitt, Carl. *Political Theology: Four Chapters on the Concept of Sovereignty*, trans. George D. Schwab. University of Chicago Press; University of Chicago, 2004.

Schmitt, Jean-Claude. *Les revenants: Les vivants et les morts dans la société médiévale*. Paris: Gallimard, 1994.

Schmitt, Jean-Claude. *Les rythmes au Moyen Âge*. Paris: Gallimard, 2016.

Schmitt, Jean-Claude. *Le saint Lévrier: Guinefort, guérisseur d'enfants depuis le XIIIᵉ siècle*. Paris: Flammarion, 1979.

Senellart, Michel. *Les arts de gouverner: Du régime médiéval au concept de gouvernement*. Paris: Seuil, 1995.

Shemesh, Aharon. *Halakhah in the Making: The Development of Jewish Law from Qumran to the Rabbis*. Berkeley: University of California Press, 2009.

Sherman, William H. *Used Books*. Philadelphia: University of Pennsylvania Press, 2008.

Sisson, Keith, and Atria A. Larson, eds. *A Companion to the Medieval Papacy: Growth of an Ideology and Institution*. Leiden: Brill, 2016.

Smith, Jamie. "Women as Legal Agents in Late Medieval Genoa." In *Writing Medieval Women's Lives*, ed. Charlotte Newman Goldy and Amy Livingstone, 113–29. New York: Palgrave, 2012.

Sobecki, Sebastian. *Unwritten Verities: The Making of England's Vernacular Legal Culture, 1463– 1549*. Notre Dame, IN: University of Notre Dame Press, 2015.

Solalinde, Antonio G. "Intervención de Alfonso en la redacción de sus obras." *Revista de Filología Española* 2 (1915): 283–88.

Squilloni, Antonella. "Il significato etico-politico dell'immagine re-legge animata. Il 'nomos empsychos' nei trattati neopitagorici 'Peri Basileias.'" *Civiltà Classica e Cristiana* 11, no. 1 (1990): 75–94.

Starobinski, Jean. *L'encre de la mélancolie.* Paris: La librairie du XXIᵉ siècle, 2012.

Stein, Peter. *Roman Law in European History.* New York: Cambridge University Press, 1999.

Steiner, Emily. *Documentary Culture and the Making of English Literature.* Cambridge: Cambridge University Press, 2003.

Stern, Josef. "The Maimonidea Parable, the Arabic *Poetics*, and the Garden of Eden." *Midwest Studies in Philosophy* 33 (2009): 209–47.

Stern, Josef. *The Matter and Form of Maimonides' Guide.* Cambridge, MA: Harvard University Press, 2013.

Stoler, Ann Laura. *Along the Archival Grain: Epistemic Anxieties and Colonial Common Sense.* Princeton, NJ: Princeton University Press, 2009.

Strawn, Brent A., ed. *Oxford Encyclopedia of the Bible and Law.* Oxford: Oxford University Press, 2015.

Sweetman, Robert. "Beryl Smalley, Thomas of Cantimpré, and the Performative Reading of Scripture: A Study in Two *Exempla.*" In *With Reverence for the Word: Medieval Scriptural Exegesis in Judaism, Christianity, and Islam,* ed. Joseph Ward Goering, Jane Dammen McAuliffe, and Barry Walfish, 256–75. New York: Oxford University Press, 2010.

Szpiech, Ryan. "From Founding Father to Pious Son: Filiation, Language, and Royal Inheritance in Alfonso X, the Learned." *Interfaces* 1 (2015): 209–35.

Taylor, Diana. *The Archive and the Repertoire.* Durham, NC: Duke University Press, 2007.

Taylor, Jamie K. *Fictions of Evidence: Witnessing, Literature, and Community in the Late Middle Ages.* Columbus: Ohio State University Press, 2013.

Teillet, Suzanne. *Des goths à la nation gothique.* Paris: Les Belles Lettres, 1984.

Teissier-Ensminger, Anne. "La loi au figuré: Trois illustrateurs du Code pénal français." *Sociétés & Représentations* 2, no. 18 (2004): 277–91.

Théry, Julien. "*Atrocitas/enormitas*: Pour une histoire de la catégorie d'"énormité' ou 'crime énorme' du Moyen Âge à l'époque moderne." *Clio@Themis. Revue électronique d'histoire du droit* 4 (2011), 1–76. http://www.cliothemis.com/IMG/pdf/Julien_TheryPDF.pdf.

Théry, Julien. "'Fama': L'opinion publique comme preuve judiciaire. Aperçu sur la révolution médiévale de l'inquisitoire (XIIᵉ–XIVᵉ siécles)." In *La preuve en justice de l'Antiquité à nos jours,* ed. Bruno Lemesle, 119–47. Rennes: Presses Universitaires de Rennes, 2003.

Théry, Julien. "Le triomphe de la théocratie pontificale, du IIIᵉ concile du Latran au pontificat de Boniface VIII (1179–1303)." In *Structures et dynamiques religieuses dans les sociétés de l'Occident latin (1179–1449),* ed. Marie Madeleine de Cevins and Jean-Michel Matz, 17–31. Rennes: Presses Universitaires de Rennes, 2010.

Thiong'o, Ngũgĩ Wa. *Globalectics: Theory and the Politics of Knowing.* New York: Columbia University Press, 2012.

Thomas, Yan. "Les artifices de la vérité en droit commun médiéval." *L'Homme* 175–176 (2005): 113–30.

Thomas, Yan. "Fictio Legis: L'empire de la fiction romaine et ses limites médiévales." *Droits* 21 (1995): 17–63.

Thomas, Yan. *Les Opérations du droit.* Paris: Gallimard/Seuil, 2011.

Thomas, Yan. "Les ornements, la cité, le patrimoine." In *Images romaines: Actes de la table ronde organisée à l'École normale supérieure, 24–26 octobre 1996,* ed. Florence Dupont and Clara Auvray-Assayas, 263–83. Paris: École Normale Supérieure, 1998.

Thomas, Yan. "El sujeto de derecho, la persona y la naturaleza: Sobre la crítica contemporánea del sujeto de derecho." In Yan Thomas, *Los artificios de las instituciones: Estudios de derecho romano*, 81–105. Buenos Aires: EUDEBA, 1999.

Thomas, Yan. "La valeur des choses. Le droit romain hors la religion," *Annales. Histoire, Sciences Sociales* 57, no. 6 (2002): 1431–62.

Tierney, Brian. *Liberty and Law: The Idea of Permissive Natural Law, 1100–1800*. Washington, DC: Catholic University of America, 2014.

Trouillot, Michel-Rolph. *Silencing the Past: Power and the Production of History*. Foreword by Hazel V. Carby. Boston: Beaconn Press, 2015.

Ullman, Walter. *The Growth of Papal Government in the Middle Ages*. London: Methuen, 1965.

Vaca Lorenzo, Ángel. *Documentación medieval del monasterio de Santa Clara de Villalobos (Zamora)*. Salamanca: Universidad de Salamanca, 1991.

Vallejo, Jesús. *Ruda equidad, ley consumada: Concepción de la potestad normativa (1250–1350)*. Madrid: Centro de Estudios Constitucionales, 1992.

Velasco, Jesús R. "Lex Animata." *Political Concepts*. Politicalconcepts.org.

Vismann, Cornelia. *Files: Law and Media Technology*, trans. Geoffrey Winthrop-Young. Stanford, CA: Stanford University Press, 2008. Originally published as *Akten: Medientechnik und Recht* (Frankfurt am Main: Fischer, 2000).

Wacks, David. *Double Diaspora in Sephardic Literature: Jewish Cultural Production Before and After 1492*. Bloomington: Indiana University Press, 2015.

Walter, Henriette. *L'Aventure des langues en Occident: Leur origine, leur histoire, leur géographie*. Paris: Robert Laffont, 1995.

Walter, Henriette, and Bassam Baraka. *Arabesques. L'Aventure de la langue Arabe en Occident*. Paris: Robert Laffont, 2006.

Warhmund, Ludwig, ed. *Rainierius Perusinus: Die Ars Notariae des Rainierius Perusinus; Quellen zur Geschichte des römisch-kanonischen Prozesses im Mittelalter*. Aalen: Scientia, 1962 [1917].

Wartburg, Walther von. *La Fragmentation linguistique de la Romania*. Paris: C. Klincksieck, 1967.

Weber, Max. *The Protestant Ethic and the Spirit of Capitalism*. New York: Scribner, 1958.

Wei, Ian P. "Guy de l'Aumône's *Summa de diversis questionibus theologie*." *Traditio* 44 (1988): 275–323.

Weis, René. *The Yellow Cross: The Story of the Last Cathars, 1290–1323*. New York: Alfred A. Knopf, 2001.

Whalen, Brett Edward. *The Two Powers: The Papacy, the Empire, and the Struggle for Power in the Thirteenth Century*. Philadelphia: University of Pennsylvania Press, 2019.

Wolfson, Harry Austryn. "The Internal Senses in Latin, Arabic, and Hebrew Philosophical Texts." *Harvard Theological Review* 28, no. 2 (1935): 69–133.

Woolgar, C. M. *The Senses in Late Medieval England*. New Haven, CT: Yale University Press, 2006.

Xifaras, Mikhaïl. "Figures de la doctrine, essai d'une phénoménologie des 'personnages juridiques.'" In *La doctrine en droit administratif: Actes du colloque de l'Association française de droit administratif*, 175–216. Paris: Litec, 2010.

Xifars, Mikhaïl. "Théorie des personnages juridiques." *Revue Française de Droit Administratif* 33, no. 2 (2017): 275–87.

Zink, Michel. *La prédication en langue romane avant 1300*. Paris: Honoré Champion, 1976.

Zumthor, Paul. "Y a-t-il une 'littérature' médiévale?" *Poétique* 66 (1986): 131–40.

INDEX

ACKNOWLEDGMENTS

Concluding a book requires a moment of introspection to summon up all the voices that have chorally contributed to the ideas, the expressions, even the motivation to continue ahead—or to put an end to it. The names that come immediately to mind are those of Aurélie Vialette, Bernard Harcourt, and Claudio Lomnitz. They have followed this tortuous process—the creation of this book—from its inception, and they have given me, with generosity and friendship, their time, their ideas, their faith, their support. Without them, this book would have vanished in the void before it was even fully conceived. To them, I am indebted more than I can express.

I want to thank my dear friends and mentors Pedro M. Cátedra and Michel Garcia, who have followed and criticized my work for many decades. Jerry Craddock laid the cornerstone, and many other stones, of this work—and in a certain way he is the reason why I started writing it—but it does not mean that he will agree with it. Juan Carlos Conde, María Jesús Díez Garretas, Enrique Gavilán, Carlos Heusch, Yonsoo Kim, Georges Martin, Nuria de Castilla, Alberto Montaner, Selby Wynn Schwartz have been with me all the way for the last few decades.

I have had the opportunity to present this project, in many different stages, on several occasions. Teo Ruiz invited me to be a distinguished visiting scholar at the Center for Medieval and Renaissance Studies at UCLA, where I first presented some ideas on dead voice; he and John Dagenais gave me important feedback. Other ideas on dead voice were also presented at the Medieval Club of New York, by invitation of Steven Kruger; and at Hofstra University, to which I was invited by Simon Doubleday. The Department of History at the University of Paris invited me to present on ghost manuscripts, for which I am indebted to François Foronda, Patrick Boucheron, and Jean-Philippe Genet. I delivered "The Aesthetics of Law," the John Kronik Memorial Lecture at Cornell University, thanks to Simone Pinet and Bruno Bosteels. Likewise, I presented some preliminary ideas on juridical language, aesthetics, and the legal discipline at Magdalen College, Oxford, and at

Amherst University; thanks go, respectively, to Juan Carlos Conde and Albert Lloret. I presented my theses on friendship and legislation at the Pázmány Péter Catholic University of Budapest, thanks to Dóra Bakucz, and at the Universidad Autónoma de la Ciudad de México, thanks to Carlos Pereda. Finally, I presented some of the conclusions on transmission and dissemination of legal thinking at the Graduate Center, CUNY, and the École Normale Supérieure de Lyon, with thanks, respectively, to José del Valle and Carlos Heusch. I presented parts of my research in the seminars of David Nirenberg, at the University of Chicago, and at the seminar of Annick Louis, at the École des hautes études en sciences sociales. I am grateful to them and their splendid students. I have had the chance to talk about all this with Rita Copeland, Michael E. Gerli, Bill Sherman, David Wallace, and Julian Weiss.

The research contained in this book is the result of continued work in many libraries and archives in the United States, France, United Kingdom, Spain, Italy, and other places. I am grateful to the librarians and staff at all those centers. Most of my work has been conducted at the Biblioteca Nacional de España in Madrid, where I have been continuously helped by the most exquisite staff and librarians of the Sala Cervantes; I include them all under the names of Julián Martín Abad and María José Rucio Zamorano.

I am not a native speaker of English, but I, nevertheless, was adamant to think and write this book in English. Eunice Rodríguez Ferguson, Sarah Goldberg, and Rachel Stein were kind enough to help me at many points during this long process. Michelle Beckett reviewed the first version of the manuscript. Bill Piper has been the best editor one could dream of. Pablo Justel has worked with me in the last moments of the production of the final manuscript. Brais Lamela took care of the index. I was lucky to have Gail Schmitt as the copyeditor of this manuscript.

Special mention goes to my dearest friend, genius, and multimedia artist, Miguel Ripoll, who has been with me for the last thirty something years of my life and who has been kind enough to design the cover of this book, as he did for a previous one.

I wish to thank Jerry Singerman in a very special way. Jerry has pushed me, helped me, been patient with me, and accompanied me in this project from day one. I completed it thanks to him, and it is an honor for me to work alongside him. His team of marvelous professionals, Lily Palladino and Zoe Kovacs, deserve my special gratitude. I also want to thank the two generous and collegial anonymous readers who helped me create a better, more readable manuscript.

My colleagues and friends at the Department of Latin American and Iberian Cultures, the Institute for Comparative Literature and Society, and the Columbia Center for Contemporary Critical Thought have been my main interlocutors for many years. I would like to thank them all, in particular the colleagues and friends in my field Seth Kimmel and Alessandra Russo. A special thanks to Rosalind Morris and Gustav Kalm, who invited me to present my project in front of the institute and gave me many important insights. I would like to thank Etienne Balibar, Patricia Dailey, Souleymane Bachir Diagne, Alex Gil, Eileen Gillooly, Stathis Gourgouris, Patricia Grieve, Eleanor Johnson, Lydia Liu, Reinhold Martin, Graciela Montaldo, Ana Ochoa Gautier, Neni Panourgià, Anupama Rao, Joey Slaughter, Gayatri Chakravorty Spivak, Dennis Tenen, and many others.

My students at Columbia have always been generous enough to listen to my scholarly obsessions and enlighten me with their questions and commentaries: Akua Banful, Nicole Basile, Noel Blanco Mourelle, Raphaëlle Burns, David Colmenares, Lexie Cook, Nicole Hughes, Miguel Ibáñez Aristondo, Pablo Justel, Gustav Kalm, Brais Lamela, Joseph Lawless, Alexandra Méndez, Charles Pletcher, Verónica Rodríguez Torres, Gianmarco Saretto, Rachel Stein, and Maristela Verástegui.

Many friends and colleagues have helped me along the way. The list could be longer, and I apologize if I have forgotten any names: Charly Barr, José Calvo González, Jeffrey J. Cohen, Emanuele Conte, Hernán Díaz, Luca Fernández, Daniela Gandorfer, Eduardo Hernández Cano, Alison Kinney, Murad Idris, Anna Krauthamer, Laurie-Anne Laget, Yitzhak Lewis, Marina Mestre, Nélida Michaud, Nada Moumtaz, Beatrice Pasciuta, Kosmas Pissakos, Dagmar Riedel, Patricia Rochwert, Mia Ruyter, Karl Steel, Hélène Thieulin-Pardo, Pier Mattia Tomassino, Sofía Torallas Tovar, and Ian P. Wei.

My sisters and brothers, Mariajosé, Javier, Blanca, Margarita, and Juanjo, have been tremendously patient with me. All members of my extended family (Javier, Mariajo, José, Sonia, Jon, nieces and nephews, and even Pipa) had to listen to my ramblings and ideas, sometimes more than once, in moments in which they were not necessarily very interested in talking about medieval law—who is? My sister Blanca, a law scholar and a judge, has helped me more than she can imagine and in more ways than I can tell, enduring my questions and ideas, always in the most supportive way. I wish I could have discussed this book with my parents, who left us when I was jotting its first words. I miss them infinitely, and I cannot write without thinking of them. My French family—Dany, Alain, and the rest of the extended Vialette-Bedos